JOHN SANFORD

Also by Jack Mearns

Deadline News
Caliphornia

JOHN SANFORD

AN ANNOTATED BIBLIOGRAPHY
(REVISED SECOND EDITION)

JACK MEARNS

CUTTING EDGE

Copyright © 2022 Jack Mearns. All Rights Reserved.

No part of this book may be reproduced, or stored in a retrieval system, or transmitted in any form or by any means, electronic, mechanical, photocopying, recording, or otherwise, without express written permission of the publisher.

ISBN-13: 978-1-954840-91-1

Published by
Cutting Edge Books
PO Box 8212
Calabasas, CA 91372
www.cuttingedgebooks.com

For
My Father

TABLE OF CONTENTS

Preface to the Second Edition ix
Introduction xi
Foreword to the First Edition. xix

A. Books, Pamphlets and Broadsides by John Sanford 1
B. Contributions to Books 125
C. Contributions to Periodicals. 150
D. Translations 162
E. Miscellanea 163

Appendix A: Index of Historical Pieces 173
Appendix B: Index of Pieces about Family
    Members and Acquaintances. 193
Appendix C: "The Master's" Circle: 1926-1933 195

PREFACE TO THE SECOND EDITION

John Sanford: An Annotated Bibliography was originally published by Oak Knoll Press in 2008. At that time, only one of Sanford's novels was in print. The advent of e-books and print-on-demand has since enabled Sanford's works to find new readership. In 2013, Bloomsbury Books released three of Sanford's works as e-books. More recently, two publishers have devised successful strategies for re-releasing Sanford's work. Richard Schober of Tough Poets essentially publishes by subscription—as Dragon Press did for Sanford's first book, *The Water Wheel*—using Kickstarter campaigns to pre-fund costs. This enables him to reissue a variety of neglected out-of-print classics tending toward the avant garde. Tough Poets has republished two Sanford novels and released *Speaking from an Empty Room*, a volume of selected letters. Lee Goldberg of Brash Books has brought his media savvy to bear on two early Sanford novels, selling more copies of the reissues than were sold of the original editions.

John Sanford's work is now experiencing something of a resurgence, making an update of this bibliography apropos. I have added descriptions of Sanford works published since 2008.

I thank Robert Fleck for seeing the original Oak Knoll edition of the bibliography into print and Lee Goldberg for publishing this second edition.

Jack Mearns
January 2022

INTRODUCTION

"Had I so interfered in behalf of the rich
... it would have been all right."
— John Brown, 1859

During this long life, John Sanford published in nine decades, a remarkable feat for anyone, but particularly remarkable for someone who came to his profession relatively late. Sanford's first published piece appeared in the expatriate little magazine *Tambour* in 1929, when he was 25 years old, and his first book was not released until 1933, when he was 28.

Little Preparation for a Career in Writing
All the more remarkable is how little formal preparation Sanford had for his career as a writer. He was a poor student in school. He did not graduate from Manhattan's DeWitt Clinton High—where his main extracurricular activity was cutting classes—when he failed English his last semester. Sanford spent a year at Lafayette College, where he unsuccessfully attempted to write for the student newspaper. This tenure was followed by the shortest of stints at Northwestern and Lehigh, at which he lasted just two weeks. Afterward, he obtained a fraudulent diploma when a relative bribed a state official; this gained him admission to Fordham Law School, from which he dropped out after less than a month. Finally, the next term, Sanford returned to Fordham, where he completed his law degree. He then joined his father's legal practice.

However, during his law studies Sanford chanced to meet a childhood acquaintance on a New Jersey golf course; this 1925 meeting would forever change Sanford's path in life. To Sanford's astonishment, the man—Nathan Weinstein, who was now going by the name of Nathanael West—announced that he was writing a book. *Writing a book*: those words were magical. Suddenly, the wayward and goal-less Sanford knew he must write one too.

Sanford formed a close friendship with West, often accompanying West on walks around New York City and listening to West discourse on art and literature, including introducing Sanford to an enduring model: an obscure short story writer named Ernest Hemingway. Sanford helped read proof on West's first novel, *The Dream Life of Balso Snell*. And Sanford shared a hunting cabin with West one summer in the Adirondacks, where West worked on *Miss Lonelyhearts* and Sanford his first novel, *The Water Wheel*. Later, West induced Sanford to change his given name, Julian Shapiro, to one less likely to damage sales due to anti-Semitism. Sanford chose the name of the protagonist in *The Water Wheel*, a decision Sanford would come to rue.

While not as self-consciously lean as Hemingway's or West's writing, Sanford's prose has an unembellished spareness that clearly shows his friend's influence. Early on, James Joyce's example can be clearly seen in Sanford's eschewing of apostrophes in contractions. Later, Joyce's inspiration endured in Sanford's continued melding of multiple narrative voices. Sanford's work is marked by a constant striving for innovation. He rarely used simile; rather, he preferred the directness and power of metaphor. He used nouns as verbs, verbs as nouns. Often his prose has subtle poetic elements, such as interior rhymes. Sanford's was a constant quest for arresting expressions.

A Second Career at Sixty-three
Sanford's other important early influence was William Carlos Williams, whose book of historical vignettes, *In the American*

Grain, Sanford read in the mid-1920s. The concept of history as literature took root in Sanford early. From the outset of his career, Sanford salted his works of fiction with historical interludes. These episodes were often a source of contention with publishers and cost him contracts. For example, *Seventy Times Seven* did not appear in England because Sanford refused to remove historical material that the publisher thought would baffle British readers.

In all, Sanford published eight novels, which showed increasing strain with the bounds of fiction, as the books became more and more dominated by teachers and preachers, who delivered sermons and lectures to Sanford's readers. Finally, in 1967, with the publication of *The $300 Man*, Sanford had exhausted the novel form as a medium. Sanford's wife, screenwriter Marguerite Roberts, asked Sanford what his novels would be like "without the novel." This embarked Sanford on what would become his second career, at the age of 63.

Three years in the writing, *A More Goodly Country* established Sanford's mature narrative voice, or rather voices. Consisting entirely of vignettes about historical events and figures, this book allowed Sanford to explore history by means of fable, parable and brief dramatic monologue. Sanford brought history to life through magnificent flights of imagination. However, so unconventional was the book that it would take another three years and more than 200 rejections before Sanford could find a publisher.

With the issuing of *A More Goodly Country* in 1975, Sanford's second career, as a non-fiction writer, was underway. There would follow eighteen more volumes of history, memoir and autobiography. It is remarkable that twelve of these books were published after Sanford reached the age of 80. At an age when most writers are retired or dead, Sanford hit his literary stride. Despite deteriorating eyesight that made writing arduous, he continued to work until just a month before his death. Sanford died in March 2003, leaving three unpublished works.

The Finest Unread Author Writing in English

Despite the beauty of Sanford's writing and the gravity and pertinence of his themes, Sanford remains mostly unknown and almost entirely unread. His books have been issued only in small editions, and only one has gone into a second printing. Early on, Sanford's work was published by the premier houses of the day—like Knopf and Harcourt, Brace. But Sanford quarreled with editors and publishers, and he refused to compromise.

As a result of Sanford's intractability, his publishers would each decide in turn that Sanford was more trouble than he was worth: one book was enough. Thus, they had little investment in his work. They did not promote his books because Sanford would never be a member of their stable. Un-promoted, his books did not sell, and the chore of publishing Sanford would pass on to another house. It is impossible not to conclude that beneath Sanford's rashness and intransigence was an unconscious effort to sabotage his career. This is the defining conflict of Sanford's writing life—his Sisyphean struggle to get his books into print and his rebellious undermining of his stature.

It was not until 1977, when Sanford had been writing for over 40 years, that the Capra Press followed *Adirondack Stories* with *View from this Wilderness,* thus becoming the first of his publishers to issue a second Sanford volume. And it was not until 1984 that Black Sparrow Press began what would be the longest run of Sanford titles from a single publisher, six in all. However, by the 1980s, Sanford was an old man, whose work appealed only to small art-house publishers. His chances of wider success had expired.

In addition to his quarrelsome ways with publishers, Sanford's lack of success must also be traced to the content of his books. From the start, one can see Sanford's obsession with the darker side of American history. In *The Water Wheel*, there is an episode musing on Philip Nolan, the Man without a Country. In *Seventy Times Seven*, there is a historical poetic interlude depicting man's inhumanity since America's earliest days. From that book onward, the harshness of Sanford's examination of the inequities in American history would only become more strident.

Literature as a Weapon
In 1936, Paramount Studios hired Sanford as a screenwriter. In late 1939, he joined the Hollywood cell of the Communist Party. The works that followed Sanford's political awakening became progressively more leftist. In a period when many American communists were reassessing their party membership, any doubts Sanford may have had only served to increase the fervor of his dedication to the cause. Even the Communists condemned 1943's *The People from Heaven* as too radical. The following *A Man Without Shoes* and *The Land that Touches Mine* were even more deeply political works, which criticized the American social and economic system as fundamentally unjust. This hard-line stance would eventually force Sanford to self-publish *A Man Without Shoes*.

In his later non-fiction historical books, Sanford's devotion to progressive causes intensified. To read 1984's *The Winters of that Country*, a blistering indictment of America, is to find oneself denounced for having profited from centuries of injustice; the book is an accusation aimed at all Americans. Even Sanford's peerless prose could induce few readers to endure such a withering rebuke of the values in which they were raised to believe. Sanford must have known that these works would find little acceptance with the general reading public, who seek diversion, not chastisement. But he could not dim his ire or the fire of his dream.

One historical figure to whom Sanford repeatedly returned is John Brown, the abolitionist whose assault on the armory at Harper's Ferry led to his execution. Sanford oft repeated Brown's statement: "Had I so interfered in behalf of the rich... it would have been all right." One could also apply that idea to Sanford's work: had he so written in behalf of the rich, he might have sold well and perhaps been a household name. Instead, Sanford chose to risk all in a quixotic attempt to right the wrongs of society, sacrificing potential success in the name of his cause. He wrote not to entertain the public, but to condemn it. He wrote to goad Americans to abandon complacency and to right society's wrongs.

The Luxury to Write What He Pleased

Soon after arriving in Los Angeles, John Sanford met fellow screenwriter Marguerite Roberts at Paramount. The couple would wed two years later, and Roberts would go on to become one of the most successful and highest-paid screenwriters in Hollywood, including twelve straight years under contract at Metro-Goldwyn-Mayer. After Sanford's year-long tenure at Paramount was up, he had a brief stint at M-G-M. Following that, he would be gainfully employed only once more, when he co-wrote Clark Gable and Carol Lombard's *Honky-Tonk* with Roberts. For the rest of his life, Sanford would be supported by his wife's earnings.

Thus, Sanford experienced a rare luxury among professional writers—the luxury to write what he pleased, without consideration of economic consequences. Sanford was not compelled to sell books to put food on the table. He did not have to seek out other writing assignments to pay the bills. Sanford abjured self-promotion. He did not do book tours, did not attend signings, did not make public appearances or give lectures. He left the selling of his works to others, as if he believed that any attempt to curry the favor of the publishing establishment or of readers would taint his work. In reaction to a pamphlet that a publisher had prepared to promote one of his books, Sanford wrote to a friend: "When I saw it, I cringed. It seemed like such a begging little job that it made me feel ashamed."

Unlike many writers of his standing, Sanford did not review books, did not write articles for magazines, did not have to interrupt the process of writing books that did not sell so that he could make ends meet. In fact, aside from several pieces in literary little magazines at the outset of his career, and during a brief editorship of *Black & White/The Clipper* in 1940-41, Sanford hardly published in periodicals at all.

On the one hand, this lack of economic necessity freed Sanford to pursue his art wherever the muse took him. Without this freedom, his life's work would not exist in its current form. On the other hand, one wonders what Sanford would have produced, if he had been forced by economics to temper his indignation and recast his reforming vision, so that his books would sell.

If he had needed to write to make money, would Sanford have been capable of writing for the popular audience, and what would have been the result? Would his missteps have been fewer? Would he have listened to the recommendations of editors and publishers and muted the excesses of politics that flawed his later fiction? Would he still have achieved the high splendor of his style under these mundane constraints? Certainly, he would have had to write more and differently to earn a living. But, could he have achieved the mass appeal that always eluded him? One wonders whether economic necessity would have improved Sanford's art or merely blunted his talent.

Nonetheless, despite its occasional excesses, John Sanford's writing has achieved a sustained beauty and passion that is rarely seen. Even his less fully realized works have passages of brilliance that commend them. And, in those works where style and content felicitously meet, Sanford is revealed as a master of his craft: his writing sparkles with the clean lines of a gem. In a letter to a novice writer, Sanford elucidated the ethos that kept him writing nearly to the end:

> There is only one book that any good writer ever writes—
> the book he's writing now. There's no past for him and
> no future. This chapter, this page, God damn it, this very
> line—that's all he has.

Although nearly unknown to the wider reading public, Sanford's work evokes fervor in critics and academics, as well as an almost fanatical devotion from a small cadre of collectors. It is, in particular, for these people this bibliography is written.

FOREWORD TO THE FIRST EDITION

Objective of this Bibliography
I intend this bibliography as a guide, in the broadest sense, to the writings of John Sanford. The primary goal, of course, is to describe Sanford's publications physically. A secondary goal, however, is to describe these publications' place in the scope of Sanford's career.

For Sanford, perhaps more so than most writers, there is a story that goes with each book. I have recounted those stories— often ones more of travail than of triumph—as a way of charting Sanford's development into the unique writer he became. My annotations address style and content of the works described as well as the often-winding road these works took toward publication.

This bibliography also includes three appendices that I hope will be of use to scholars. Appendix A indexes, by subject, book appearances of Sanford's historical pieces. These include pieces in Sanford's non-fiction books as well as pieces in his novels that are typographically distinct from the narrative. Appendix B indexes pieces about family members and acquaintances from Sanford's historical books. Scenes from his autobiography are not included.

Appendix C presents a description of "The Master's" Circle: Sanford's friend and mentor George Brounoff's knot of intellectuals in the late 1920s and early 1930s, which included Nathanael West, whom Sanford brought in.

A Note on Sources
This book is the product of over twelve years of association with John Sanford, including several hundred hours of conversation with him. I have also drawn from his files of correspondence with his publishers, which are now housed in his archive at the Howard Gotlieb Archival Research Center at Boston University; the copyright registration materials for his books; and his autobiography, *Scenes from the Life of an American Jew*.

Physical descriptions of books are based on examination of Sanford's own copies, housed at Boston, and volumes in my own collection of Sanford's work. Bonnell and Bonnell's bibliography of Conrad Aiken has been an indispensable model for this project.

Acknowledgments
I thank John Martin for providing specifics about Black Sparrow Press publications and Bob Bason for his help with Capra Press items. I also thank Ralph Sipper for steering this book into print. I express boundless thanks my wife for her indulgence. And I am grateful to John Sanford, for his amused tolerance of my obsession with his work.

The following people and institutions also provided help: Tom Andrews; Barricade Books; Jim at Books Again; Maria L. Morelli at the Howard Gotlieb Archival Research Center, Boston University (for J. S.'s letters to Jesse Greenstein); Carroll & Graf; Noel Young at Capra Press; Chan Gordon at The Captain's Bookshelf; University of Delaware Library (for J. S.'s letters to Richard Johns); Farrar, Straus & Giroux; Dan Giancola; Willis G. Regier at University of Illinois Press; Anthony M. Tedeschi at Lilly Library, Indiana University (regarding Capra Press); Anne-Mari Karttunen at Joensuu University; Steven G. Kellman;

Susan L. Cash at The Kent State University Press; Ruth J. Hutnik at Lafayette College; Sarah Almond at Library of America; *The Literary Review*; Joseph McBride; Nora Gorman at Northwestern University Press; Lin Rolens at Oyster Press; Sabrina R. Paris at Pearsons Education (regarding Prentice-Hall); Per Petterson; Pushcart Prize; Jean Rose at the Random House Group (regarding Jonathan Cape); Robert W. Smith; Harry Ransom Humanities Research Center, The University of Texas at Austin (for J. S.'s letters to Angel Flores); and The University of Wisconsin Press.

A. BOOKS, PAMPHLETS AND BROADSIDES BY JOHN SANFORD

A1   THE WATER WHEEL   1933

a. First edition:

THE WATER WHEEL | *Julian L. Shapiro* | [Dragon Press ornament 2.7 x 1.3 cm.] | THE DRAGON PRESS | *Duffield and Green*

19 x 12.2 cm. *1-20⁸ 21².* Pp.*1-10*, 11-26, *27-28*, 29-86, *87-88*, 89-125, *126-128*, 129-157, *158-160*, 161-204, *205-206*, 207-281, *282-284*, *285-324*.

P.*1* half title: […] *The Dragon Series | Edited by Angel Flores*; p.*2* blank; p.*3* title; p.*4* copyright: […] *First Edition | Designed by* | M. A. FRIEDMAN [J. S.'s cousin Melvin] | *Printed at the Plant of* | THE HADDON CRAFTSMEN, INC.; p.*5* disclaimer; p.*6* blank; p.*7* dedication: *This book is for* | O. B. [Olga Brounoff]; p.*8* blank; p.*9* section title; p.*10* blank; pp.11-26 text; p.*27* section title; p.*28* blank; pp.29-86 text; p.*87* section title; p.*88* blank; pp.89-125 text; p.*126* blank; p.*127* section title; p.*128* blank; pp.129-157 text; p.*158* blank; p.*159* section title; p.*160* blank; pp.161-204 text; p.*205* section title; p.*206* blank; pp.207-281 text; p.*282* blank; p.*283* section title; p.*284* blank; pp.285-324 text.

Dark green cloth boards; lettered in gold across the spine: THE | WATER | WHEEL | SHAPIRO, and at the foot: DRAGON | PRESS. Top edges cut; fore edges roughly cut; bottom edges roughly trimmed; endpapers. Bright yellow dust jacket printed in green, gray and black, in swirling rings of water surrounding a black vortex, designed by J. S.'s friend the painter Lester Rondell; back quotes praise from Samuel Putnam, William Carlos Williams and Manuel Komroff. Yellowish white wove paper.

Published 27 March 1933 at $2.50; number of copies uncertain [500-1,500].

Note: Portions of *The Water Wheel* were revised from pieces published in *The New Review* as "Prose" (C7) and "The First Chapter of a Novel" (C11), and in *Contempo* as "The Dime: A Cruel Story" (C15).

J.S. began writing the book in 1928 and finished it in 1932. *The Water Wheel* was originally accepted by Mohawk Press but then subsequently rejected. It was finally published in the Dragon Press Series by Angel Flores, a professor at Cornell University. J. S. had been introduced to Flores by Nathanael West, who also was expected to be a Dragon Press author. An early working title was *Among the Rocks*, but Flores felt this contained too much "Eliotite symbolism." Later in life, J. S. claimed he remained unsure of the meaning of the title—which had been suggested by West—guessing it might have represented the protagonist's being swirled by forces over which he does not have control. J. S. worked on this book in the summer of 1931, when he and West rented a hunting cabin together in the Adirondacks at Viele Pond.

Dragon Press Series books typically were printed in editions of 500 copies. However, in a letter to *Pagany* editor, Richard Johns (1/10/33), J. S. wrote that Duffield and Green, the distributor for the book, "made Flores triple the print order." And in an undated letter to Angel Flores, J. S. wrote, "Haddon [Craftsmen, the book's binder] is waiting for your O.K. in order to proceed. In addition, would you specify to them whether you want all 1500 copies printed and bound, or whether you want only 500 bound and the rest set up to wait for further orders." J. S. later recalled that, when the Dragon Press went out of business in 1933, the Haddon Craftsmen came after him for bills relating to the book that Flores had not paid. Whether all ordered copies were bound, and whether all bound but unsold copies survived remains unclear. By any standard, *The Water Wheel* is a scarce book.

Stylistically, *The Water Wheel* owes much inspiration to James Joyce, with unconventional typography and wordplay. This includes running two words together and capitalizing another word created by this joining—e.g., "wiDEWet" eyes and "SpaniSHAMerican" war. Also, Sanford made a triangle of legal terms that wreaked havoc with typesetting: the compositors repeatedly broke the triangle over two pages, ruining the effect, until Sanford finally wrote on the proof, "Goddammit, get this right!"

The content is highly autobiographical, including the setting of J. S.'s father's law offices and descriptions of salons in the apartment of J. S.'s friend George Brounoff. The character of the boarder is based on Olga Brounoff, sister of George and dedicatee of the book. At Viele Pond, West chided Sanford over how recognizable the Olga character was. The protagonist is named John Sanford.

The tone of *The Water Wheel* is palpably one of self-loathing. In a letter to Matthew Bruccoli—who in 1975 had proposed reprinting *The Water Wheel* in Southern Illinois University's Lost American Fiction Series, although no such edition appeared—J. S. wrote:

> The writing of the Water Wheel was self-punishment deliberately undertaken in order to lighten a burden of guilt I felt in relation to O.B., to whom the book is

dedicated. There's no confession for a Jew, there's no symbolic penance or outside absolution: A Jew must suffer for such of his acts as he knows to have been wrong, and his suffering lasts until his heart informs him that his God has relented—and a worthy Jew, I might add, never lets himself off lightly…. I exposed every villainy I could find in myself, every lack, every meanness, and so far from wanting pity, I courted scorn and odium. In large measure, judging by the reviews, I got them both.

There is little similarity of *The Water Wheel* to J. S.'s later writing, although the author's preoccupation with history is evident even here, as seen in the protagonist's musings on the Man without a Country, Philip Nolan. Also, quotations from Robert Juet's *The Discovery of the Hudson River* would return much later to form the titles of J. S.'s autobiography.

b. First reprint edition (Tough Poets), [2020]

THE WATER WHEEL | *Julian L. Shapiro* | (John Sanford) |Tough Poets Press | Arlington, Massachusetts

21 x 14.8 cm. *1-10*, 11-22, *23-24*, 25-33, *34*, 35-69, *70*, 71-91, *92*, 93-109, *110*, 111-181, *182*, 183-208, *209-210*.

P.*1* blank; p.*2* BOOKS BY JOHN SANFORD | [twenty-four titles arranged by category—Novels and Stories, Creative Interpretations of History, Autobiography and Memoir]; p.*3* half title; p.*4* blank; p.*5* title; p.*6* Copyright © by The Dragon Press | Copyright © renewed 1960 by John Sanford | Introduction copyright © 2019 by Jack Mearns […] | ISBN 978-0-578-64021-1 | This edition published with permission from | The Estate of John Sanford in March 2020 by: | Tough Poets Press | […]; p.*7* disclaimer; p.*8* blank; p.*9* dedication; p.*10* blank; pp.11-22

Introduction: Literary Remains of an Unappreciated Genius by Jack Mearns; p.*23* fly title; p.*24* blank; pp.25-33 text; p.*34* blank; pp.35-69 text; p.*70* blank; pp.71-91 text; p.*92* blank; pp.93-109 text; p.*110* blank; pp.111-181 text; p.*182* blank; pp.183-206 text; p.207-208 Acknowledgments: Profound thanks are extended to the following for their generous financial support which helped to defray some of the book's production costs [names of Kickstarter campaign contributors]; p.*209* blank; p.*210* CPSIA information [...].

Glossy white stiff paper wrappers printed in greenish yellow, light green and black; lettered in black down the spine: THE WATER WHEEL • JULIAN L. SHAPIRO TOUGH POETS PRESS; lettered on the upper cover [in yellow:] THE | [in black] [bowed up:] WATER WHEEL | [bowed down:] JULIAN L. SHAPIRO | RONDELL; the cover approximately reproduces the design of the original Dragon Press dust jacket; on the bottom cover is a 1933 photograph of a seated J. S.—proud new author—with a copy of the first edition open in his hands; edges cut flush; perfect binding. Yellowish white wove paper.

Published 16 March 2020 at $16.99; print on demand.

A2   THE OLD MAN'S PLACE   1935

a. First edition:

[in orangish red:] The | Old Man's Place | [in black:] by JOHN B. SANFORD ~ published by | ALBERT and CHARLES BONI, INC. | [in orangish red:] NEW YORK | [oval publisher's device of Pan 1.3 x 1 cm.]

18.6 x 12 cm. 1^4 2-17^8. Pp.*1*-8, 9-101, *102*, 103-167, *168*, 169-209, *210*, 211-255, *256*, 257-263, *264*.

P.*1* half title; p.*2* blank; p.*3* title; p.*4* copyright: [...] | [rule] | PRINTED IN U. S. A. BY HADDON CRAFTSMEN INC. | TYPOGRAPHY BY M. A. FRIEDMAN [J. S.'s cousin Melvin]; p.*5* dedication: *This book is for* | 'THE GOVERNOR' [Philip D. Shapiro, J. S.'s father]; p.*6* blank; p.*7* fly title; p.*8* blank; pp.9-101 text; p.*102* blank; pp.103-167 text; p.*168* blank; pp.169-209 text; p.*210* blank; pp.211-255 text; p.*256* blank; pp.257-263 text; p.*264* blank.

Light gray cloth boards; printed in orangish red across the spine, in a dark navy-blue panel, 2.2 x 18.8 cm.: THE | OLD | MAN'S | PLACE | [small ornament] | JOHN B. | SANFORD | [large blue floral ornament in red box] | [in red box near the foot in blue:] ALBERT | AND | CHARLES | BONI. Top edges stained black; fore edges roughly cut; bottom edges cut; endpapers. Cream colored paper jacket printed vividly in black and bluish green, with three menacing, dark figures looming over a tiny farmhouse in the background; designed by Worch; back presents a staged letter "FROM THE AUTHOR TO THE PUBLISHER" from Warrensburg, New York, and dated 1 August 1935. Yellowish white wove paper.

Published October 1935 at $2.50; 2,346 copies.

Note: J. S.'s archive contains an advance proof copy of *The Old Man's Place*, which consists of tall galleys bound in plain tan boards, with black fabric tape on the spine. The front panel of the dust jacket is glued to the upper cover; the jacket's spine is glued to the lower cover. This is the only copy I am aware of, although Boni reported that 154 copies were bound in paper and distributed to the book trade.

The Old Man's Place was based on stories about a group of poachers who terrorized the Warrensburg area one summer. These were told to J. S. by Harry Reoux, the owner of Viele Pond.

The first draft was written in two months in the fall of 1931 on the roof of the Sutton Hotel, which was managed by Nathanael West, and in whose unoccupied rooms West allowed fellow writers to stay for free. The book was placed at Boni by J. S.'s cousin Melvin Friedman, who designed the typography. J. S. revised the manuscript during the summer of 1935. The original title in the contract with Boni was *The Trampled Vineyard* (a misquote from Julia Ward Howe), although an author's note in *Contact* said J. S. "is almost finished with a book to be called 'Adirondack Novel.'"

Under the influence of West, and hoping to boost sales by avoiding an anti-Semitic reaction to his name, J. S. published this book under a pseudonym, taking the name of his *Water Wheel* protagonist. (J. S. would later legally change his name to John Sanford in 1941.) The back of the jacket furthers this transformation with its swaggering letter from "Jack" Sanford, which mixes fact and fiction in describing his Jack London-esque adventures. *The Water Wheel* is not listed as a previous book, and thus *The Old Man's Place* is sometimes erroneously described as J. S.'s first book.

J. S. received his law degree in 1927, passed the bar, and joined his father's law practice. But after the Crash of 1929, the practice dwindled, and J. S. devoted himself full time to writing. Early in 1935, J. S.'s father had a heart attack and was no longer able to maintain what remained of his practice. J. S.'s aunt prevailed upon her nephew to give up writing and return to the law. J. S. refused. This refusal was pivotal, in that *The Old Man's Place* brought J. S. to the attention of a Hollywood agent and earned him a contract at Paramount Studies as a screenwriter. This willful gambit meant J. S. could thereafter support his father at a level the law practice never would have enabled. However, J. S. suffered lifelong guilt over his choice of writing over helping his father.

The copyright for *The Old Man's Place* was taken out in Boni's name. Boni even asserted ownership of the name John B. Sanford and sought to prohibit J. S. from publishing any more books under that name. J. S. and Boni later fought an epic battle over this copyright. J. S. sought to have it transferred into his name, but Boni refused because the book technically was still in print. In 1948, J. S. arranged for Pickwick Books in Hollywood to order all 350 remaining copies. He then demanded Boni either reprint the book or relinquish the copyright. Boni gave the copyright over to J. S., and J. S. stored the unsold copies.

In March 1982, Black Sparrow Press sold 256 of J. S.'s copies for $30. An additional 25 copies were specially signed and numbered by J. S. on the front free endpaper. These were sold at $60. This arrangement explains why such remarkably well-preserved copies of this book appear on the market.

Stylistically, *The Old Man's Place* is a vast departure from *The Water Wheel*. Its prose is straightforward, largely unadorned and vigorous. Although one holdover from the previous book clearly displays Joyce's continuing influence on J. S.: the running together of words—e.g., "brightgreen" and "kitchenknife." This book is also notable for its almost complete lack of interiority of the narrative, the polar opposite of *The Water Wheel*'s obsessively self-conscious voice. In content, *The Old Man's Place* begins J. S.'s trio of books about the Adirondacks, in which he tried to create fiction "as American as [Mathew] Brady's pictures." This small-town setting provides the basis for an examination of the violence at the core of the American psyche.

In later years, J. S. regretted that the characters in this book were presented as fundamentally flawed misfits, rather than as being corrupted by their experience in World War One. In hindsight, J. S. wished he had made *The Old Man's Place* an antiwar novel.

In 1962, Marguerite Roberts wrote three versions of a never-produced screenplay of the novel, entitled *The Hero Suit*, drastically changing the plot. In 1972, *The Old Man's Place* was released as a motion picture called *My Old Man's Place* (see E4a), which was more faithful to the source novel.

b. First reprint edition (Permabooks), [1953]

The | Old Man's | Place | BY JOHN B. SANFORD | PERMABOOKS | *A division of Doubleday & Company, Inc. | Garden City, New Jersey.*

18 x 10.4 cm. *1-6, 7-160*.

P.*1* overview of three main characters; p.*2* BOOKS BY JOHN B. SANFORD | [three titles: *The Land that Touches Mine* is listed, but *The Water Wheel* is not; neither is *A Man without Shoes*]; p.*3* title; p.*4 Permabooks edition 1953, | by special arrangement with the author |* PRINTING HISTORY | *Albert and Charles Boni edition published 1935 | Permabooks edition published November, 1953 | First printing* […] October, 1953 | […] | Printed in the United States; p.*5* dedication; p.*6* blank; pp.*7-160* text.

Glossy yellowish white stiff paper wrappers; lettered in black across the brownish yellow spine: 25¢, and down: THE OLD MAN'S PLACE [in white:] JOHN B. SANFORD [in black:] A PERMA STAR [star] P251; lettered on the upper cover [in a field of brownish yellow extending 5.7 cm. from the top] [in black:] The brutal story of three moral outcasts — | of the evil they plot and the doom they meet | [in white:] THE OLD | MAN'S PLACE | COMPLETE AND UNABRIDGED John B. Sanford; in the top right corner is the price in black on a white box and a publisher's device in whitish yellow on a black box; the bottom is a portrait in lurid colors of an innocent mail-order bride meeting three desperate and violent men; printed in brownish yellow, yellow, black and red on the lower cover; edges cut flush; all edges stained red; perfect binding. Yellowish white wove paper.

Published November 1953 at $.25; in 1955 the contract was taken over by New American Library; number of copies not obtainable.

c. Second reprint edition (Signet), [1957]

The Hard Guys | {Original Title: *The Old Man's Place*} | John B. Sanford | [publisher's device] | A SIGNET BOOK | Published by THE NEW AMERICAN LIBRARY.

17.9 x 10.6 cm. *1-4, 5-128.*

P.*1* overview of plot and biographical note; p.*2* advt. for other Signet books; p.*3* title; p.*4* [...] | First printing, August, 1957 | [rule] | [dedication] | [rule] | [three lines printed in a single-ruled box:] *SIGNET BOOKS are published by* | *The New American Library of World Literature, Inc.* | *501 Madison Avenue, New York 22, New York* | PRINTED IN THE UNITED STATES OF AMERICA; pp.5-128 text.

Glossy yellowish white stiff paper wrappers; lettered in black across the top of the spine: • | 1432, and down the spine: THE HARD GUYS John B. Sanford; the upper cover, printed in red, brown, grayish blue and shades of yellow, is a portrait of a decidedly less innocent mail-order bride meeting a more menacing trio of men, dominated by the bride's rear in a tight red skirt and her bare calves above black high heeled shoes; upper cover lettered at top left [in red:] The | HARD GUYS | [in black:] (Original title: The Old Man's Place) | John B. Sanford, at bottom left [in black:] Three Toughs | A Mail-Order Bride | —And Sudden Violence! | [in red:] A SIGNET BOOK | Complete and Unabridged, in upper right [in black:] 1432 | [bowed up:] SIGNET | [unprinted in black oval:] 25¢ | [bowed down with an upward curving black rule around it, in black:] BOOKS; lower cover printed in bright yellow and lettered in red and black; edges cut flush; all edges stained orangish red; perfect binding. Yellowish white wove paper.

Published August 1957 at $.25; 155,977 copies sold by June 1965.

Note: Tom Dardis (see B13) writes that J. S.'s blacklisting created serious hurdles to publishing this edition. Berkley Books had contracted with J. S. for a reprint. However, Berkley was owned by the arch-conservative actor John Wayne. Although the "small and struggling" Berkley was permitted editorial freedom, "it was the name Sanford that was unacceptable" to the firm's ownership. "It was made clear that we *couldn't* publish him" because "for Wayne to have his own publishing firm bring out a book by a man who had dared the lightning defying the House Committee would invite him to considerable joshing if not open hostility from his friends on the Right." Dardis then arranged for New American Library to take over the contract. Dardis concludes that, contrary to the general belief that book publishing was not affected by the blacklist, "the 'unfriendly' writers had extraordinary difficulties in obtaining publication in their native land."

d. Third reprint edition (Brash Books), [2021]

THE OLD MAN'S | PLACE | [in gray:] John Sanford | [publisher's device of a B with a fedora perched on it] RASH | BOOKS.

21.6 x 13.9 cm. *i-vi*, vii-xviii, *xviii*,1-154, *155-158*.

P.*1* half title; p.*2* Books by John Sanford | [chronological list of 23 titles] | As Julian L. Shapiro | *The Water Wheel*; p.*3* title; p.*4* Copyright © 1935, 2021 by John Sanford | Introduction Copyright © 2021 by Jack Mearns | [disclaimer] | ISBN-13: 978-1-7358517-3-0 | Published by | Brash Books [...]; p.*v* dedication; p.*vi* blank; p.vii-xiv Introduction to the New Edition by Jack Mearns; pp.xv-xvi Books by John Sanford | [categorical listing of 25 titles]; p.xvii Publisher's Note [warning crime fiction readers about J. S.'s unconventional stylistic elements]; p.*xviii* blank; pp.1-154 text; p.*155-157* blank; p.*158* Made in the U.S.A. | [...].

Glossy yellowish white stiff paper wrappers; lettered in white down the dark gray spine: JOHN SANFORD [in bronze:] THE OLD MAN'S PLACE [across spine] [unprinted: publisher's hatted B device]; the upper cover, printed in bronze, yellow, black and shades of gray shows a stone house in a field surrounded by trees with fall foliage ablaze; upper cover lettered [in white:] JOHN SANFORD | [in a kind of weathered white with streaks of gray, in perspective with letters diminishing in size toward the right:] THE OLD MAN'S | PLACE; lower cover printed in dark gray and lettered in white and bronze; edges cut flush; perfect binding. Yellowish white wove paper.

Published 2 April 2021 at $17.99; print on demand.

e. First e-book edition (Brash Books), [2021]

[title page as in A2d]

Published 3 May 2021 at $4.99; 152 pp.

A3   SEVENTY TIMES SEVEN   1939

a. First edition:

[in purplish black:] [large block print of barn in background with footsteps leading to it through snow, 9 x 6.7 cm.] | [in gothic script:] Seventy [shaded S] times | seven *A NOVEL BY* | JOHN SANFORD | NEW YORK • *ALFRED • A • KNOPF* • LONDON | 19 [publisher's device of a borzoi 1.8 x 1 cm.] 39.

20.4 x 13 cm. *1-13^8*. Pp.*i-x, 1-2, 3-195, 196-198.*

P.*i* blank; p.*ii* [enclosed in heavy-ruled box whose top and bottom lines end at text:] *RECENT BORZOI NOVELS* | [six titles on twelve lines] | [publisher's borzoi device] | PUBLISHED BY ALFRED • A • KNOPF; p.*iii* half title; p.*iv* blank; p.*v* title; p.*vi* copyright: [...] Manufactured in the United States of America. Published simultaneously in | Canada by the Ryerson Press. | FIRST EDITION; p.*vii* dedication: *For* [script F] MARGUERITE [Marguerite Roberts, J. S.'s wife, whom he had married just prior to the book's release]; p.*viii* blank; p.*ix* epigraph: [five lines from the Bible Book of Matthew 18:21-22]; p.*x* disclaimer; p.*1* fly title; p.*2* blank; pp.*3-195* text; p.*196* FROM WHARTON'S *CRIMINAL LAW* | [two quotations from sections 455 and 456 pertaining to "omission to perform acts of mercy," 17 lines] | [4 legal cases on 4 lines]; p.*197* blank; p.*198* [borzoi in double ruled oval, with thicker outer rule] | [notes on typography, printing and paper manufacturer].

Buckram covered boards, tan with darker and light brown threads woven in; printed in purple down the spine: [wavy ribbon pattern consisting of 20.5 loops of alternating thin and heavy lines, with unprinted center area for title], lettered down the spine: *SEVENTY TIMES SEVEN* • *JOHN SANFORD*, lettered across the spine in third loop from the foot: KNOPF; printed on upper cover: purple strip 1.4 cm high and the width of cover, [unprinted in the strip, in script:] *Seventy* [S is shaded and is higher than strip, with top 1 cm. printed in purple] *times seven*, printed on lower cover at foot: [borzoi device, 2.7 x 1.7 cm.]. Top edges speckled with purple; top and bottom edges cut; fore edges roughly cut; endpapers; flat spine. White glossy paper jacket printed in gray, bright red and purple, with painting by Lawrence which is a larger version of the woodcut on the title page; photograph of Sanford on back flap; ad for New Borzoi Novels on back, which says of *Seventy Times Seven*, "Written in a form that is as perfected as it is new and unusual, this extraordinary novel tells a story at once brutal and absorbing and reveals a talent both large and mature. No reader of novels can afford to miss it." Yellowish white wove paper.

Published 13 March 1939 at $2.00; number of copies not obtainable.

Note: Some copies have an extra set of endpapers at front and rear. Knopf issued an unknown number of advance reading copies of *Seventy Times Seven*, which consist of the finished pages of the novel, bound in gray paper wrappers printed in sepia. I have also observed a variant binding in light gray cloth, which is in all other respects identical.

Seventy Times Seven was the second of J. S.'s novels to be set in Warrensburg, NY, in the Adirondacks. It is expanded from J. S.'s story "I Let Him Die," published in *Pagany* with "Jasper Darby's Passion" as "Two Stories" (C12). The historical poem was reprinted in *Black & White* (C18).

Originally titled *I Let Him Die*, the novel was slated to be published by Knight in spring 1938 but was later pulled by J. S. when Knight could not guarantee a publication date. Additionally, J. S. was under contract with Knight to write the first biography of Ernest Hemingway (see E6f), a project J. S. never seriously pursued.

Contemporaneous with the Knopf publication, Constable had planned to issue *Seventy Times Seven* in Britain. However, J. S. refused to remove the historical blank verse section as well as "objectionable" material, so Constable did not publish the book.

Seventy Times Seven was initiated after J. S. aborted work on a novel first called *A Lingering Illness* and later called *David Holloway* (see E6e). Begun in early 1936, before J. S.'s move to California, much of *Seventy Times Seven* was written in the back yard of J. S.'s future wife, screenwriter Marguerite Roberts, dedicatee of the book. The ending was suggested by screenwriter and director Joseph Mankiewicz.

In style and content, *Seventy Times Seven* represents J. S.'s arrival at the top of his craft. As with his previous novel, *Seventy Times Seven* explores the violence inherent in America. However, through the addition of a historical blank verse section, J. S. roots contemporary violence in the violence perpetrated since whites set foot on the continent. These interpolations of historical material that amplifies and grounds the plot of the novel would become J. S.'s *sine qua non*.

b. First reprint edition (Avon), [1954]

[across opposing pages:] [left side: four-line epigraph from Psalm 139:8] | *Make My Bed* | Other books by John Sanford | [five titles, including *The Water Wheel* and *The Land that Touches Mine*, but excluding *A Man without Shoes*]; [right side:] *in Hell* | (Seventy Times Seven) | by John Sanford | complete and unabridged | AVON PUBLICATIONS, INC. | 575 Madison Avenue—New York 22, N.Y.

16.2 x 10.3 cm. *1-4, 5-159, 160*.

P.*1* three racy blurbs about the plot; pp.*2-3* title; p.*4* dedication | disclaimer | copyright [...] | Published by arrangement with the author | Printed in the U.S.A.; pp.5-158 text; p.159 [quotations from Wharton's *Criminal Law*] | [legal cases] | THE END; p.*160* advt.

Glossy yellowish white stiff paper wrappers; printed down the medium blue spine [in black:] JOHN SANFORD [in white:] Make My Bed in Hell by the author of | THE OLD MAN'S PLACE, and across near the foot of the spine [in pink:] 574 | [between two half circles:] AVON | III; printed in black on upper cover at top, in bright red strip 1.2 cm. high, [Avon device of two half circles with AVON in between, and [in white:] on top half 25¢ and on bottom 574], [in white:] by the author of THE OLD MAN'S PLACE; painting in light blue, pink and shades of greenish brown of a man and a woman in prelude to amorousness in what could be a hayloft, lettered across top [in yellow:] Make My Bed | [in white:] (SEVENTY TIMES SEVEN), [in yellow:] in Hell, and at the foot [in white:] by JOHN SANFORD | [in yellow:] complete and unabridged; lower cover printed in black and red, lettered in yellow and white; edges cut flush; all edges stained red; perfect binding. Yellowish white wove paper.

Published 14 April 1954 at $.25; 202,243 copies.

Note: this edition appears to be a reduced and repaginated photo-offset of A3a (1939), with same publisher's ornaments as in the original.

c. Second reprint edition (Avon), [1957]

Identical to A3b, except for a slightly wider leaf, 16.2 x 10.6 cm., and quoted criticism on p.*1*.

Glossy yellowish white stiff paper wrappers; lettered down the spine [in black on yellow:] John Sanford [in reddish orange on white:] MAKE MY BED IN HELL, across yellow foot of spine [in black:] 35¢ | [Avon device in reddish orange] | [in black:] T-189; upper cover printed on left in black, red and shades of blue with portrait of a hard-faced, smoldering-eyed man; a woman lies across the base of the cover, her red blouse torn, her brassiere exposed; lettered on left half [in white:] "Combination of Hemingway | and Caldwell" —*The New Yorker* | [in black:] AVON | [in red in a black box:] 35¢ | [in black:] T-189 | [in red:] JOHN SANFORD | [in black:] Complete and Unabridged | Originally published as | SEVENTY TIMES SEVEN; lettered in black on reddish orange, right half: MAKE | MY | BED | IN | HELL; lower cover repeats the woman's portrait in black on red at bottom, lettered in red, black and yellow; edges cut flush; all edges stained yellowish orange; perfect binding. Yellowish white wove paper.

Published August 1957 at $.35; 111,970 copies.

d. Third reprint edition (Brash Books), [2021]

MAKE MY BED | IN HELL | [in gray:] John Sanford | [publisher's device of a B with a fedora perched on it] RASH | BOOKS.

21.7 x 14 cm. *i-viii*, 1-159, 160-170, *171-174*.

P.*1* half title; p.*2* Books by John Sanford | [chronological list of 23 titles] | As Julian L. Shapiro | *The Water Wheel*; p.*3* title; p.*4* Copyright © 1939, 2021 by John Sanford | Afterword Copyright © 2021 by Jack Mearns | Previously published as "Seventy Times Seven." | [disclaimer] | ISBN-13: 978-1-7358517-2-3 | Published by | Brash Books [...]; p.*v* dedication; p.*vi* blank; p.*vii* [two lines from Psalm 139.8]; p.*viii* blank; p.*ix* Publisher's Note [warning crime fiction readers about J. S.'s unconventional stylistic elements, such as the historical poem]; p.*x* blank; pp.1-158 text; p.159 [quotations from Wharton's *Criminal Law*] | [legal cases] | p.*160* blank; pp.161-170 Afterword by Jack Mearns | pp.*171-173* blank; p.*174* Made in the U.S.A. | [...].

Glossy yellowish white stiff paper wrappers; lettered in white down the dark gray spine: JOHN SANFORD [in blue:] MAKE MY BED IN HELL [across spine] [unprinted: publisher's device]; the upper cover, printed in dark gray and shades of bluish gray, shows the back of a dismayed-looking figure in the foreground, regarding a snow-covered barn; upper cover lettered [in black:] JOHN SANFORD | [in lightening shades of gray:] MAKE MY | BED IN HELL; lower cover printed in dark gray and lettered in white and lavender; edges cut flush; perfect binding. Yellowish white wove paper.

Published 30 April 2021 at $17.99; print on demand.

e. Second hardcover edition (Brash Books), [2021]

[title page as in A3d]

21.7 x 14 cm. Identical to A3d, except for having printed paper boards that reproduce the paperback's spine and covers; ISBN-13: 978-1954841093; endpapers; flat spine.

Published 19 May 2021 at $27.99; print on demand.

f. First e-book edition (Brash Books), [2021]

[title page as in A3d and A3e]

Published 1 June 2021 at $4.99; 159 pp.

A4   THE PEOPLE FROM HEAVEN   1943

a. First edition:

THE PEOPLE | FROM HEAVEN | by | JOHN SANFORD | [four line quotation from Christopher Columbus] | NEW YORK | HARCOURT, BRACE AND COMPANY

18.6 x 12.2 cm. 1-15^8. Pp.*i-vi*, 1-2, 3-232, *233-234*.

P.*i* half title; p.*ii By the same author* | [three titles]; p.*iii* title; p.*iv* COPYRIGHT, 1943, BY | JOHN SANFORD […] | *first edition* | […] | PRINTED IN THE UNITED STATES OF AMERICA;

p.*v* dedication: TO NATHANAEL WEST | 1903-1940; p.*vi* blank; p.*1* fly title; p.*2* blank; pp.3-44 text; pp.45-56 historical piece; pp.57-65 text; pp.66-72 historical piece; pp.73-80 text; pp.81-85 historical piece; pp.86-109 text; p.110 historical piece; p.111 text; pp.112-118 historical piece; pp.119-123 text; pp.124-130 historical piece; pp.131-148 text; pp.149-157 historical piece; pp.158-168 text; pp.169-176 historical piece; pp.177-199 text; pp.200-201 historical piece; pp.202-232 text; pp.*233-234* blank.

Navy blue cloth boards with a wavy texture; stamped in white across the spine: THE | PEOPLE | FROM | HEAVEN | JOHN | SANFORD, and at the foot: Harcourt, Brace | and Company. All edges cut; endpapers. Yellowish white dust jacket, printed in light olive green and black, designed by E. McKnight Kauffer, with a black and a white pointing hand; unattributed photograph of J. S. by Marguerite Roberts on back flap. Yellowish white wove paper.

Published 28 October 1943 at $2.50; number of copies not obtainable.

Note: Harcourt issued an unknown number of advance proof copies of *The People from Heaven*, which consist of page proofs bound in greenish blue paper wrappers, string-tied on the left, with wording hand-written in black ink on the upper cover.

The novel grew from "The Fire at the Catholic Church," which appeared in *Contact* (C13). It also incorporates material from "Once in a Sedan and Twice Standing Up," which also appeared in *Contact* (C14). In *The People from Heaven*, J. S. achieved the style that would remain his favored method for the rest of his novels, interposing historical vignettes, which he would later say gave the color of the air—infusing the text with historical undercurrents.

These historical pieces appear in *The People from Heaven*: "I'll Bring You Back Chicago" (1492 A.D.)—The People from Heaven (1607 A.D.)—Dutch Treat (1619 A.D.)—Captain Shrimp, and Certain Others (1620 A.D.)—The First Knee on Canada (1632 A.D.)—Land of Beans and God (1691 A.D.)—God in the Hands of an Angry Sinner (1741 A.D.)—The Man in the Black Coat (1775 A.D.)—The Blue and the Gray-and the Black (1863 A.D.). These pieces previously appeared in *The Clipper*: "I'll Bring You Back Chicago" (C21), "The People from Heaven" (C22) and "The First Knee on Canada" published as "First Knee in Canada" (C23). Portions of this novel were reprinted in *Negro Digest* as "The Lincolns Never Shoot" (see C24). Quotes also appear in *A Class of its Own* (B24).

The novel was on the cutting edge of fiction, and few publishers could see any hope of profit in it. Under the terms of his contract for *Seventy Times Seven*, J. S. submitted *The People from Heaven* to Knopf. Knopf replied, "We all feel the book is a mistake...too difficult to read, to understand, and to sell." Duell, Sloan and Pearce worried that the book's graphicness would make the book impossible to send through the mails. Reynal and Hitchcock wrote, "You've combined so many experimental techniques that I am afraid even a better than average reader would come up with a feeling of frustration." Even the Communist Party tried to dissuade J. S. from publishing the book as is. They feared it would inspire Blacks to revolt, a premature uprising doomed to failure.

Through a hard-fought campaign and partially on the basis of a promised next novel, John Woodburn, an editor at Harcourt, was able to convince his firm to publish the book. Through its focus on history, in particular the links between the earliest white settlers' extermination of the Indian and America's exploitation of enslaved Africans, *The People from Heaven* set J. S.'s writing on the path it would follow for the rest of his career. It is an unflinching examination of America's legacy of racial hatred and violence.

b. First reprint edition (Liberty Book Club), [1947]

THE PEOPLE | FROM HEAVEN | by | JOHN SANFORD | [four line quotation from Christopher Columbus] | LIBERTY BOOK CLUB | NEW YORK

18.5 x 12.2 cm. 1^8 2-4^{16} 5^8 6-8^{16} 9^8. Pagination identical to A4a.

Beige woven cloth boards; lettered in purple across the spine: THE | PEOPLE | FROM | HEAVEN | JOHN | SANFORD, and at the foot: L • B • C. Top and bottom edges cut, fore edges roughly cut; endpapers. Yellowish white dust jacket, printed in gray-blue and white, with an angel wing at the top, lettered in gray-blue on back. Yellowish white wove paper.

Published 1947 at $2.75; number of copies not obtainable.

Note: This edition was printed with the Harcourt plates and is identical to A4a, with the exception of the publisher information on the title page and the removal of *first edition* and changed printer information on the copyright.

c. First paperback reprint edition (University of Illinois Press), [1995]

The People | from Heaven | [rule] | JOHN SANFORD | Introduction by Alan Wald | University of Illinois Press | Urbana and Chicago

20.3 x 13.3 cm. 1^{16} 2^8 3^{16} 4^8 5^{16} 6^4 7^2 8-10^{16} 11^2 12^{16}. Pp.*i-viii*, ix-xxxvi, *1-2*, 3-232, *233-236*.

P.*i* THE RADICAL NOVEL RECONSIDERED | A series of paperback reissues of mid-twentieth-century | U.S. left-wing fiction [...] | *Series Editor* | Alan Wald, University of Michigan; p.*ii* BOOKS IN THE SERIES [four titles on eight lines]; p.*iii* half title; p.*iv* blank; p.*v* title; p.*vi* © 1943, 1971, 1995 by John Sanford [...] | Manufactured in the United States of America | P 5 4 3 2 1 | *This book is printed on acid-free paper.* | [...] | ISBN 0-252-06491-7 (pbk.) | [...]; p.*vii* dedication; p.*viii* epigraph [three lines from Christopher Columbus]; pp.*ix-x* preface; pp.xi-xxxvi introduction; pp.*1-232* identical to A4a and A4b; p.*233* author and editor biographical data; pp.*234-236* blank.

Glossy yellowish white stiff paper wrappers; printed thin red band 1.1 cm. across the top, front to back; lettered across the top of the spine [in white, on black oval, on red band:] [small ornament] RNR [small ornament]; down the spine [in black:] THE PEOPLE FROM HEAVEN [in red:] SANFORD [in black:] UNIVERSITY OF | ILLINOIS PRESS; on upper cover at the top: [RNR device] lettered [in white on red band:] THE RADICAL NOVEL RECONSIDERED | [in black:] THE PEOPLE | FROM HEAVEN | [color illustration by Jack Davis surrounded by a black and brown rule, 10.6 x 10.6] | JOHN SANFORD | Introduction by Alan Wald; lettered in black on lower cover; edges cut flush; perfect binding. Yellowish white wove paper.

Published 1 February 1996 at $15.95; 1,750 copies.

Contents: Preface by J. S.—Introduction by Alan Wald [the rest as in A4a and A4b].

Note: The text of this edition was photo offset printed from A4a.

A5   A MAN WITHOUT SHOES   1951

a. First edition:

[in bright red:] A MAN | WITHOUT | SHOES | *A NOVEL* BY JOHN SANFORD | [floral ornament] | *Los Angeles* : THE PLANTIN PRESS : 1951

25 x 16.2 cm. *1*^{4} *2-29*^{8} *30*^{4}. Pp.*i-viii*, 1-79, *80*, 81-452, *453-456*.

P.*i* half title; p.*ii* blank; p.*iii* title; p.*iv* COPYRIGHT, 1951, BY | JOHN SANFORD | [...] | PRINTED IN THE U. S. A.; p.*v* dedication: IN MEMORY OF | SARAH AND HARRIS FRIEDMAN [J. S.'s paternal aunt and uncle]; p.*vi* Other books by John Sanford | [four titles]; p.*vii* epigraph: "The people are a powerful source of power." [unattributed quotation from Paul Robeson]; p.*viii* blank; pp.1-79 text; p.80 blank; pp.81-452 text; p.*453* blank; p.*454* [woodcut of printers at work 4.4 x 2.6 cm.] | TWO THOUSAND COPIES OF | A MAN WITHOUT SHOES | PRINTED IN EHRHARDT TYPE | BY SAUL & LILLIAN MARKS AT THE | PLANTIN PRESS, LOS ANGELES | THIS IS NUMBER | [hand-written number] | AND IS SIGNED BY THE AUTHOR | [signed]; pp.*455-456* blank.

Paper boards printed in beige and brown in a woven wicker pattern; spine of coarse green cloth; beige paper spine label 6.3 x 4.2 cm., lettered across in orangish red, within a garland border: A Man | Without | Shoes | [wavy line] | *John Sanford*. Top edges cut, bottom edges roughly trimmed, page ends uncut. Tan dust jacket printed in orangish red and brown; back flap is an order blank, listing J. S.'s home address in Encino. Yellowish white wove paper.

Published 15 June 1951 at $10.00; 2,000 copies.

Note: A single trial copy was bound with a light blue cloth spine and a larger spine label. It is in J. S.'s archive at Boston University.

Originally titled *Johnson, Daniel*, this novel has a star-crossed history. Initially sought by Harcourt while still a concept, the finished novel was rejected by them. The book was next accepted by Reynal and Hitchcock in 1945. But Curtice Hitchcock, the liberal member of the house, was killed in a car crash, and the contract was canceled in 1947. In June 1950, after 33 rejections, including two prior ones by Little, Brown, the book was accepted by Little, Brown, one of whose editors called the book "the closest thing to the great American novel that I have seen yet, a major contribution to our literature." However, the Korean War broke out within days, and the book's vehement left-leanings again made it commercially unpublishable.

J. S. originally had had an agent to shop *Man* around. However, eventually the agent quit, and J. S. relied upon his cousin Mel Friedman, who had placed his first two books with publishers. However, the strain of his string of rejections—uniformly over the political content of the book—shows in a letter from J. S. to Friedman (6/12/49):

Dear Mel:

Your letter was a cold sheet of paper, no doubt the wrapping off that stiff hunk of meat you call a heart.

But that you piss ice-water is no new thing. What is is your sudden appearance on the side of publishers, spouting their advice about how to improve a book: cut the balls off, draw the blood, pull the teeth, and strangle it, and we'll be glad to print it.

Get another boy. And while I'm on the subject, I think I'll get another myself. Please return my manuscript.

Sincerely,

J. S. finally contracted with Saul Marx's Plantin Press to privately publish the book. J. S. had become acquainted with Marx as the printer for the periodicals *Black & White* and *The Clipper*. The book has never been reprinted by a commercial publisher. In 1953, Doubleday considered putting out *Man*, but poor sales of *The Land that Touches Mine* (A6) led them to decline.

Because *A Man without Shoes* was self-published, no periodical would review it. J. S. recorded that a mere 382 copies of *A Man without Shoes* were distributed by 1982: 268 sold either personally or through local booksellers and 114 given away to friends or as promotional copies. J. S. reported that in 1956 five copies were sold through a bookstore without a number; all others were signed and numbered. The remainder of the books were put into storage until March 1982, when Black Sparrow arranged to reissue them with a new 8-page introduction by J. S. tipped in (see B10). Additionally, Black Sparrow stamped the base of the dust jacket's front with its device and name, stamped out the price on the front flap, and stamped out J. S.'s address on the back flap, printing Black Sparrow's above. Approximately 1,500 copies were issued at $25.00.

J. S. signed and numbered nearly all of these in two marathon sessions, although he reported Black Sparrow noted 75 damaged copies. I have observed unsigned and unnumbered copies in mixed states: with and without the Black Sparrow introduction, some of which have the original dust jacket, and some of which have the altered one.

Much of the novel contains historical material. These separate historical pieces appear in *A Man without Shoes*: Buckeye Johnny Appleseed—O Those Wabash Blues—Marse Linkum—Like Sap in a Tree—Had I So Interfered on Behalf of the Rich—A Man Name of James Wilson Marshall—Paul Bunyan and Friend—The State of Washington—On the Little Big Horn—Father of Waters—Vicksburg '63—Bob Anderson, My Beau Bob—This Will Have a Very Happy Effect. The following pieces first appeared in *New Masses*: "Had I So Interfered on Behalf of the Rich," published as "Marse Brown" (C25), and "Marse Linkum" (C26).

In style, *A Man without Shoes* is more fluid than *The People from Heaven*, melding the historical with the contemporary narrative. In a letter to Albert Maltz, who had questioned including the historical prose poems, J. S. noted, "*Anything* belongs in a novel that in any way contributes to it. These poems, all representing an unconscious assimilation by [the protagonist] of his country's history and meaning, add much to his understanding, stature, direction and sympathies, and they need no defense."

In content, the novel is J. S.'s first explicitly leftist book, focusing much attention on Sacco and Vanzetti and containing an extended section in which the protagonist recounts the contents of Marxist economics lectures he attends. This is perhaps the book's fatal flaw. In striving so hard to communicate the philosophy that would soon lead to his blacklisting, J. S. neglects the demands of plot. He descends to delivering a lecture to the reader and abandons dramatizing the message he wants the reader to receive. A letter from Pascal Covici at Viking (2/28/49) illustrates this point:

> The first 75 pages delighted me. It was good story telling, excellent characterization, amusing and emotional writing. Then the characters, to me, become marionettes and you pull them wherever your propagandizing leads you, with sermons and speeches and long wordy conversations which lead nowhere, nothing particularly illuminating or newly interpretive. Yet, interspersed, there is some good novel writing but almost completely lost in the shouting exhortations of your thesis.

A Man without Shoes was broadcast on radio in its entirety (see E2b).

b. First e-book edition (Bloomsbury Reader), [2013]

A MAN | WITHOUT | SHOES | JOHN SANFORD | [publisher's device with a reversed script B and forward script R] | BLOOMSBURY READER | LONDON • NEW DELHI • NEW YORK • SYDNEY

ISBN: 9781448213252

Published 12 September 2013 at $6.50; 452 pp.

A6   THE LAND THAT TOUCHES MINE   1953

a. First edition:

THE LAND THAT | TOUCHES MINE | *A Novel* by | JOHN SANFORD | [publisher's device of an urn with fruit on top and J and C on either side beneath the rim, enclosed in a double circle with the inner rule heavier, 1.6 cm.] | [epigraph from Abraham Lincoln: 8 lines] | LONDON | JONATHAN CAPE 30 BEDFORD SQUARE

19.2 x 12.1 cm. A^8 B-O^8. Pp.*1-6*, 7, *8-14*, 15, *16-18*, 19-33, *34-36*, 37-49, *50*, 51, *52-54*, 55-90, *91-92*, 93-126, *127-128*, 129-156, *157-158*, 159-183, *184*, 185-186, *187-188*, 189-222, *223-224*.

Pp.*1-2* blank; p.*3* half title, p.*4* blank; p.*5* title; p.*6* FIRST PUBLISHED 1953 | PRINTED IN GREAT BRITAIN IN THE CITY OF OXFORD | AT THE ALDEN PRESS | BOUND BY A. W. BAIN & CO. LTD., LONDON; p.*7* contents; p.*8* blank; p.*9* epigraph: [8 lines from Bartolomeo Vanzetti]; p.*10* blank; p.*11* dedication: *This book | is for my mother* [who died when J. S. was ten years old]; p.*12* blank; p.*13* fly title; p.*14* blank; p.*15* historical piece; p.*16* blank; p.*17* section title; p.*18* blank; pp.19-32 text;

p.33 historical piece; p.*34* blank; p.*35* section title; p.*36* blank; pp.37-49 text; p.*50* blank; p.51 historical piece; p.*52* blank; p.*53* section title; p.*54* blank; pp.55-88 text; pp.89-90 historical piece; p.*91* section title; p.*92* blank; pp.93-124 text; pp.125-126 historical piece; p.*127* section title; p.*128* blank; pp.129-154 text; pp.155-156 historical piece; p.*157* section title; p.*158* blank; pp.159-183 text; p.*184* blank; pp.185-186 historical piece; p.*187* section title; p.*188* blank; pp.189-222 text; pp.*223-224* blank.

Periwinkle cloth boards, printed in lavender across the spine: THE | LAND | THAT | TOUCHES | MINE | [publisher's device of one long curving line, with two shorter lines on either side of its middle, 2.1 cm.] | JOHN | SANFORD, and at the foot: [publisher's urn device]; stamped across the upper cover: THE LAND THAT TOUCHES MINE. Top and fore edges cut; bottom edges roughly trimmed; endpapers. Yellowish white dust jacket printed in lavender, gray and orange, with unprinted back. Yellowish white wove paper.

Published 11 May 1953 at 12 s. 6 d.; 2,000 copies.

Note: There was a second impression of 1,000 copies issued 1 July 1953, making the Cape edition the only one of J. S.'s books to go into a second printing.

    J. S.'s archive contains an advance uncorrected proof copy of *The Land that Touches Mine*, which consists of page proofs bound in light brownish yellow paper wrappers printed in black. This is the only copy I have seen.

    J. S.'s working title for the novel was *The Bandage*. The publication history of *The Land that Touches Mine* is intimately tied with that of *A Man Without Shoes*. By 1949, J. S. was showing both books to potential publishers. In June 1950, *The Land that Touches Mine* was accepted with *A Man Without Shoes* by Little,

Brown. However, after the outbreak of the Korean War, the agreement was withdrawn.

In 1951, J. S. and his wife, Marguerite Roberts, were subpoenaed to testify before the House Committee on Un-American Activities in Los Angeles. Both took the Fifth Amendment, refusing to name names, and both were blacklisted. Unable to work in Hollywood, the couple soon left for Europe, fearing that, if they delayed, their passports would be confiscated.

J. S. took along with him the manuscript for *The Land that Touches Mine*. At the urging of his wife, he offered it to Jonathan Cape, who accepted the book. According to Tom Dardis (see B13) Cape "dared" Doubleday to issue an American edition. This is the only book of J. S.'s to be published outside the U. S.

As in *The People from Heaven*, *The Land that Touches Mine* uses historical pieces to punctuate the action of the novel. These historical pieces appear: The Only Good Indian—I Only Want the Land that Touches Mine—The Unspotted Lambs of the Lord—Ever Thus to Tyrants—A Juror: "I'd Hang All the Damn Buggers."—"It Has Been a Splendid Little War."—Champagne for Our Real Friends.

Centered on the theme of man's inhumanity to man, which J. S. depicts as stemming from the earliest conquest of America by Europeans and their introduction to North America of the institution of slavery, *The Land that Touches Mine* is another explicitly radical book. On the whole, *Land* is a more successful novel than *A Man without Shoes*, as its politics is more at the service of the narrative, rather than vice versa. Still, at times, one can observe J. S. struggling too hard to impart his message, in this case using a character who is a teacher to lecture on politics to the captive audience of the reader.

In 1954-1955, Marguerite Roberts wrote a stage adaptation of *The Land that Touches Mine* that was never produced.

b. First American edition:

[epigraph from Abraham Lincoln: 11 lines] | THE LAND | THAT TOUCHES | MINE | A NOVEL BY JOHN SANFORD

20.3 x 13 cm. *1-8*^{16}. Pp.*i-ii*, 1-16, 17-33, *34-36*, 37-52, *53-54*, 55-96, *97-100*, 101-138, *139-140*, 141-172, *173-176*, 177-206, *207-210*, 211-251, *252-254*.

Pp.*i-ii* blank; p.*1* half title; p.*2* blank; p.*3* BY JOHN SANFORD | [five titles, including *The Land that Touches Mine* but excluding *A Man without Shoes*]; p.*4* DOUBLEDAY & COMPANY, INC., GARDEN CITY, N.Y. 1953; p.*5* title; p.*6* […] | Copyright, 1953, by John Sanford | […] | Printed in the United States at | The Country Life Press, Garden City, N.Y. | First Edition | Designed by Diana Klemin; p.*7* dedication; p.*8* blank; p.*9* epigraph [12 lines from Bartolomeo Vanzetti]; p.*10* blank; p.*11* contents; p.*12* blank; p.*13* fly title; p.*14* blank; p.*15* historical piece and section title; p.*16* blank; pp.17-33 text; p.*34* blank; p.*35* historical piece; p.*36* section title; pp.37-52 text; p.*53* historical piece; p.*54* [historical piece continued, 4 lines] section title; pp.55-96 text; pp.*97-98* historical piece; p.*99* section title; p.*100* blank; pp.101-138 text; p.*139* historical piece; p.*140* [historical piece continued, 2 lines] section title; pp.141-172 text; pp.*173-174* historical piece; p.*175* section title; p.*176* blank; pp.177-206 text; pp.*207-208* historical piece; p.*209* section title; p.*210* blank; pp.211-251 text; pp.*252-254* blank.

Bright yellow cloth boards, stamped in orangish red [down the spine:] THE LAND THAT TOUCHES MINE | [across the spine at the foot:] JOHN SANFORD | DOUBLEDAY. Top edges cut; bottom edges roughly cut; foredges roughly trimmed; endpapers; flat spine. Yellowish white dust jacket printed in grayish blue, pale yellow, white and black; designed by Ted [Edward]

Gorey; front depicts a man and a woman, and in the background a close-up of a bandaged hand; with a photo of J. S. on back. Yellowish white wove paper.

Published 28 May 1953 at $3.00; number of copies not obtainable.

Note: Publication of this American edition was arranged by Jonathan Cape. It was one of the few bright spots for the blacklisted Sanfords, now in internal exile in the U.S. However, sales were poor. By 31 October 1953, 1,441 copies had sold. And by 30 April 1954, 423 of those had been returned.

    J. S. would adapt *The Land that Touches Mine* for the screen in 1960 (see E3i). But, while his wife remained unable to work for films, he could not bring himself to write books. It would be more than ten years until his next novel appeared. And in it the bitterness of that fallow decade would be evident.

c. First reprint edition (Tough Poets), [2021]

[epigraph from Abraham Lincoln: 10 lines] | THE LAND | THAT TOUCHES | MINE | A NOVEL BY JOHN SANFORD | Tough Poets Press | Arlington, Massachusetts

21 x 14.8 cm. Pp. *1-6*, 7-22, *23-30*, 31-44, *45-46*, 47-59, *60-62*, 63-96, *97-100*, 101-131, *132-134*, 135-160, *161-164*, 165-188, *189-192*, 193-225, *226*, 227-228, *229-234*.

Pp.*1* blank; p.*2* Books by John Sanford | [categorical listing of 25 titles]; p.*3* title; p.*4* [...] | Copyright © 1953 by John Sanford | Copyright © renewed 1981 by John Sanford | Introduction copyright © 2021 by Jack Mearns [...] | ISBN 978-0-578-93795-3 | This edition published with permission from | The Estate of John Sanford in 2021 by: | Tough Poets Press | [...]; p.*5* dedication; p.*6* blank; pp.7-22 Introduction by Jack Mearns; p.*23* [10 lines from Bartolomeo Vanzetti]; p.*24* blank; p.*25* contents; p.*26* blank; p.*27* fly title; p.*28* blank; p.*29* historical piece; p.*30* section title; pp.31-44 text; p.*45* historical piece; p.*46* section title; pp.47-59 text; pp.*60-61* historical piece; p.*62* section title; pp.63-96 text; pp.*97-98* historical piece; p.*99* section title; p.*100* blank; pp.101-131 text; pp.*132-133* historical piece; p.*134* section title; pp.135-160 text; pp.*161-162* historical piece; p.*163* section title; p.*164* blank; pp.165-188 text; pp.*189-190* historical piece; p.*191* section title; p.*192* blank; pp.193-225 text; pp.*226* blank; pp.227-228 Acknowledgments: Profound thanks are extended to the following for their generous financial support which helped to defray some of the book's production costs [names of Kickstarter campaign contributors]; pp.*229-233* blank; p.*234* CPSIA information [...].

Glossy white stiff paper wrappers printed in yellow and shades of brown and orange; lettered down the spine [in white:] John Sanford [in yellow:] THE LAND THAT TOUCHES MINE; lettered on the upper cover [flush right:] [in white:] John | Sanford [in yellow:] THE | LAND | THAT | TOUCHES | MINE; the upper cover reproduces a photograph [circa 1938 by Rondal Partridge] of a young man in overalls gazing at his shadow, which lies across arid land; on the bottom cover is a photograph of a wary-looking J. S. taken for his 1951 passport; edges cut flush; perfect binding. Yellowish white wove paper.

Published 10 August 2021 at $15.99; print on demand.

A7 EVERY ISLAND FLED AWAY 1964

First edition:

JOHN SANFORD | EVERY | [snowflake ornament] | ISLAND | [snowflake] | FLED | [snowflake] | AWAY | *New York* W • W • NORTON & COMPANY • INC •

21.2 x 14.1 cm. $1\text{-}6^{16}$. Pp.*1-8, 9-187, 188-192*.

P.*1* half title: EVERY | ISLAND | FLED | AWAY | [publisher's device of gull in an oval 2.6 x 1 cm.]; p.*3* NOVELS BY JOHN SANFORD | [7 titles, including *A Man without Shoes* and *Every Island Fled Away*]; p.*3* title; p.*4* COPYRIGHT © 1964 BY JOHN SANFORD | *First Edition* | [...] | Published simultaneously in the Dominion of | Canada by George J. McCleod Limited, Toronto | PRINTED IN THE UNITED STATES OF AMERICA | FOR THE PUBLISHERS BY THE VAIL-BALLOU PRESS, INC. | 123456789; p.*5* dedication: [snowflake ornament] | TO MY FATHER, WITH LOVE | [snowflake]; p.*6* blank; p.*7* fly title; p.*8* epigraph: ... and the mountains were not found. | Rev. 16.20; pp.9-187 text; pp.*188-192* blank.

One-third yellowish gray cloth and reddish orange paper boards; printed across spine [in red:] SANFORD | [in black:] EVERY | [snowflake ornament] ISLAND | [snowflake] | FLED | [snowflake] | AWAY | [in red:] NORTON; stamped in black on the upper cover: [device of flying bird carrying an arrow 3.5 x 3.2 cm.]. Top edges cut; bottom and fore edges roughly trimmed; endpapers. Yellowish white dust jacket printed in orangish red, black and gray, repeating bird in flight with arrow on front; photo of a decidedly surly J. S. on back flap. Yellowish white wove paper.

Published 23 October 1964 at $3.95; number of copies not obtainable.

Note: *Every Island Fled Away* marks the return of J. S. to writing, after his wife was able to return to films from the blacklist; she was one of the first blacklisted writers to do so. Sales were poor: by 31 March 1965, 1,561 copies had sold; by 30 September of that year, 652 of those copies had been returned. The book was remaindered nine months after original release. Jonathan Cape explored the possibility of publishing the book in England, but they did not follow through because of anticipated small sales.

When one follows the trail of J. S.'s submissions for *Every Island*, it is clear what a small world the publishing industry was, and how the burned bridges and bad blood of his *A Man without Shoes* submissions haunted his *Island* efforts fifteen years later.

The bitterness of the blacklist years is evident in this sequel to *The Land that Touches Mine*. It also bears some similarities to *The People from Heaven*, although the setting has been changed from Warrensburg to the Northern California Coast. *Every Island Fled Away* is a dark, spare book, almost entirely devoid of exposition, and lacking historical pieces.

In content, the book anticipates the tumult of the 1960s, with a small town divided over a young man's refusal to register for the draft. J. S. used a minister as his protagonist to sit in judgment over the town. The minister is the brother of the teacher-protagonist in *The Land that Touches Mine*.

A8   THE $300 MAN   1967

First edition:

[in bold:] THE | $300 | MAN | [not bold:] by | John Sanford | Prentice-Hall, Inc. | Englewood Cliffs, N. J.

21.2 x 14.1 cm. *1-11*^{8}. Pp.*i-viii*, 1-161, *162-168*.

P.*i* half title; p.*ii* Books by John Sanford | [7 titles]; p.*iii* title; p.*iv* [...] | © 1967 by John Sanford | [...] • Printed in the United | States of America • T92029 | [...]; p.*v* dedication: For Maggie [J. S.'s wife, Marguerite Roberts], *with love*; p.*vi* blank; p.*vii* fly title; p.*viii* blank; pp.1-161 text; p.*162* blank; p.*163* ABOUT THE TYPE | The text in this book was set in 11 point Jan – | son Linotype, leaded 4 points. [...]; pp.*164-168* blank.

One-quarter orangish bronze cloth and blue paper boards; lettered in blue on the spine [across:] Sanford | [down:] *THE $300 MAN* | [across the foot:] Prentice | Hall. All edges cut; top edges stained blue; endpapers. Yellowish white dust jacket printed in deep blue, bright orange, white and black; photo of J. S. on back. Yellowish white wove paper.

Published 30 March 1967 at $4.95; number of copies not known.

Note: By 30 March 1967, 3,065 copies had sold; one year later 1,647 of those copies had been returned. The book was remaindered 15 September 1968, with 5,416 copies on hand.

Originally titled *The Hero Suit*, the novel was based on a screenplay by Marguerite Roberts of the same name, a dramatization of *The Old Man's Place* (A2).

The $300 Man returns to themes from *The Land that Touches Mine* and *Every Island Fled Away*, this time with a soldier returned from war seeking to make amends to the man who was drafted in his place when he originally was given a fraudulent medical deferment. Inspired by Roberts's screenplay for a previous novel, *The $300 Man* is something of a rehash, presenting familiar characters, somewhat changed since the earlier works. This novel was poorly received by critics; it marked the end of J. S.'s career as a novelist. J. S. was 63 years old.

Joseph McBride (see B30) reports that Prentice-Hall had intended to bring all of J. S.'s novels back into print; however, poor sales nixed that plan.

A9   A MORE GOODLY COUNTRY   1975

First edition:

A | *More Goodly* | COUNTRY | *A personal history of America* | John Sanford | HORIZON PRESS | NEW YORK

23.4 x 15.3 cm. 1^8 $2\text{-}3^{16}$ 4^2 $5\text{-}6^8$ 7^4 $8\text{-}12^{16}$ 13^2. Pp.*i-ii, 1-5*, 6-11, *12*, 13-285, *286*.

P.*i* half title; p.*ii other books by John Sanford* | [8 titles]; p.*1* title; p.*2* Copyright © 1975 by John Sanford | [...] | ISBN 0-8180-0814-8 | Manufactured in the United States of America; p.*3* dedication: to | William Carlos Williams | 1883-1963 | *in bronze above a doorway*; p.*4* blank; pp.*5*-11 contents; p.*12* blank; pp.13-285 text; p.*286* blank.

Light olive-green cloth boards; stamped in gold down the spine [in a ruled box:] John | Sanford [in a ruled box:] A *More Goodly* | COUNTRY, and across the foot: HORIZON | PRESS; stamped at the foot of upper cover: [J. S.'s signature above a diagonal line]. All edges cut; endpapers. White dust jacket printed in black, brown, olive green, and yellowish green; photo of J. S. on back flap, from same shoot as photo for *The $300 Man*. Yellowish white wove paper.

Published 28 March 1975 at $12.95; number of copies not obtainable.

Contents: 1000 North America-A Place Called Here—1000 Leif Ericson-Vicar of Christ—1492 Christopher Columbus, I-The Log of the *Santa Maria*—1492 Christopher Columbus, II-The Wake of the *Santa Maria*—1519 The Mississippi-River of the Holy Spirit—1521 Juan Ponce de Leon-A Remedy for Time—1540 Francisco de Coronado-Draw Me Not without Reason—1542 Hernando de Soto-Adelantado of Florida—1587 Virginia Dare-First Lady—1607 Jamestown-The People from Heaven—1609 Henry Hudson-The Men in the Moon—1617 Pokahontas-Lady Rebekah—1619 Slavery in Virginia-Where All the Blues Began—1628 Plimmoth Plantation, I-A Man of Pretie Parts—1632 Plimmoth Plantation, II-Nor His Ass—1632 The Jesuits-The First

JOHN SANFORD

Knee on Canada—1638 Anne Hutchinson-Those Total Depravitie Blues—1646 Annotations-Winthrop's Journal—1652 John Cotton-Death of a Clergyman—1660 The Quakers-Pass Not Over the Brook—1691 Witchcraft, I-The Deuce in Massachusetts—1691 Witchcraft II-Evil from Us Deliver—16__ *The Scarlet Letter*-Ad Libs by a Fictitious Character—1703 Deerfield-Lovers of the Uppermost Seats—1728 Cotton Mather-Blues for a Christian—1741 Heaven and Earth-God in the Hands of an Angry Sinner—1745 George Washington-King George—1755 Gen. Edward Braddock-What Will the Duke Say?—1759 Society of Friends-Gadfly—1774 George Washington-First Gent of Virginia—1775 Runaway Slave-The Man in the Black Coat—1775 One of the Daughters-D.A.R.—1776 The Declaration-Rebellion of the Well-Fed—1776 George Washington-The Boys in Buff and Blue—1787 Constitutional Convention-Bystander in Philadelphia—1787 Federalism-The People: A Great Beast—1788 Rip Van Winkle-In the Kaatskills—1790 Benjamin Franklin-Old Man on a $100 Bill—1793 George Washington-A Constitutional in Philadelphia—1799 *Benito Cereno*-A Visitor from the *Bachelor's Delight*—1809 Abraham Lincoln-The Kentucky Abraham—1809 Thomas Paine-The Bones of a Pamphleteer—1823 James Monroe-A License to Steal—1826 Thomas Jefferson-Notes for a Speech on the 4th of July—1830 Slavery-The Peculiar Institution—1836 The Alamo-Gone to Texas—1836 A Mexican Shepherd-Under a Lone Star—1836 Samuel Colt-New and Useful—1837 Elijah P. Lovejoy-A Round Trip to Alton—1845 Margaret Fuller-The Bluestocking—1845 Andrew Jackson-Oh, Lord! Old Massa's Dead!—1846 The Donner Party-Winter Carnival—1847 John Chapman-Buckeye Johnny Appleseed—1847 Ralph A. Blakelock-A Dreamer Perishes—1848 John Quincy Adams-The Last of the Superbas—1848 John Jacob Astor-The Landlord—1848 Sutter's Mill-Alta California—1849 Edgar Allan Poe-In Bronze above a Doorway—1851 John James Audubon-Every Bird of

Every Sort—1852 Harriet Beecher Stowe-The Lord Himself Wrote It—1854 Runaway Slave-The Law Must Be Executed!—1856 Charles Sumner-The Head which is Gold—1857 Dred Scott-Like the Sap in a Tree!—1858 Lincoln-Douglas Debates-Twenty-one Hours in Illinois—1859 At Harper's Ferry-Oh, Dear Dangerfield—1859 John Brown-Had I So Interfered in Behalf of the Rich—1859 John D. Rockefeller-Petra, *Rock* + Oleum, *Oil*—1861 Abraham Lincoln-Illinois Central Caboose—1861 Abraham Lincoln-First Inaugural—1861 Fort Sumter-Tall Talk in South Carolina—1861 Robert E. Lee-Chivalry vs. Shovelry—1862 Henry Thoreau-A Call of Nature—1862 J. Pierpont Morgan-A Lesson in Business—1862 Abraham Lincoln-At the Telegraph Office—1863 Vicksburg-Hundred Years' War—1863 Soldier, Union Army-The Blue and the Gray-and the Black—1863 The Address-Cemetery at Gettysburg—1864 Gen. N. B. Forrest-Low Company in Tennessee—1864 Col. J. M. Chivington-Inquiry into a Massacre—1865 Mathew Brady-War for All to See—1865 Abraham Lincoln-Second Inaugural—1865 Fall of Richmond-Appomattox, 95 Miles—1865 The Surrender-Army of Northern Virginia—1865 John Wilkes Booth-Play within a Play—1865 Mary Lincoln-Good Friday at Ford's Theatre—1865 Abraham Lincoln-Seven Cars in Black Bunting—1865 Abraham Lincoln-Marse Linkum—1866 Chinese in California-The Pig-Business—1868 Thaddeus Stevens-This Quiet and Secluded Spot—1869 The Lobby-The Nast People—1869 Union Pacific-Deseret—1870 R. E. Lee and *Traveller*-A Pair of Confederates—1872 George Catlin-Painter of the Painted Indian—1874 Henry Ward Beecher-On a Couch in the Vestry—1875 Frank Lloyd Wright-Gifts for Her Son—1875 *Sequoia Gigantea*-The Mighty Fallen—1876 Crazy Horse—Hoka Hey!—1876 Gen. George Custer-On the Little Bighorn—1877 The Molly Maguires-Class Struggle—1878 Boss Tweed-Wrong-way Alger-boy—1885 The King Ranch-The Running *W*—1885 U. S. Grant-Last in Peace—1885 The Vanderbilts-Monument to Manure—1886 Emily

JOHN SANFORD

Dickinson-Revenge of the Nerves—1886 The Haymarket, I-A Juror: *I'd Hang all the Damn* Buggers—1886 The Haymarket, II-Patrolman Mathias Degan—1888 T. S. Eliot-The Verdict—1890 Paul Bunyan-Legend with Added Material—1891 Russell Sage-The Go-between—1892 The Strike-Homestead, Pennsylvania—1892 Jay Gould-Always for Erie—1892 Walt Whitman-A Hell on Wheels—1892 An Emigrant-Origin of an American—1893 An Immigrant-Ellis Island—1893 John Altgeld-Eight Dirty Radicals—1893 Mark Twain-Give a Dog a Bad Name—1894 Jacob Coxey-Coxey's Army—1894 Pullman Strike, I-Kingdom Come, Ill.—1894 Pullman Strike, II-If Christ Came to Chicago—1894 Pullman Strike, III-The Big Train—1896 McKinley and Bryan-A Word Fitly Spoken—1896 Mrs. Stephen Crane-Cora, *Mi Corazon*—1898 At Havana-U. S. S. *Maine*—1898 Theodore Roosevelt-It Has Been a Splendid Little War—1899 Ernest Hemingway-The Blood-letter—1900 Stephen Crane-His Name Was Heart's Pain—1901 Theodore Roosevelt-The American—1903 At Kittyhawk-The Machine—1903 Josiah Willard Gibbs-Where No Road Ran—1903 The Panama Canal-The Ditch which He Made—1904 Jazz-Those Easy Airs for Everyman—1905 Albert Einstein-A Wandering Jew—1906 Henry Adams-The Education of *Pteraspis*—1906 Harry K. Thaw-Only Poorer Grades of Meat Are Fried—1906 The First Broadcast-The Word in Space—1907 Ex-Gov. Frank Steunenberg-A Murder in Idaho—1909 Frederic Remington-A Parsifal of the Plains—1909 John Marin-A Water-Color—1909 Down East-The State of Maine—1910 Winslow Homer-To the Passenger-pigeon—1910 Christian Science-Faith in Things Unseen—1911 The Triangle Factory Fire-Twelve Dozen Girls—1912 U. S. S. *Maine*-The Ship that Sank Twice—1914 I. W. W.-No Ashes for Utah—1914 In Mexico-To Die for One's Country—1914 John Reed-A Land to Love—1915 The Leo Frank Case-How Doth the Gaberdine in Georgia?—1915 Anthony Comstock-Vice and Versa—1916 Henry James-A *Conversazione* at Henry's—1916

Hetty Green-Witch of Wall Street—1916 Tom Mooney-Market, Corner of Steuart—1917 Woodrow Wilson-Professor of History—1917 Albert Pinkham Ryder-Metaphors in Oil—1917 The Bisbee Deportations-It Don't Apply in Arizona—1917 V. I. Lenin-Old Nick on Nevsky Prospekt—1918 Dixieland-The Black and the Blues—1918 Randolph Bourne-Encounter on 8th Street—1919 Woodrow Wilson-Those Dear Ghosts—1919 The Palmer Raids-Undesirable Aliens—1919 Alexander Berkman-The Anarchist—1919 Eugene Debs-Champagne for Our Real Friends—1919 Eugene O'Neill-Superman with Qualms—1919 The Black Peril-Those Abe Lincoln Blues—1920 The Flivver-Mother and Children—1920 The Wall Street Explosion-The September Horse—1921 The Unknown Soldier-Mute Inglorious Richard Roe—1921 The Sacco-Vanzetti Case-The District Attorney—1922 A Black Schoolboy-A voice from Harlem—1922 Sinclair Lewis-The Man Who Wrote Blank Prose—1923 Warren Harding-The Private Car *Superb*—1923 Pancho Villa-A Gringo: *Do You Speak English?*—1924 Calvin Coolidge-A Vermont Sap-bucket—1924 Louis Sullivan-A Loyal Little Henna-haired Milliner—1925 The Ford Plant-Assembly-line—1926 Eugene Debs-On the Banks of the Wabash—1927 Isadora Duncan-*Die Erste Barfuss Tanzerin*—1927 Sacco and Vanzetti, I-Blues for Two Greenhorns—1927 Sacco and Vanzetti, II-Blues for Two Dead Italians—1927 Charles Lindbergh-The Mechanic—1931 The Depression-Thoughts on a Breadline—1932 Letter from the Grave-From Washington on His 200th Birthday—1932 Hart Crane-Voyages, VII—1933 Judge Webster Thayer-Doomsday for a Deemster—1933 The Depression-Apples of Sodom—1935 Huey Long-Every Man a King—1935 Billy Sunday-*You're Out!* The Umpire Cried—1937 Anti-Fascist Meeting-The Spanish unAmerican War—1939 Willa Cather-On the Enchanted Bluff—1940 Emma Goldman-Castle-builder in Union Square—1940 F. Scott Fitzgerald-Seven Bucks Found in a Toilet—1940 The Funny Papers-Tragic Strip—1941 Mount Rushmore-Headstone—1941

JOHN SANFORD

Pearl Harbor-East Wind Rain—1945 Statue of Liberty-Big Dumb Broad—1945 F. D. Roosevelt, I-The Sugar-tit Man—1945 F. D. Roosevelt, II-Old Flame at Warm Springs—1945 F. D. Roosevelt, III-Among the Roses—1945 Eleanor Roosevelt-Among the Roses, cont'd—1945 Hiroshima-The Thousand-mile Stare—1945 H. S. Truman-Jehovah—1945 Charlie Chaplin-The Revelation—1945 Ezra Pound-In Short the Usual Subjects—1945 U. S. A.-Prayer for a Dead Mother.

Note: The Fitzgerald piece is erroneously listed in the contents as Seven Bucks Found It in a Toilet. *A More Goodly Country* repeats several pieces from earlier books, as well as pieces previously published in periodicals: First Lady A5; The People from Heaven A4 & C22; Where All the Blues Began, revised from Dutch Treat in A4; The First Knee on Canada A4 & C23; God in the Hands of an Angry Sinner, revised from A4; The Man in the Black Coat, revised from A4; Buckeye Johnny Appleseed A5; Alta California, revised from A Man Name of James Wilson Marshall in A5; Like Sap in a Tree! A5; Had I So Interfered in Behalf of the Rich, revised from A5 & C25; Tall Talk in South Carolina appeared as Bob Anderson, My Beau Bob in A5; Hundred Years' War, revised from Vicksburg '63 in A5; Army of Northern Virginia, revised from This Will Have a Very Happy Effect in A5; Marse Linkum A5 & C26; The Mighty Fallen appeared as "The Bark was Three Feet Thick" in C30; On the Little Bighorn, revised from A5; A Juror: *I'd Hang All the Damn* Buggers A6; Legend with Added Material, revised from Paul Bunyan and Friend in A5; It Has Been a Splendid Little War A6; Champagne for Our Real Friends, revised from A6; A Voice from Harlem appeared in A5 as part of What I Want to Be When I Grow Up. A Letter from the grave was reprinted in the *Congressional Record* (see C31). In Mexico-To Die for One's Country was reprinted in *Concept* (see C34). The following were reprinted in "The Sacco and Vanzetti Papers" in *American Letters and Commentary* (see C56): Judge

41

Webster Thayer-Doomsday for a Deemster, The Sacco and Vanzetti Case-The District Attorney, Sacco and Vanzetti, I-Blues for Two Greenhorns, and Sacco and Vanzetti, II-Blues for Two Dead Italians.

J. S. liked to say *A More Goodly Country* took him four years to write and three years to place. In this first book of non-fiction, J. S. gave himself wholly over to the historical pieces that had imbued his novels with background color. Begun when J. S. was 63 years old, *A More Goodly Country* would represent his embarkation on a new career, that of a non-fiction writer.

Despite J. S.'s previous critical praise, the publishing industry was not eager to accept an entire volume of personal musings on American history. Variously titled *Always for Erie* and *The American Room*, the book was rejected 236 times, before finally being accepted by Horizon Press, in J. S.'s third submission to the house. (J. S. had earlier terminated a contract with Kennikat Press.) With publication just preceding the nation's bicentennial year, the book was ripe for success. However, J. S. refused to attend book signings, and he turned down several invitations for television and radio appearances. By 3 March 1976, only 3,200 copies had been shipped.

On 28 September 1977, J. S terminated his contract with Horizon, and Capra Press took on unsold copies. Capra issued the book with a new dust jacket, printed in bronze, but left the book unchanged, except for affixing a *"Distributed by |* CAPRA PRESS | [address]" sticker over the printed "HORIZON PRESS" on the title page. The price was lowered to $10.00; it is not known how many copies were sold like this. In April 1982, Black Sparrow Press took on about 800 remaining copies and sold them in the original Horizon dust jacket at $10.00. Laid into these copies was a small pamphlet, *"A More Goodly Country*: A New Introduction" by J. S. (see A13). On 1 July 2002, John Martin closed the Black Sparrow Press, and David R. Godine took over unsold copies, offering them in the original Horizon dust jacket at $22.95.

In style and content, *A More Goodly Country* shows the author's range, as he takes on topics as diverse as Leif Ericson, the atomic bomb, and the funny pages. Varying his style and voice depending on the period and the perspective, J. S. brings history alive. Additionally, *A More Goodly Country* allowed J. S. to transcend the limitations imposed by the novel form. No longer would he have to rely on teachers and preachers to harangue his audience. Now, he could instruct by parable, by allegory, by brief cautionary tale, often using the perspective of a peripheral figure to illuminate a well-known individual's character.

A10   ADIRONDACK STORIES   1976

a. First (limited, signed, lettered) edition:

[three lines enclosed in four ornaments like picture corners:] ADIRONDACK [swash A] | STORIES [swash S] | JOHN SANFORD | CAPRA PRESS | SANTA BARBARA | [small ornament] 1976 [small ornament]

22.8 x 14.9 cm. *1-7*^{8}. Pp.*1*-8, 9-27, *28*, 29-39, *40*, 41-47, *48*, 49-55, *56*, 57-107, *108-112.*

P.*1* blank; p.*2 Also by John Sanford:* | [9 titles]; p.*3* title; p.*4* Copyright © 1976 by John Sanford | [...] | ISBN 0-88496-065-X | ISBN 0-88496-066-9 pbk. | CAPRA PRESS | [...]; p.*5* dedication: *For my sister Ruth,* | *who looked in on us for* | *a while that summer.*; p.*6* blank; p.*7* contents; p.*8* blank; pp.9-12 foreword; pp.13-27 text; p.*28* blank; pp.29-39 text; p.*40* blank; pp.41-47 text; p.*48* blank; pp.49-55 text; p.*56* blank; pp.57-105 text; pp.106-107 notes; p.*108* blank page, with photo taken by J. S.'s sister, Ruth, of J. S. and "Pep" West in front of their Adirondack cabin tipped in, captioned in J. S.'s hand; p.*109 Printed and bound by Macintosh & Young in Santa Barbara for* | *Capra Press. Display typography by*

Bill Horton, linotype by Achilles | Friedrich. 100 copies handbound by Emily Paine, numbered and | signed by the author. | [lettered in brown ink] | [author's signature in blue ink]; pp.*110-112* blank.

Deep grayish green cloth boards, with yellowish white wove paper spine label, printed down the spine in black: *Adirondack Stories* [small ornament] John Sanford; on upper cover is affixed a color reproduction of a detail from Winslow Homer's watercolor *The Hunt Club*, 13.7 x 13.5 cm. All edges cut; endpapers; flat spine. Clear acetate dust jacket. Light mint green paper covered slipcase, stamped in black on front: [enclosed in four ornaments like picture corners:] ADIRONDACK [swash A] | STORIES [swash S] | JOHN SANFORD. Yellowish white wove paper.

Published 1 August 1976; price not obtainable; 26 copies.

Contents: Foreword—The Fire at the Catholic Church—Once in a Sedan and Twice Standing Up—I Let Him Die—Jasper Darby's Passion—Adirondack Narrative—The King of the Minnies—Notes on the Stories.

Note: The stories in this volume represent some of J. S.'s earliest published writings. The Fire at the Catholic Church appeared in *Contact* (C13) and was incorporated into A4. Once in a Sedan and Twice Standing Up appeared in *Contact* (C14) and was incorporated into A4. I Let Him Die and Jasper Darby's Passion appeared together in *Pagany*, under the title Two Stories (C12) and both were incorporated into A3. Adirondack Narrative appeared in *Pagany* as An Adirondack Narrative (C10). The King of the Minnies appears separately here for the first time but became an episode in A3. The foreword and The Fire at the Catholic Church were reprinted in *The Pushcart Prize, II* (see B8).

b. First (limited, signed, numbered) edition:

[title page as in A10a]

Collation and pagination identical to A10a, except for p.*108*, which has no photo, and p.*109*, which is numbered in brown ink, rather than lettered.

Yellowish copper colored cloth boards; otherwise identical to A10a.

Published simultaneously with A10a at $10.00; 100 copies.

Contents: As in A10a.

Note: An undetermined number of copies were designated "Presentation Copy" in brown ink on p.*109*, rather than numbered. These presumably were not offered for sale.

c. First trade paperback edition:

22.8 x 14.9 cm. [no discernable gathers]. Pagination as in A10b, except for p.*109*, which has no number or author signature.

Stiff yellowish white paper wrappers; lettered in black down the spine [at head:] *Adirondack Stories* [at foot:] JOHN SANFORD; and across head of the upper cover: *ADIRONDACK* [swash A] | *STORIES* [swash S], and foot: JOHN SANFORD. The middle of the front cover, and extending across to the lower cover, is a color reproduction of a detail from *The Hunt Club*, 20.1 x 13.8 cm. Edges cut flush; endpapers; perfect binding; yellowish white wove paper.

Published simultaneously with limited edition at $4.50; number of copies not obtainable.

Contents: As in A10a and A10b.

A11   VIEW FROM THIS WILDERNESS   1977

a. First (limited, signed) edition:

View | From | This | Wilderness | American Literature as History | JOHN SANFORD | [thin rule] | *Neither could they go up to the top of Pisgah, | to view from this wilderness a more goodly | country to feed their hopes.* | —WM. BRADFORD | HISTORY OF PLYMOUTH PLANTATION | [thin rule] | foreword by PAUL MARIANI | CAPRA PRESS / *Santa Barbara*

22.8 x 14.7 cm. *1-6*^{16}. Pp.*1-12*, 13-23, *24*, 25-183, *184-192*.

P.*1* half title; p.*2 Books by John Sanford* | [11 titles]; p.*3* title; p.*4* Copyright © 1977 by John Sanford | [...] | Manufactured in the United States of America | Several of these pieces originally appeared in *A More Goodly Country,* | published in 1975. For permission to reprint them here, grateful | acknowledgment is made to Mr. Ben Raeburn of Horizon Press | [thin rule] | [...] ISBN 0-88496-112-5 | [thin rule] | CAPRA PRESS | [...]; p.*5* dedication: Joseph Moncure March 1899-1977 [J. S.'s second writing partner at Paramount Studios, who introduced J. S. to Marguerite Roberts] | Dalton Trumbo 1905-1976 [member of the Hollywood Ten] | Edwin Rolfe 1909-1954 [Hollywood Communist, who fought in the Spanish Civil War] | Henry Bamford Parks 1904-1972 [New York University history professor and author of *The American Experience*] | [thin rule] | IN THEIR MEMORY; p.*6* blank; pp.*7-12* contents; pp.*13-23* foreword; p.*24* blank; pp.*25-184* text; pp.*185-186* blank; p.*187* This first edition was designed by Marcia Burtt | in Santa Barbara, California. Display type by | Foster & Horton; Caslon Old Face body type | by Charlene McAdams; calligraphy by Emily | Paine; camera work by Santa Barbara | Photoengravers; printed and bound | by R. R. Donnelley & Sons in | Crawfordsville, Indiana. | Author's photo by Wayne McCall. | [number in brown ink] | [J. S.'s signature in blue ink] | [date in J. S.'s hand in blue ink]; pp.*188-192* blank.

One-quarter brown cloth and light brown paper boards; printed in copper down the spine: View From This Wilderness • Sanford, and across near the foot: [publisher's goat head device] | CAPRA | PRESS. All edges cut; endpapers. Yellowish white dust jacket printed in black and brown; photo of J. S. on back flap. Yellowish white wove paper.

Published 11 September 1977 at $25.00; 100 copies.

Contents: Foreword by Paul Mariani—Christopher Columbus c. 1446-1506 First Words in the New World—William Hickling Prescott 1796-1859 Quetzalcoatl—Thomas Harriot 1506-1621 Going Home to Eden—Nathaniel Ward 1578-1653 The Simple Cobler of Aggawam—John Winthrop 1588-1649 Annotations on Winthrop's *Journal*—Thomas Morton c. 1590-1646 An Infamouse and Scurillous Booke—John Eliot 1604-1690 The Medicine-Man—Capt. John Mason 1600-1672 A Brief History of the Pequot War—Père Paul Le Jeune 1635-? Of Sorcery and Smoke—Increase Mather 1639-1723 As Once to Israel— Nathaniel Hawthorne 1804-1864 Ad Libs by a Fictitious Character—Edward Taylor 1645-1729 How Far from then Forethought of—Roger Williams 1603-1683 Mark Them Which Cause Divisions—Jonathan Edwards 1703-1758 Heaven Was His Country—John Peter Zenger 1697-1746 The World of Movable Type—Sam Adams 1722-1803 A Yell of Rebellion—James Otis 1725-1783 Near the Grave of Paul Revere—James Madison

1751-1836 The Virginia Plan—Tom Paine 1737-1809 The Bones of a Pamphleteer—Thomas Jefferson 1743-1826 Rebellion Is as the Sin of Witchcraft—John Marshall 1755-1835 A Case that Was Never Tried—J. H. St. John de Crèvecoeur 1735-1813 Letters from an American Farmer—Meriwether Lewis 1774-1809 Ah Sinful Nation—Susanna Rowson 1761-1824 *Charlotte Temple,* a Tale of Truth—Col. Davy Crockett 1786-1836 Cock-Fight at Natchez—Paul Bunyan 1837-? Legend with Added Material—Washington Irving 1783-1859 In the Kaatskills—Ralph Waldo Emerson 1803-1882 Does Thy Blue Eye?—Henry Wadsworth Longfellow 1807-1882 The Jewish Cemetery at Newport—Francis Parkman 1823-1893 He Called His Rifle *Satan*—Edgar Allan Poe 1809-1849 In Bronze Above a Doorway—John Woolman 1720-1772 A Small Fire—Phillis Wheatley c. 1753-1784 Ah! Whither Wilt Thou Go—Herman Melville 1819-1891 A Visitor from the *Bachelor's Delight*—Mark Twain 1835-1910 Give a Dog a Bad Name—Harriet Beecher Stowe 1811-1896 The Lord Himself Wrote It—Roger Taney 1777-1864 The Language of the Law—Abraham Lincoln 1809-1865 A Few Appropriate Remarks—Henry David Thoreau 1817-1862 A Call of Nature—Henry Timrod 1829-1867 No Marble Column—Albion Winegar Tourgée 1838-1905 The Lost Cause—Joel Chandler Harris 1848-1908 Brer Nigger—Hinton Rowan Helper 1829-1909 Have You Any Wool?—Emily Dickinson 1830-1886 Revenge of the Nerves—Rebecca Harding Davis 1831-1910 Life and Death in the Iron Mills—Constance Fenimore Woolson 1840-1894 Henry James and Lady— Helen Hunt Jackson 1831-1885 An Epigraph for a Short Story—Horatio Alger, Jr. 1832-1899 Navigator of the Windward Passage—William Dean Howells 1837-1920 The Red Letter *A*—Philander Deming 1829-1915 A Garland for the Unrenowned—John Hay 1838-1905 The Elegant Capt. Farnham—Sidney Lanier 1842-1881 A Mouthful of Blood—Walt Whitman 1819-1892 A Hell on Wheels—Ambrose Bierce 1842-1913? An Occurrence at the Styx River Ferry—Henry James 1843-1916 A *Conversazione* at

Henry's—Emma Lazarus 1849-1887 Persons that Pass—Henry Demarest Lloyd 1849-1903 About John D. (Baptist)—Henry George 1939-1897 I Am for Men—Sarah Orne Jewett 1849-1909 The State of Maine—Lafcadio Hearn 1850-1904 On Raising the Coast of Japan—Mary Baker Eddy 1821-1910 Faith in Things Unseen—Henry Adams 1838-1918 The Education of *Pteraspis*— Kate Chopin 1851-1904 A Walk to the Gulf—William Cowper Brann 1855-1898 The Idols of Texas—Booker T. Washington 1856-1924 What's that Nigger Doing on the Stage?—Woodrow Wilson 1856-1924 Summer White House, 1916: Two Studies— Theodore Roosevelt 1858-1919 The Naturalist—Alfred Thayer Mahan 1840-1914 The Flag Follows Trade—Owen Wister 1860-1938 Evil Has No First Name, Good Has No Last—Hamlin Garland 1860-1940 A Flat on 105th St.—Stephen Crane 1871-1900 His Name Was Heart's Pain—Frederick Jackson Turner 1861-1932 The Future Is the Past—O. Henry 1862-1910 Pool-Shooter in a Billiard Room—Arthur Brisbane 1864-1936 One Whose Father Rhapsodized—Herbert Croly 1869-1930 The Promise of American Life—Gustavus Myers 1872-1942 The Great American Fortunes—Benjamin N. Cardozo 1870-1938 Hear, O Israel!—Frank Norris 1870-1902 Far Above Our Poor Power—Vernon Louis Parrington 1871-1929 A Sword to Fight With—Jack London 1876-1916 The Locomotive of History— Theodore Dreiser 1871-1945 Loose Fish from Indiana—Robert Frost 1874-1963 The Past in the Present—Gertrude Stein 1874-1946 All Stiff and Yet All Trembling—Sherwood Anderson 1876-1941 The Train that Went Nowhere—Willa Cather 1876-1947 On the Enchanted Bluff—Upton Sinclair 1878-1968 Socialism—Carl Sandburg 1878-1967 All the Coasts of Palestine—Wallace Stevens 1879-1955 In My Room—William Carlos Williams 1883-1963 On Rereading *In the American Grain*—Sinclair Lewis 1885-1951 The Man Who Wrote Blank Prose—Ezra Pound 1885-1972 In Short the Usual Subjects—Ring Lardner 1885-1933 What Sarah E. Spooldripper Knew—Randolph Bourne 1886-1918 Encounter on

8th St.—Lincoln Steffens 1866-1936 The Muckraker Who Looked Up—John Reed 1887-1920 A Land to Love—Robinson Jeffers 1887-1962 Una—Marianne Moore 1887-1972 The Accuracy of the Vernacular!—Bartolomeo Vanzetti 1888-1927 Last Words for Scorning Men—Nicola Sacco 1891-1927 Don't Cry, Dante—Heywood Broun 1888-1938 After the Crucifixion—Edna St. V. Millay 1892-1950 Dead Letter from a Dead Lover—Eugene O'Neill 1888-1953 Superman with Qualms—Katherine Anne Porter c.1890– The Fools Forgather at Vera Cruz—Archibald MacLeish 1892– *Pilar*, Out of Key West—E. E. Cummings 1894-1963 Lumberman of the Distinct—Jean Toomer 1894-1967 I Am Not a Negro—Edmund Wilson 1895-1972 Momus from Old Nassau—F. Scott Fitzgerald 1896-1940 Seven Bucks Found in a Toilet—T. S. Eliot 1888-1965 The Verdict—John Dos Passos 1896-1970 Workingmen and People Like That—William Faulkner 1897-1962 Listen to the Ghosts—Hart Crane 1899-1932 Voyages, VII—Thomas Wolfe 1900-1938 A Feast Not Made for Laughter—Ernest Hemingway 1899-1961 The Blood-Letter—Nathanael West 1903-1940 Miss Lonelyhearts in the Adirondacks—Countee Cullen 1903-1946 High School on 59th St.—John Steinbeck 1902-1968 The *East of Eden* Letters—Lionel Trilling 1905-1975 Maxim Has Broken—Leonard Ehrlich 1905 – God's Angry Man—John O'Hara 1905-1970 The End of Lantenengo St.—Richard Wright 1908-1960 Creche 4596, Pere Lachaise—James Agee 1909-1955 Death in a Hack—Conrad Aiken 1889-1973 At the Grave of Malcolm Lowry—John Berryman 1914-1972 The Mississippi: At the Head of Navigation.

Note: Twenty-six copies were denoted "Presentation copy" in brown ink on p.*187* rather than numbered. These presumably were not offered for sale. Also, a small number of copies exist on which the dust jacket lacks the brown printing.

View from this Wilderness repeats several pieces from A9: Winthrop's Journal; Ad Libs by a Fictitious Character;

The Bones of a Pamphleteer; Legend with Added Material; In the Kaatskills; In Bonze Above a Doorway; A Visitor from the *Bachelor's Delight*; Give a Dog a Bad Name; The Lord Himself Wrote It; A Call of Nature; Revenge of the Nerves; A Hell on Wheels; A *Conversazione* at Henry's, revised; The State of Maine, revised; Faith in Things Unseen; The Education of *Pteraspis*; His Name Was Heart's Pain; On the Enchanted Bluff; The Man Who Wrote Blank Prose; In Short the Usual Subjects; Encounter on 8th Street; A Land to Love; Superman with Qualms; Seven Bucks Found in a Toilet; The Verdict; and The Blood-Letter. Last Words for Scorning Men, Don't Cry, Dante, and After the Crucifixion were reprinted in "The Sacco and Vanzetti Papers" in *American Letters and Commentary* (see C56).

Originally titled *Voices of the People*, the book failed to find acceptance with mainstream publishers. A report from an editor at Houghton-Mifflin repeats a common refrain about J. S.'s work:

> John Sanford's book VOICES OF THE PEOPLE is a difficult book to classify…. Sanford is an original, no doubt about it. His writing is fine and so are his perceptions. There are bits… that are truly powerful. And as a recreation of American literary experience… the book, unexpectedly, does begin to add up. But how in hell could you sell it?

View from this Wilderness was finally published by Capra when J. S. was 73 years old. After almost fifty years of writing, it represented the first time the same publisher had issued a second of his books. According to J. S., *View* received only one review: in it, Robert Kirsch of the Los Angeles *Times* called the book "a masterpiece." J. S. felt that Capra did not promote the book enough. In its first year, *View* sold only 1,328 copies.

J. S.'s reading of *View from this Wilderness* was broadcast on radio in 1978 (see E2c).

b. First trade edition:

This edition is identical to A11a, except there is no number, signature or date on p.*187.*

Published simultaneously with A11a at $10.00; 5,342 copies.

A12   TO FEED THEIR HOPES 1980

a. First edition:

JOHN SANFORD | To Feed Their Hopes | [leaf ornament] A BOOK OF AMERICAN WOMEN | Foreword by Annette K. Baxter | University of Illinois Press | URBANA CHICAGO LONDON

22.8 x 14.8 cm. *1-7*^{16}. Pp.*i-vi*, vii-xv, *xvi*, xvii-xix, *xx*, xxi-xxii, *1-2*, 3-198, *199-202*.

P.*i* half title; p.*ii* BOOKS BY JOHN SANFORD | [11 titles]; p.*iii* title; p.*iv To Feed Their Hopes* is the third part of a trilogy | on American history to be called *The Top of Pisgah.* The first | two parts have been published as: | [...] | © 1980 by John Sanford | Manufactured in the United States of America | [...] | ISBN 0-252-00804-9; p.*v* epigraph [three lines from William Bradford, as in A11 p.*3*]; p.*vi* blank; pp.vii-xv contents; p.*xvi* blank; pp.xvii-xix foreword; p.*xx* blank; p.xxi-xxii preface; p.*1* fly title; p.*2* blank; pp.3-197 text; p.198 dedication: Marguerite Sanford 1905 – | DEDICATION PAGE | *You've never written me a love letter.* | — Maggie | But it has all been a love-letter ....; pp.*199-202* blank.

One-quarter navy blue cloth and blue-gray cloth boards; stamped in silver down the spine: SANFORD [leaf ornament] To Feed Their Hopes [leaf] UNIVERSITY OF ILLINOIS PRESS. All edges cut; endpapers. Yellowish white dust jacket printed in deep blue, white and light blue; photo of J. S. on back flap. Yellowish white wove paper.

Published 19 November 1980 at $10.95; 4,000 copies.

Contents: Foreword by Annette K. Baxter—Preface by J. S.—Virginia Dare 1587-(?) First Lady—Pokahontas 1595-1617 Lady Rebekah—Anne Hutchinson 1590(?)-1643 Those Total Depravitie Blues—Mary Dyer (?)-1660 Pass Not Over the Brook—Katharine Tekakwitha 1656-80 Katharine, Bride of Christ—Virgin Bride of the Lord – The Underground Stream—Mrs. Prudence Whitwell 1740-73 Used Only Once—Phyllis Lyndon 1746-73 Burying-Ground on Farewell Street—Sarah Johnson 1766-90 Her Soul a Very Sun—Ann Putnam and Abigail Williams, 1692 Two of Salem's Afflicted Children—Pearl Prynne, in *The Scarlet Letter*-Ad Libs by a Fictitious Character—Eunice Williams 1696-1786 A Prisoner of the Indians—Martha Washington 1731(?)-1802 When I Cast My Eyes Toward Belvoir—Mrs. Benedict Arnold 1760-1804 After Great Suffering—Sally Hemings 1773-1835 Black Sally—Susan and Betsy Roberts c. 1775-(?) Sisters on the Natchez Trace—Charlotte Temple, in *Charlotte Temple* (1791) A Tale of Truth—Nancy Ward c. 1738-1822 A White Indian—Nancy Hanks Lincoln 1784(?)-1818 A Resting Place in Indiana—Sacajawea 1788(?)-1884(?) Charbonneau's Woman—Ann Rutledge 1813-35 The Silver Figment—Mrs. Edgar Allan Poe 1821-47 A Doll that Bled—Maria Clemm 1790-1871 Mother of Virginia, Mother-in-Law of Poe—Talahina Houston 1795(?)-1835 To His Squaw in Indian Territory—Molly Maguire (?)-(?) Immigrant from the Emerald Isle—Margaret Fuller 1810-50 The Bluestocking—Emma Crockett 1857-(?) In Alabama, at the Age of Eighty—Evangeline St. Claire, in *Uncle Tom's Cabin* (1852) Little Eva: A Genre Painting—Polly Ann Henry (?)-(?) John Henry Had a Little Woman—Woman Posing, Unidentified 1859

Print from a Wet-Plate Negative—Clara Albers 1859 Small Grave on the Great Plains—Isabel Banford, in *Pierre, or The Ambiguities* (1852) Thy Sister, Isabel—Harriet Beecher Stowe 1811-96 The Lord Himself Wrote It—Mary Lincoln 1818-82 Good Friday at Ford's Theatre—Mrs. Mary Surratt 1820-65 A Hanging: Four Exposures—Mrs. George Armstrong Custer 1842-1933 I Dreamed of You—Lydia Hamilton Smith 1913-84 Housekeeper of Thaddeus Stevens—Margaret Carrington 1831-70 Expedition to Absaraka—Mrs. Henry Adams 1843-85 Hooded Figure—Mrs. Cornelia Clinch Stewart 1802-86 The Merchant as Merchandise—Statue of Liberty 1886 – A Mighty Woman with a Torch—Emily Dickinson 1830-86 Revenge of the Nerves—Emma Lazarus 1849-87 Persons that Pass—Maria Mitchell 1819-89 The Region of Truth—Mrs. Herschel Gruenberg 1870(?)-1947 Aunt Sarah—Mary Hallock Foote 1847-1938 Woman by the Train Tracks—Maggie's Mother, in *Maggie* (1893) Like a Devil on a Japanese Kite—Mrs. Theodore (Elizabeth) Tilton 1835-97 A Work of the Flesh—Mariana Andrada 1830-1902 Mariana *La Loca*—Kate Chopin 1851-1904 A Walk to the Gulf—Olivia Langdon Clemens 1845-1904 A Fall on the Ice—Louise Clappe (Dame Shirley) 1819-1906 Letters from the California Mines—Ida Saxton McKinley 1847-1907 A Trip to Buffalo and the Falls—Sarah Orne Jewett 1849-1909 On Reading a Collection of Her Letters—A Neighbor Woman, Name Unknown 1908 The Precious Stone—Cora (Mrs. Stephen) Crane 1865-1910 Cora, *Mi Corazon*—Mary Baker Eddy 1821-1910 Faith in Things Unseen—Three Women, Unnamed 1910 Tar-Paper Shack—Auld Acquaintance (P. G.) 1910 Childe Julian, Boy King—Jennie, in *Jennie Gerhardt* (1911) The Wood Dove—Triangle Fire Victims 1911 Twelve Dozen Girls—Unknown Woman, Triangle Fire 1911 In Evergreen Cemetery—A Corsetière's 1912 A Dress Form Named...—Unknown Woman, Harlem 1912 This Empty Room—Zenobia Frome, in *Ethan Frome* (1911) The Heroine—Martha 1885-1914 Agony in Another Garden—A Teacher at P. S.

81, Manhattan 1913 Miss Blauvelt—Harriet (Chai Esther) Shapiro 1881-1914 A Disease of the Heart—Mrs. Abraham Nevins 1857(?)-1934 Mother of Your Mother—Unknown Woman, Washington Heights 1915 420 Convent Ave., Apt. D—New Orleans Prostitute 1915 In the "Queer Zone"—Unknown Girl, Harlem 1915 The Falling Sickness—Audrey Munson (?)-(?) Model for a Bronze of Pomona—Hetty Green 1834-1916 Witch of Wall Street—Sister Ruth 1908- and Brother Julian—Unknown Woman, Long Branch 1917 A Summer by the Sea—Unknown Woman, United States 1921 Wife of the Unknown Soldier—Ella Downey, in *All God's Chillun Got Wings* (1924) The Wife of Nigger Jim—Mrs. Virgil Adams, in *Alice Adams* (1921) My Dear, Beautiful Girl—Maimie Pinzer 1885-1922(?) My Dear Mrs. Howe—Fanny Quincy Howe 1870-1933 Letters to a Scarlet Woman—Auld Acquaintance (D. U. S.) 1924 Woolworth Building, 28th Floor—Mrs. Jack Gardner 1840-1924 Self-Abasement on Brimmer St.—California, in *Roan Stallion* (1924) The Stallion's Wife—Mary Litogot Ford 1839-76 Speaking of Neatness, He Said—Isadora Duncan 1877-1927 *Die Erste Barfuss Tanzerin*—Mrs. Nicolo (Rosina) Sacco (?)-(?) August, 1927—Auld Acquaintance (L. G.) 1927 The Hand-Me-Down—Ina Coolbrith 1841-1928 Poet Laureate of California—Lady Brett Ashley, in *The Sun Also Rises* (1926) The Christ-Killer—Hadley Richardson Hemingway 1892-1979 The Mountains in the Distance—Auld Acquaintance (O. B.) 1928 A Poem Set to Music—Auld Acquaintance (S. L.) 1929 The Pleasures of Sin for a Season—Marian Forrester, in *A Lost Lady* (1923) A Sense of Elation—Willa Cather 1873-1947 The Lost Lady—Auld Acquaintance (R. P.) 1931 A Woman Arrayed in Purple—Ruby Lamar, in *Sanctuary* (1931) Walpurgis-Nacht—Auld Acquaintance (L. T.) 1932 Let Her Take Thee with Her Eyelids—Unidentified Woman 1936 Okie Madonna—Mrs. Thomas Eakins 1852-1938 Portrait of a Lady with a Setter Dog—Curley's Wife, in *Of Mice and Men* (1937) Do You Like to Feel Velvet?—Elizabeth

McCourt (Baby Doe) 1854-1935 The Seven Ages of Baby Doe, *A Photographic History*—Ellen Lang 1880(?)-1935(?) The Form of a Servant—Auld Acquaintance (H. L.) 1935 A Nine-Page Letter—Louise Bryant 1890(?)-1936 The Wife of John Reed—Bessie Smith 1896(?)-1937 Dreams of Flight—Harriet Monroe 1860-1936 On a Visit to Arequipa—Edith Wharton 1862-1937 Narrative in Three Photographs—Unknown Girl, Carmel Highlands 1938 Someone Named Anne or Anna—Elizabeth Drexel Lehr c. 1875-1940 Harry Died in Baltimore in 1929—Nancy Astor 1879-1964 Mistress of Cliveden—Aimee Semple McPherson 1890-1944 Sister—Zelda Fitzgerald 1900-1948 The Fiction of F. S. Fitzgerald—Wallis Warfield Simpson 1896- The Shopper—Emma Goldman 1869-1940 Castle-Builder in Union Square—Florence Kahn Beerbohm 1876-1951 The First Lady Max—Edna St. Vincent Millay 1892-1950 Dead Letter from a Dead Lover—Rosie Ackerman c. 1885-(?) From the Old Country—Ella Reeve Bloor 1862-1951 A School for Young Ladies of Good Family—Grace Hemingway 1872-1951 Mother of Six—Mrs. Ada Russell 1863-1952(?) Ada Lived Till about 1952—Ethel Rosenberg 1916-53 A Letter to Julius—Mabel Dodge Luhan 1879-1962 How Things Die on One!—Agnes Smedley 1894(?)-1950 By the Time This Reaches You—Aline Bernstein 1882-1955 A Lingering Illness—Zora Neale Hurston 1903-60 A Pilgrim to the Horizon—Mrs. Woodrow Wilson 1872-1961 The Well-Dressed Dead—Emily Hale 1891-1969 A Thousand Letters From *Our Friend*—Dorothy Thompson 1893-1961 The Last Terrible Remembering—Marion Davies 1897-1961 The Mistress of Citizen Hearst—Dorothy Comingore 1913(?)-1965(?) The Mistress of *Citizen Kane*—Lucy Young, a Wailike Indian c. 1846-(?) Listen to Him Dream—Sylvia Beach 1887-1962 12, Rue de L'Odéon—Sylvia Plath 1932-63 To Her Friend, Who Said—Flannery O'Connor 1925-64 The Deadly Butterfly—Elisabeth Morrow 1903-34 The Flightless One—Dorothy Parker 1893-1967 The Long Suicide—Ayn Rand 1905- Speaking as John

Galt:—Carson McCullers 1917-67 This Side-Show—Gertrude Stein 1874-1946 All Stiff and Yet All Trembling—Alice B. Toklas 1877-1967 Precious Precious Gertrude—Helen Keller 1880-1968 The Three Monkeys—Carlotta Monterey 1888-1970 Mrs. Eugene O'Neill—Eudora Welty 1909- The Neighbors—Caresse Crosby 1892-1970 I Promise You—Auld Acquaintance (I. L.) 1910-70 A Judas with Tits—Marianne Moore 1887-1972 The Accuracy of the Vernacular!—Aunt Jo 1882-1972 The Painted Woman— Unknown Woman, Santa Barbara 1970 The Word is Very Nigh Unto Thee—Josephine Baker 1906(?)-75 Catch a Nigger by the Toe—Minnie Blumfield 1886(?)-1977 Wyandottes, Plymouth Rocks—Joan Crawford 1908-77 A Coat of Arctic Fox—Katherine Anne Porter 1890(?)- The Fools Forgather at Vera Cruz—Georgia O'Keeffe 1887- A Painting Called *White Barn, No. 1*—Agnes von Jurowsky 1892- In the Late Summer of that Year—Eleanor Roosevelt 1884-1962 Among the Roses—Alice Roosevelt Longworth 1884-1980 With Her Feet Up on the Handlebars— Sara Delano Roosevelt 1854-1941 Just the Sweetest Dearest Mama—Golda Meir 1898-1979 A Voyage to Palestine, 1921— Marguerite Sanford 1905- Dedication Page.

Note: *To Feed Their Hopes* repeats several pieces from previous books: First Lady (A5 & A9); Lady Rebekah (A9); Those Total Depravitie Blues (A9); Ad Libs by a Fictitious Character (A9 & A11); The Blue Stocking (A11); The Lord Himself Wrote It (A9 & A11); Good Friday at Ford's Theatre, revised from (A9); Revenge of the Nerves (A9 & A11); Persons that Pass, revised from (A11); A Walk to the Gulf (A11); Cora, *Mi Corazon* (revised from A9); Faith in Things Unseen (A9 & A11); Twelve Dozen Girls (A9); Witch of Wall Street (A9); *Die Erste Barfuss Tanzerin* (A9); Castle-Builder in Union Square (A9); Dead Letter from a Dead Lover (A11); All Stiff and Yet All Trembling (A11); The Accuracy of the Vernacular! (A11); The Fools Forgather at Vera Cruz (A11); Among the Roses (revised from A9). August, 1927 was reprinted in "The Sacco and Vanzetti Papers" in *American Letters and Commentary* (see C56). The Pleasures of Sin for a Season was reprinted as "Sonia: 1929" in the *Los Angeles Times* (see C57).

To Feed Their Hopes had been announced by Capra Press, but J. S. withdrew the book because he believed Capra was not committed deeply enough to promoting its sales. The book was also accepted by Stein & Day, but J. S. withdrew because he objected to the terms of the contract. A blistering rejection from Southern Illinois University Press showed what J. S. was up against: even with two books of personal reflections on history already published, his style and approach to history were still so unique that he appalled readers at publishing houses who were expecting something within the norm. *To Feed Their Hopes*—an entire book of reflections on women—shows J. S.'s enduring fascination and preoccupation with women.

To Feed Their Hopes was optioned by Elaine Kendall and Elaine Moe in 1983 for dramatic adaptation. This became the stage musical *An American Cantata* (see E5a).

b. First paperback edition (University of Illinois Press), [1995]

JOHN SANFORD | A Book of | American Women | Foreword by Annette K. Baxter | University of Illinois Press | URBANA AND CHICAGO

22.8 x 14.8 cm. [no discernable gathers]. Pagination as in A12a.

P.*i* half title; p.*ii* OTHER BOOKS BY JOHN SANFORD | [22 titles]; p.*iii* title; p.*iv* Illini Books edition, 1995 | © 1980 by John Sanford | Manufactured in the United States of America | P 5 4 3 2 1 | *This book is printed on acid-free paper.* | […] | ISBN 0-252-06533-0 (pbk.) | […]; pp.*v*-xxii identical to A12a, except for the addition of year of death for Marguerite Sanford p.xv; p.*1* fly title; pp.*2-202* identical to A12a, except for the addition of year of death for M. S. p.198.

Glossy yellowish white stiff paper wrappers; printed in white, red and gray, with names of the women portrayed in the book forming a geometric, crisscrossing pattern; down the spine [in white:] *A Book of American Women* SANFORD [publisher's device of a red "i" on a white shield]; on upper cover [in white:] *A BOOK OF* | [shadowed:] *American* | *Women* [the A and W of both words overlap] | *John* | *SANFORD*. Edges cut flush; perfect binding; yellowish white wove paper.

Published 28 December 1995 at $15.95; 1,750 copies.

Contents: as in A12a.

Note: In January 2006, the publisher declared the book out of print, with a total of 420 copies sold.

A13 A MORE GOODLY COUNTRY: 1982 A NEW INTRODUCTION

First edition:

[in orange:] A MORE GOODLY COUNTRY | [in black:] *a new Introduction by* | [in orange:] John Sanford

23.5 x 15.2 cm. 1^2. Pp.*1-4*.

P.*1* [title] | [text] | [short black rule] | Copyright © 1982 by John Sanford.; pp.*2-3* text; p.*4* [text] | [long black rule] | [publisher's sparrow device] BLACK SPARROW PRESS | BOX 3993 SANTA BARBARA, CA 93105.

Yellowish white wove paper printed in orange and black; folded at left.

Published April 1982; distributed gratis; approximately 800 copies.

Contents: A New Introduction.

Note: This pamphlet was laid into copies of *A More Goodly Country* (A9) sold by Black Sparrow. It details the travails J. S. experienced in the long process of getting the book published.

A14 BLACK SPARROW PRESS ANNOUNCES THE SPRING 1984 PUBLICATION OF THE WINTERS OF THAT COUNTRY   1984

First edition:

[in light blue:] [line of floral ornaments across page] | [in black:] BLACK SPARROW PRESS | announces | the Spring 1984 | publication | of | [in light blue:] THE WINTERS | OF THAT COUNTRY | [in black:] tales of | the man-made seasons | JOHN SANFORD | [in light blue:] [line of floral ornaments across page] | [in black:] [shorter line of pinwheel ornaments] | [in light blue:] [shorter line of floral ornaments] | [in black:] [three shorter lines of pinwheel ornaments] | [in light blue:] [shorter line of floral ornaments] | [in black:] [shorter line of pinwheel ornaments] | [in light blue:] [line of floral ornaments across page]

22.8 x 13.9 cm. *1*^{2}. Pp.*1-4*.

P.*1* title; p.*2* one of the tales ... [text]; p.*3* text; p.*4* [information about editions of the book] | [contact information for distributors] | [address for Black Sparrow Press].

Stiff tan paper printed in light blue and black; folded at left.

Published February 1984; distributed gratis; 2,000 copies.

Contents: The Ugly Sky.

Note: This pamphlet was distributed as an advertisement for the upcoming book. It was also laid into the limited hardcover copies of *The Winters of that Country* (A15). This pamphlet represents the first separate printing of The Ugly Sky, which would soon appear in *The Winters of that Country*.

A15   THE WINTERS OF THAT COUNTRY   1984

a. First (limited, signed, lettered) edition:

[greenish gray-blue rule extending to facing page] | [in red:] JOHN | [in gray:] THE [in red:] SANFORD | [in gray:] WINTERS | OF THAT | COUNTRY | [in red:] TALES OF THE MAN MADE SEASONS | [short greenish gray-blue rule, flush right] | [in gray:] BLACK SPARROW PRESS | SANTA BARBARA-1984

22.7 x 14.8 cm. $1^2\,2^1\,3\text{-}11^{16}$. Pp.*i-ii, 1-12*, 13-161, *162-179*, 180-349, *350-356*.

P.*i* ALSO BY JOHN SANFORD | NOVELS AND OTHER FICTION | [9 titles] | INTERPRETATIONS OF AMERICAN HISTORY | [4 titles] | SCENES FROM AN AMERICAN LIFE | *The Color of the Air, Part 1* (Spring 1985); p.*ii* blank [except for extension of rule from title page]; p.*1* title; p.*2* [...] | Copyright © 1984 by John Sanford | [...] | ISBN 0-87685-615-6 | ISBN 0-87685-616-4 (signed) | ISBN 0-87685-614-8 (pbk.); p.*3* [author's signature in blue ink]; p.*4* blank; p.*5* dedication: To a more perfect Union; p.*6* epigraph: [4 lines from Bradford's *History of the*

Plymouth Plantation]; pp.*7-9* contents; p.*10* blank; p.*11* fly title; p.*12* blank; pp.13-161 text; pp.162-179 alternating text and photographs; pp.180-349 text; p.*350* blank; p.*351* Printed in March 1984 in Santa Barbara & Ann Arbor | for the Black Sparrow Press by Graham Mackintosh and | Edwards Brothers Inc. Design by Barbara Martin. | This edition is published in paper wrappers; there are | 300 hardcover trade copies; 200 hardcover copies | numbered and signed by the author; and 26 copies hand– | bound in boards by Earle Gray lettered and signed by | the author. [letter in red ink] | [publisher's sparrow device 1.4 x 1.3 cm.]; p.*352* author biography; p.*353* photo of J. S.; pp.*354-356* blank.

Ripple-patterned gray, black and silver cloth spine, with sand-colored paper label, printed down the spine [in red:] JOHN SANFORD [in orange:] THE WINTERS OF THAT COUNTRY; sand-colored paper boards; upper cover has a geometric pattern printed in gray and greenish gray-blue, the bottom part of which extends to the lower cover, that frames the text: [flush right in orange:] JOHN | [in red:] THE | [in orange:] SANFORD | [in red:] WINTERS | OF THAT | COUNTRY | [in orange:] TALES OF THE MAN MADE SEASONS. All edges cut; endpapers; flat spine. Clear acetate dust jacket. Yellowish white wove paper.

Published 16 May 1984 at $40.00; 26 copies.

Contents: On the Waters of Darkness—Of the People of Apalache—A Prisoner of Hirrihigua—Off Nombre de Dios, in the Gulf of Darien—The Price of the Dog—Master of the *Salomon*—All Learned and Virtuous Men—Mutiny Aboard the *Discovery*—Passengers on the *Mayflower*—I Am, Sir, yr. Most Obedt. Servt.—The Troubles in New-England—Voyage of the *James*, 1675-76—Bacon's Rebellion—Journal of the *Arthur*, Capt. Rob't. Doegood—Leisler's Rebellion—On the Care and Feeding of Slaves—Livingston Manor—Voodoo on Broadway—It Being a Pleasant Cuntry—Impressment, 1769—The Boston

JOHN SANFORD

Massacre, 1770—The Boston Tea Party, 1773—A Martial Air at a Hanging—Of the Goings on of that Winter—The British Prison Ship *Jersey*—The Last Gentleman—The Longest Summer's Day—All But One of Them—A Letter to Capt. Lawrence—I Didn't Mean to Kill My Boy—The Inventor—I Have Made My Way Alone—A Servile Rebellion—The Stain of Settlement—The *Amistad*, Formerly the *Friendship*—A Place of Flowers—Poor Mexico, So Far from God—A Book for Know-Nothings—The Dorr Rebellion—A Rope with Two Ends—In Dixie's Land—The Conscription Act—The Prince of Cincinnati—*Allons, Enfants de la Patrie*—Turn Right on a Dirt Road—War Means Fighting—A Military History of Slavery—The Performance Will Be Honored—Christmas Eve in Pulaski, Tennessee—A Flood Upon the Earth—The World's Hard Eye—In the San Joaquin—The View from Mt. McGregor—Harangue in Desplaines Street—The Customhouse Years—The Feudal System in Illinois—Devices in the Oval Room—The Revolutionary—Labor War at a High Altitude—Discharge without Honor—The Bombing of the *Los Angeles Times*—The School at Carlisle—The Baldwin-Felts Detective Agency—Birds of Passage—The Night Witch Did It—Causes of Death—A River of the Air—Two Black Caskets and Eleven White—Warren K. Billings—An Album of Photos and Postcards—The Troop Trains—A Swim in Lake Michigan—In Wooded Washington—Dick the Bootblack—A Blizzard of Picayunes—Bartolomeo Vanzetti—The Man Who Looked Like a President—That Little Baldplate from Simbirsk—The Burning of Jim Ivy—A Speech in Canton, Ohio—The Water-Bringer of Los Angeles—Rosina Sacco and Luigia Vanzetti—The Gastonia Strike—Al Capone et al—The God with the Glass Head—The Management of Labor—On the Way to Joy Road—Freight Train on the Southern—A Cruell and Feirce Storme—*My Dear General Pershing*, She Wrote—*Shikata Ga Nai*—Of One Who Missed the Second Creation—The Ugly Sky—Baby Brother—Oh God, When I Go Down—On Refusing to Answer—He Rode Upon a Cherub—Who Killed Cock Robin—My Lai 4—The Wicked Walk on Every Side—The Moor of Princeton—A Messenger of God—Father to the Man—The War that Was Fought in Your Home.

Note: Voyage of the James should read Voyage of the *James* (p.7). The Little Baldplate from Simbirsk should read The Little Baldpate from Simbirsk (p.9). The Ugly Sky previously appeared in Black Sparrow Press Announces the Spring 1984 Publication of The Winters of that Country (A14). The Night Witch Did It and A Speech in Canton, Ohio, previously appeared in *Blast 3* as "The Leo Frank Case, 1913-1915" and "Eugene V. Debs, 1855-1926," respectively (see B11). *Shikata Ga Nai* was reprinted in *Daybook of Critical Reading and Writing* (see B25). The Ugly Sky was reprinted in the *Santa Barbara News-Press* (see C37). The following were reprinted in "The Sacco and Vanzetti Papers" in *American Letters and Commentary* (see C56): Bartolomeo Vanzetti, and Rosina Sacco and Luigia Vanzetti.

The Winters of that Country is the first book to spring from a long relationship with the Black Sparrow Press. Originally attracted by the storied unsold copies of *A Man without Shoes*, Black Sparrow would publish more of J. S.'s books than any other publisher.

In content, *The Winters of that Country* is a book as brutal as they come—full of riots, lynchings, labor unrest, the persecution of the weak and poor by the strong and rich, and the desecration of the environment. It is a blistering book, yet one of consummate beauty. This work, published when he was 80 years old, shows J. S. at the pinnacle of his form.

b. First (limited, signed, numbered) edition:

[title page as in A15a]

22.7 x 14.8 cm. Collation and pagination identical to A15a, except for p.*351*, which is numbered in red ink, rather than lettered.

Brilliant blue cloth spine; spine label and boards identical to A15a. Clear acetate dust jacket.

Published simultaneously with A15a at $30.00; 200 copies.

Contents: As in A15a.

c. First trade edition:

[title page as in A15a and A15b]

22.7 x 14.8 cm. 1^2 $2\text{-}10^{16}$. Pp.*1-12*, 13-161, *162-179*, 180-349, *350-356*.

P.*1* publication history; p.*2* blank [except for extension of rule from title page]; p.*3* title; p.*4* copyright; pp.*5-356* [identical to A15a and A15b, except that p.*351* has no letter or number].

Light tan cloth spine; spine label and boards identical to A15a and A15b. Clear acetate dust jacket.

Published simultaneously with limited edition at $20.00; 300 copies.

Contents: As in A15a and A15b.

d. First paperback edition:

[title page as in A15a, A15b and A15c]

22.7 x 14.8 cm. Collation and pagination identical to A15c.

Stiff sand colored paper wrappers; printed down the spine [in red:] JOHN SANFORD [in orange:] THE WINTERS OF THAT COUNTRY [in red:] *Black Sparrow Press* [greenish gray-blue and gray rules that extend design from upper cover]. Upper and lower cover identical to A15a, A15b and A15c. Edges cut flush; endpapers; perfect binding; yellowish white wove paper.

Published simultaneously with hardcover edition at $12.50; 2,471 copies.

Contents: As in A15a, A15b and A15c.

Note: On 1 July 2002, David R. Godine took over unsold copies, offering them at $13.95.

A16 WILLIAM CARLOS WILLIAMS JOHN 1984 SANFORD: A CORRESPONDENCE

a. First (limited, signed) edition:

William Carlos Williams | John Sanford | A Correspondence | [thin red rule] Commentary by | John Sanford | (Julian Shapiro) | Foreword by | Paul Mariani | [thin red rule] | Oyster Press | Santa Barbara | 1984

22.2 x 14.9 cm. $1\text{-}3^8\ 4^4\ 5^2$. Pp.*1-4*, 5-11, *12-14*, 15-53, *54-60*.

Pp.*1-2* blank; p.*3* title; p.*4* Copyright © 1984 by John Sanford | Oyster Press gives special thanks to the National | Endowment for the Arts for continued patience and | for a grant which made this book possible. | Published by Oyster press, Lin Rolens, Editor, | [...] | [thin rule] | Distributed by Capra Press [...] | ISBN 0-933114-04-4 (paper) | ISBN 0-933114-05-2 (cloth) | ISBN 0-933114-06-0 (signed); pp.5-11 foreword; p.*12* blank;

p.*13* dedication: To Bill [W. C. Williams] | *from Pep* [Nathanael West] *and Julian* [Shapiro a.k.a. J. S.]; p.*14* blank; pp.15-16 commentary; pp.17-53 text; p.*54* blank; p.*55* afterword; p.*56* blank; p.*57* Designed and Printed by Graham Macintosh for | Oyster Press in November 1984. Set in Bembo, this | edition is limited to 2500: 2000 in paper wrappers | and 500 hardcover copies of which 75 have been | numbered and signed by John Sanford. | [number in blue ink] | [signature in blue ink]; pp.*58-60* blank.

Navy blue cloth boards, lettered in gold down the spine: WILLIAMS / SANFORD :: A CORRESPONDENCE. All edges cut; endpapers; flat spine. Yellowish white textured paper dust jacket printed in a marbled pattern in red, blue, white, black and shades of beige; no price printed on front flap. Yellowish white wove paper.

Published November 1984; price not obtainable; 75 copies.

Contents: Foreword by Paul Mariani—Commentary by J. S.—Correspondence—Afterword by J. S.

Note: J. S. cited Williams's *In the American Grain* as a paramount influence on his sense of America. Certainly, one can see those literary reflections on American history as a stimulus for J. S.'s own treatment of history. In addition, Williams was a revered idol and editor for J. S. at *Contact*. Williams also provided crucial praise for J. S.'s early writing. J. S. wrote in the Commentary to this edition, "The correspondence, sparse as it was... could hardly fail to govern the rest of my life."

The original letters printed in this volume were owned by J. S., and he donated them to the Williams archive at Yale University. However, Williams's heirs initiated a legal dispute over the letters' publication. The dispute was resolved when J. S.

assigned the copyright for this volume to the Williams heirs in April 1985.

b. First trade edition:

[title page as in A16a]

22.2 x 14.9 cm. Collation and pagination identical to A16a, except for p.57, which has no number or author signature. Binding and jacket identical to A16a, except that jacket has a price [printed in black on a white field] on the front flap.

Published simultaneously with A16a at $17.00; 425 copies.

Contents: As in A16a.

c. First paperback edition:

[title page as in A16a and A16b]

22.2 x 14.9 cm. $1\text{-}3^8\ 4^4\ 5^1$.

Pagination identical to A16b, except there is no pp.59-60.

Stiff yellowish white unprinted paper wrappers. Edges cut flush; perfect binding; yellowish white wove paper. Dust jacket is identical to A16a and A16b, but it has been glued to the spine and cut down flush to top and bottom of leaves; price printed in red.

Published simultaneously with hardcover edition at $8.00; 2,000 copies.

Contents: As in A16a and A16b.

A17 AN INTERVIEW WITH JOHN SANFORD: AN AMERICAN CLASSIC 1985

a. First (limited, signed) edition:

ROBERT W. SMITH | [rule] | An Interview with John Sanford: | An American Classic

21.6 x 13.8 cm. 1^6. Pp.*i*, 544-554.

Pp.*i* title; p.544 [drawing of J. S. by Pat Kenny] | [text]; pp.545-553 text; p.554 [text] | © Robert W. Smith | Works of John Sanford | Fiction | [9 titles] | Non-fiction | [6 titles on 7 lines].

Slightly stiff yellowish white paper wrappers; printed in black with facsimile of cover of the journal issue; [signed in black ink:] John Sanford/Julian Shapiro | The [swash T] LITERARY [swash L] REVIEW [swash R] | [rule] | SUMMER 1985 • VOLUME 28 • NUMBER 4 • $4.50 | [thin double rule] | [drawing of J. S. by Kenny, in box] | An Interview with and Writing by John Sanford | Nina Berberova's Prize-Winning Novella | Essays and Poetry. Edges cut flush; wire staples at left. Yellowish white wove paper.

Published in 1985; number of copies uncertain; presumably distributed gratis

Contents: Interview by Robert W. Smith.

Note: This pamphlet appears to be an offprint from *The Literary Review* (see C35); however, *The Literary Review* was not aware of its existence and suggested it was a private undertaking of the author. Robert Smith reported that J. S. sent him 25 copies, 5 of which were signed. Thus, it appears that J. S. arranged for these;

how many total [likely no more than 50], and how many of those were signed [likely no more than 20-25] cannot be determined.

b. First regular (limited) edition:

[as in A17a, except upper cover is not signed]

21.6 x 13.8 cm. Slightly stiff yellowish white paper wrappers; printed in black. Edges cut flush; wire staples at left. Yellowish white wove paper.

Published in 1985; number of copies uncertain [likely no more than 25-30]; presumably distributed gratis.

A18   THE COLOR OF THE AIR   1985

a. First (limited, signed, lettered) edition:

[magenta square] | JOHN | SANFORD | [yellow rule extending onto facing page] | [in magenta:] THE COLOR | OF THE AIR | [in black:] SCENES | FROM | THE | LIFE | OF | AN | AMERICAN | JEW | VOLUME 1 | [yellow rule] | BLACK SPARROW PRESS [square] SANTA BARBARA [square] 1985

22.8 x 14.9 cm. $1^2\ 2^1\ 3\text{-}4^{16}\ 5^8\ 6\text{-}13^{16}$. Pp.*i-ii, 1-18,* 19-301, *302-308.*

P.*i* ALSO BY JOHN SANFORD | NOVELS AND OTHER FICTION | [9 titles] | INTERPRETATIONS OF AMERICAN HISTORY | [4 titles] | LETTERS | [1 title on 2 lines] | AUTOBIOGRAPHY | [2 titles on 4 lines]; p.*ii* blank [except for extension of design elements from title page]; p.*1* title; p.*2* [...] Copyright © 1985 by John Sanford | [...] Printed in the United States of America [...] | ISBN 0-87685-644-X (vol. 1) | ISBN 0-87685-643-1 (pbk. : v. 1.) | ISBN 0-87685-645-8 (lim. ed. : v. 1);

p.3 [author's signature in blue ink: John Sanford/Julian Shapiro]; p.4 blank; p.5 dedication: In honor of my father and mother | *Philip D. Shapiro* | 1878-1972 | *Harriet Nevins Shapiro* | 1881-1914 | and with love; p.6 blank; p.7 epigraph: A very good land to fall with | and a pleasant land to see | — R. Juet: *Discovery of the Hudson*; p.8 blank; p.9 A Note on the Title; p.*10* blank; pp.*11-15* contents; p.*16* blank; p.*17* fly title; p.*18* blank; pp.19-301 text; p.*302* blank; p.*303* Printed in August 1985 in Santa Barbara & Ann Arbor | for the Black Sparrow Press by Graham Mackintosh & | Edwards Brothers Inc. Design by Barbara Martin. | This edition is published in paper wrappers; there | are 300 cloth trade copies; 150 hardcover copies have | been numbered and signed by the author; & 26 copies | handbound in boards by Earle Gray lettered & | signed by the author. [letter in red ink] | [publisher's sparrow device 1.6 x 1.5 cm.] | p.*304* photo of J. S.; p.*305* author biography; pp.*306-308* blank.

Dark blue cloth spine patterned in black, with gray-blue paper label printed with one yellow and two white bands, lettered down the spine [in black:] JOHN | SANFORD [in magenta:] THE COLOR | OF THE AIR; light gray-blue paper boards; upper cover has a medium gray-blue geometric pattern extending to lower cover; upper cover printed: [small dark blue square] | [white rule extending to lower cover] | [in black:] JOHN | [white rule extending to lower cover] | [in black:] SANFORD | [yellow rule extending to lower cover] | [in magenta:] THE COLOR | OF THE AIR | [white rule extending right] | [black lettering alternating with white rules:] SCENES | FROM | THE | LIFE | OF | AN | AMERICAN | JEW | [white rule] | VOLUME 1 | [yellow rule extending to lower cover] | [small dark blue square]. All edges cut; endpapers; flat spine. Clear acetate dust jacket. Yellowish white wove paper.

Published 25 September 1985 at $40.00; 26 copies.

Contents: The Color of the Air, I—Father (1878-1972)—Mother (1881-1914)—Abraham Nevins (c.1857-1926)—Leah Nevins, née Jacobson (c.1859-1934)—Sinai Shapiro (c.1845-1911)—Rachel Shapiro, née Lieberman (c. 1845-1934)—Harry W. Perlman (1902)—Philip and Harriet Shapiro, née Nevins (1903)—May 31, 1904—2 West 120th Street—*And Then Zipporah Took a Sharp Stone* (1904)—The Gainsboro Years (1904-09)—Summer at Tannersville, a Photo (1905)—The Color of the Air, II—Undesirable Citizens (1907)—The Panic of 1907—Sister Ruth, the Starved Cuban (1908)—The Precious Stone (1908)—The Cabonak Years (1909-12)—A Place of Spells (1909)—The Paternal Relation (1909)—Dissent (1909)—The Maternal Relation (1909)—Morris Avenue, Long Branch, N.J. (1909)—Rubeola (1910)—Phyllis G. (1910)—Childe Julian, Boy King (1910)—Childe Julian, Etc., cont'd. (1910)—The Color of the Air, III—Uncle Jerome, "Romie" (1894-1946)—Garfield Avenue, Long Branch, N.J. (1910)—A Book Called *Patriotic America* (1910)—Pages and Pictures of American History—*Meet Me at the Fountain* (1910)—Leather Buttons (1910)—Miss Moorhead (1910-11)—A Letter from Your Mother, Nov. 1, 1911—The Seal of Yale College (1911)—Aunt Ida (c. 1890-1969)—Cottage Place, Long Branch, N.J. (1912)—Uncle Lulu (c. 1885-1900)—Aunt Rae (c.1879-1962)—Uncle Dave Nevins (c.1884-1947)—Miss Blauvelt, Teacher (1913)—The Color of the Air, IV—Hark, Hear the Merry Mandolin (1913)—The Failing Years (1912-14)—The Seaside Summers (1909-14)—A Nice Quiet Law Practice (1909-14)—Of Boats and Trains (1911)—Emma Trentini (1912)—By Motor-Coach to Morristown (1912)—The Black Box (1912)—The Cripple (1911)—An Ill Wind (1912)—The Man Who Knew Gyp the Blood (1912)—Uncle Dave (1913)—The Color of the Air, V—The Character Committee (1914)—Easter in Atlantic City (1914)—The Hotel and Boardinghouse Years (1912-14)—The Dowry (1914)—Variable Winds (1903-14)—The Last Summer of Chair Esther (1914)—The Color of the Air, VI—July 29, 1914—By Automobile to Brooklyn (1914)—Mourner's

JOHN SANFORD

Kaddish (1914)—The Eleven-Month Year (1914-15)—The *Schul* on 116th Street (1914-15)—Mary Phagan (1915)—The Flat on 117th Street (1914-15)—The Crib (1915)—The School on 119th Street (1914-15)—Uncle Dave Nevins (1914-15)—Grandpa Nevins (1914-15)—What the Trunk Contained (1914)—The Three Blows (1914-17)—The Color of the Air, VII—The Nevins Household (1914-15)—A New Member of the Family (1880?-1935?)—Sartor Resartus in Harlem (1914)—The Silver Son-in-law (1914-15)—Poor Misfortunate Boy (1914-15)—The *Fresser* (1914-15)—*Sol y Sombra* (1914)—The Nevins Household (1914-20)—White Bread (1914-20)—Sister Ruth and Brother Julian (1916)—Beneath a Tiffany Chandelier (1914-20)—Dissent (1915)—The Color of the Air, VIII—Harlem (1915)—The Widower (1914-15)—Son-in-law Phil (1914-20)—*Gummelappen* (1914-20)—Zoological Gardens (1915)—Long Branch, N.J. (1915)—*And Grant Thee Eternal Peace* (1915)—Brother's Keeper (1916)—Dissent (1916)—On the Way Home (1916)—Seventy-five Flies (1916)—The Flyswatter (1916)—The Presidential Campaign of 1916—The Mick from the Moy (1916)—Two Years at P.S. 10 (1915-17)—The Color of the Air, IX—*God Helping Her, She Can Do No Other* (1917)—Claudia Muzio (1917)—The Steamboat House (1917)—A Pair of Shoes, Size 2 (1917)—*Fear Ye Not, Stand Still* (1917)—Mildred A. (1917)—The Poor Misfortunate Boy (1917)—How to Know and Check the Spread of (1917)—You and Your Bonehead Friends (1917-18)—Dictatorship of the Proletariat (1917)—The Years at De Witt (1917-21)—Well, Romie is Home Again (1917)—The Manly Art of Self-Defense (1917)—The Color of the Air, X—Homage to Jacob Mendelson (1916-17)—The Fishes and the Feits (1918)—Episodes in a Bathroom (1918)—*Mens Sana in Corpore Sano* (1918)—The Painted Woman (1918-20)—Green Mountain Camp (1920)—Julian Dear, He Wrote (1920)—A Faithful and Dutiful Son (1920)—While You Looked the Other Way (1920)—The Rift (1920)—The Color of the Air, XI—To Join the Gypsies (1920)—The Dotey Squad (1921)—High School on

59th St. (1917-21)—Childe Julian: Working Stiff (1921)—*How Far from Then Forethought of* (1921)—First Semester at Lafayette (1922)—Transcontinental: A Bumming-Trip (1922)—The Color of the Air, XII—Second Semester at Lafayette (1922-23)—*The Time of Figs Was Not Yet* (1923)—The Campus on the 28th Floor (1923)—*Falsus in Uno* (1923)—An Inkling of Savannah (1923)—A Girl Named B. (1923)—*Wanderjahr* (1924)—Question and Answer (1924)—Fordham Law School (1924-25)—Of Things Past (1925)—Aaron's in Town (1860-1938)—The Autumn of 1925—A Trip to Californy (1925)—The Color of the Air, XIII—North Pole, South Pole (1925)—Another Friend from Lafayette (1925)—Blue (1925)—The Fall of 1926—The Winter of 1926—The Death of Grandpa Nevins (1926)—Ignorance I (1926)—Ignorance II (1926)—Ignorance III (1926)—The Color of the Air, XIV—Walks in the Dark (1926-27)—Sunsets, Dooryards, Sprinkled Streets (1926-27)—The Final Year on the 28th Floor (1926-27)—Of Things Past (1926-27)—An Hour with Silver Phil (1927)—On a Bench in Washington Square (1927)—The Fine Arts (1927)—Room 1021 (1927)—*Jealousy Is Cruel as the Grave* (1927)—A Walk with the Adversary (1927)—The Bed in Room 1021 (1927)—When Shall We Three Meet Again (1927)—A Letter Dated June 7, 1927—Midsummer Night (1927)—August 22, 1927—August 23, 1927—August 24, 1927—Even at This Late Day (1927)—The Color of the Air, XV—S.S. *Caronia* (1927).

Note: There are the following misprints:
p.28, l.29—"unindured"
p.46, l.14—"neighbor who loved"
p.63, l.11—"defenceless"
p.64-5—a line of text appears to be missing
p.74, l.23—"you 'd"
p.127, l.15—"thoght"
p.143, l.17-8—"still wearing crape on your sleeve"
p.175, l.21—"learn of Mr. Mendelson"

p.207, l.10-1—there appears to be an inadvertent line break
p.233, l.4 "fflloor"

The Color of the Air commences J. S.'s epic autobiography. In it, he intersperses historical pieces that give the context of the narrative. J. S. writes, "Each deals with a phase or force in the history of the country [...] furnish[ing] 'the color of the air,' a fast color, for history does not fade." In volume 2 of his autobiography, J. S. would describe these pieces as giving "the political element in which the principal character lives."

The following pieces are repeated from previous books: Draw Me Not Without Reason (A9); First Lady (A5, A9 & A12); The Precious Stone, revised from A Neighbor Woman, Name Unknown 1908 The Precious Stone in A12; Childe Julian Boy King appeared as Auld Acquaintance (P. G.) 1910 Childe Julian, Boy King (A12); The First Knee on Canada, revised from A4 & A9; Miss Blauvelt, Teacher (1913) appeared as A Teacher at P. S. 81, Manhattan 1913 Miss Blauvelt in A12; Lovers of the Uppermost Seats (A9); Rebellion of the Well-Fed (A9); Under a Lone Star (A9); A Round Trip to Alton (A9); Sister Ruth and Brother Julian (1916), revised from Sister Ruth 1908 – and Brother Julian in A12; A Dreamer Perishes (A9); The Landlord (A9); Oh, Dear Dangerfield (A9); At the Telegraph Office (A9); The Dotey Squad (1921), revised from an episode in A5; High School on 59th St. (1917-21) appeared as Countee Cullen 1903-1946 High School on 59th St. in A11; Childe Julian Working Stiff (1921), revised from an episode in A5; How Far from Then Forethought of (1921), revised from 1927 Sacco and Vanzetti, I-Blues for Two Greenhorns in A9; Transcontinental: A Bumming Trip (1922) reprints a portion of an episode from A5; The Winter of 1926, revised from Auld Acquaintance (L. G.) 1927 The Hand-Me-Down in A11; Play Within a Play (A9); Deseret (A9); Ignorance III (1926-27) repeats a portion of an episode from A5; Hoka Hey! (A9); A Juror: *I'd Hang All the Damn Buggers* (A6 & A9). Scenes

1 through 9 previously appeared in *The Literary Review* (C36) and scenes 1 through 13 appeared in *Jewish Spectator* (C39). *And then Zipporah Took a Sharp Stone* (1904) reprints a portion of the invitation to J. S.'s *bris* (see E1a), and Homage to Jacob Mendelson (1916-17) reprints the invitation to his bar mitzvah (see E1b).

Sales, again, were unexceptional. By October 1986, Black Sparrow reported the following sales: 1017 paperback, 109 hardcover, 77 numbered, 24 lettered.

The Color of the Air begins audaciously, with an—intended? unintended?—metaphorical equation of the author's pen with the sword of one of Coronado's conquistadors. An inscription on that sword read "Draw me not without reason. Sheathe me not without honor." This, it seems, is the challenge the 80-year-old J. S. presented to himself in undertaking a multi-volume autobiography.

The Color of the Air's style is unusual for an autobiography. J. S. eschewed traditional exposition and opted instead in favor of dramatizing his life in scenes replete with dialog. This at times provokes amazement in readers, over J. S.'s apparent ability to recall detailed conversations from decades ago. J. S. has confessed that it would, of course, be impossible to remember such conversations. Instead, he constructed scenes based on a recalled phrase, or simply knowing what he was doing at a particular time. He filled these scenes with dialog that "may have happened, could have happened, *should* have happened." The result is a dramatic and evocative narrative that brings his personal history to life, in a way rarely found in memoirs.

In structure, *The Color of the Air* is unique in its organization into scenes. Sometimes lengthy, sometimes brief, the structure of the book mimics the structure of recollection. Memories do not form a seamless flow. Rather, they represent discrete bits of material—more mosaic than stream.

The content of *The Color of the Air* is often poignant, as the aged J. S. writes of himself in the second person, "you." The chagrin the author felt as he examined his youthful self's misdeeds is palpable: "Seen from this future, that past belongs to someone else—it isn't yours, you tell yourself. It isn't yours at all. How can that be you there…?" (p. 266). In particular, it appears J. S. could never forgive himself for his child's ignorance of his mother's mortal sickness. Her lingering illness, her death, and the aftermath of her death form the heart of the narrative. In his foreword to the autobiography's final volume, *The Season, It Was Winter*, J. S. wrote: "Looking back on what you were, you have the sense of watching an independent image in a glass, a past self unattached to the self outside, and, unable to intervene, you can only be a witness to its callow conduct, its errors, cocksure, thoughtless, and rash" (p. 19).

Stylistically, *The Color of the Air* is exquisite. J. S. was at the peak of his authorial powers. Just one of innumerable examples is a passage about his mother on her honeymoon from p. 28. It displays an intricate web of interior rhymes—rhyming words in the middle of phrases rather than at the ends. J. S. maintained that, though these rhymes would likely not be detected by readers, they would nonetheless be compelling at an unconscious level. They give J. S.'s prose the ring of poetry. "Unknown to you now forever what she wore, what she *said*, what thoughts *wound* through her *head*, and wonder though you *may*, never to be *found* her frame of *mind*—was she *grave* or *gay*, did she please with what she *gave* him, did she think her husband *kind*?" [italics mine]

The Color of the Air was given the PEN award for best nonfiction by a Southern California writer in 1985. (See A19 for J. S.'s acceptance speech.)

b. First (limited, signed, numbered) edition:

[title page as in A18a]

Collation and pagination identical to A18a, except for p.*303*, which is numbered in red ink, rather than lettered.

Bright yellow cloth spine; spine label and boards identical to A18a. Clear acetate dust jacket.

Published simultaneously with A18a at $30.00; 150 copies.

Contents: As in A18a.

c. First trade edition:

[title page as in A18a and A18b]

22.8 x 14.9 cm. *1^2 2-3^{16} 4^8 5-12^{16}*. Pp.*1-18*, 19-301, *302-308*.

P.*1* publication history; p.*2* blank [except for extension of design elements from title page]; p.*3* title; p.*4* copyright; pp.*5-308* [identical to A18a and A18b, except that p.*303* is not lettered or numbered].

Royal blue cloth spine; spine label and boards identical to A18a and A18b. Clear acetate dust jacket.

Published simultaneously with limited edition at $20.00; 300 copies.

Contents: As in A18a and A18b.

d. First paperback edition:

[title page as in A18a, A18b and A18c]

22.8 x 14.8 cm. Collation and pagination identical to A18c.

Stiff yellowish white paper wrappers; printed in medium gray-blue and light gray-blue; spine with white and yellow rules extending from upper cover, lettered down [in black:] JOHN | SANFORD [in magenta:] THE COLOR | OF THE AIR [in black:] *Black Sparrow Press*. Upper and lower covers identical to A18a, A18b and A18c. Edges cut flush; endpapers; perfect binding; yellowish white wove paper.

Published simultaneously with hardcover edition at $12.50; 2,506 copies.

Contents: As in A18a, A18b and A18c.

Note: On 1 July 2002, David R. Godine took over unsold copies, offering them at $16.95.

A19   [THE CREATIVE PROCESS]   1986

a. First (signed, limited) edition:

A KEEPSAKE FOR JOHN SANFORD ON THE OCCASION OF HIS | EIGHTY-SECOND BIRTHDAY—MAY 31, 1986 | [THE CREATIVE PROCESS] | [text] | [signed and numbered in blue ink] | Remarks given by John Sanford on the occasion of receiving the PEN AWARD | for the best work of non-fiction (*The Color of the Air: Scenes from the Life of* | *An American Jew*) by a southern California author in 1985. | Beverly Hills Hotel, April 25, 1986

Broadside. 34.2 x 25.4 cm. Textured light gray paper, printed in purple.

Published 31 May 1986; 15 copies; distributed gratis.

Note: This broadside was published by J. S.'s friend Tom Andrews, a professor of English at Westmont College. These remarks are J.

S.'s acceptance speech for the first literary award he was given. In them, he avers he is as baffled as anyone about how he comes to create his works.

b. First regular (limited) edition:

[as in A19a, except not signed or numbered]

Broadside. 34.2 x 25.4 cm. Textured light gray paper, printed in purple.

Published 31 May 1986; 15 copies; distributed gratis.

A20   THE WATERS OF DARKNESS   1986

a. First (limited, signed, lettered) edition:

[at a 30-degree angle upward to the right:] [in black:] JOHN | [blue square] SANFORD | [in red:] THE | WATERS | OF | DARKNESS | [blue square] [in black:] VOLUME 2 | [horizontal:] SCENES | FROM | THE | LIFE | OF | AN | AMERICAN | JEW | [blue rule extending onto facing page] | BLACK SPARROW PRESS [small square] SANTA BARBARA [small square] 1986

22.8 x 14.9 cm. $1^2\ 2^1\ 3\text{-}4^{16}\ 5^2\ 6\text{-}12^{16}$. Pp.*i-ii, 1-16*, 17-289, *290-296*.

P.*i* ALSO BY JOHN SANFORD | NOVELS AND OTHER FICTION | [9 titles] | INTERPRETATIONS OF AMERICAN HISTORY | [4 titles] | LETTERS | [1 title] | AUTOBIOGRAPHY | [3 titles on 6 lines]; p.*ii* blank [except for extension of design elements from title page]; p.*1* title; p.*2* [...] Copyright © 1986 by John Sanford | [...] Printed in the United States of America [...] | ISBN 0-87685-671-7 (pbk. : v. 2) | ISBN 0-87685-672-5 (hard : v. 2) | ISBN 0-87685-673-3 (signed : v. 2); p.*3* [author's signature in blue ink: John Sanford/

Julian Shapiro]; p.*4* blank; p.*5* dedication: This book is for my cousin | Mel Friedman | who has also been my friend [and who provided significant support for J. S.'s early writing career by placing with publishers and designing J. S.'s first two books]; p.*6* blank; p.*7* epigraph: Water is a movable and wandering thing | — Blackstone's *Commentaries*; p.*8* blank; p.*9* A Note on the Inserts; p.*10* blank; pp.*11-13* contents; p.*14* blank; p.*15* fly title; p.*16* blank; pp.17-289 text; p.*290* blank; p.*291* Printed in April 1986 in Santa Barbara & Ann Arbor | for the Black Sparrow Press by Graham Mackintosh & | Edwards Brothers Inc. Design by Barbara Martin. | This edition is published in paper wrappers; there | are 300 cloth trade copies; 150 hardcover copies | have been numbered and signed by the author; & 26 | copies handbound in boards by Earle Gray have been | lettered & signed by the author. [letter in red ink] | [publisher's sparrow device 1.7 x 1.7 cm.] | p.*292* photo of J. S.; p.*293* author biography; pp.*294-296* blank.

Black cloth spine patterned in pink, blue and mauve, with mauve and yellowish white paper label lettered down the spine [in black:] JOHN | SANFORD [in magenta:] THE WATERS | OF DARKNESS; yellowish white paper boards; upper cover has a mauve geometric pattern and dark blue rules extending to lower cover; printed at thirty degree angle [in dark blue:] JOHN | [small black square] | [in dark blue:] SANFORD | [in bright red:] THE | WATERS | OF | DARKNESS | [dark blue square] [in black:] VOLUME 2 | [each line preceded by a dark blue rule extending to lower cover:] SCENES | FROM | THE | LIFE | OF | AN | AMERICAN | JEW. All edges cut; endpapers; flat spine. Clear acetate dust jacket. Yellowish white wove paper.

Published 27 June 1986 at $40.00; 26 copies.

Contents: The Color of the Air, I—Round-trip to England (September 1927)—The Apprentice (1927-1929)—The Color of the Air, II—The Summer that Began in May (1929)—And Ended in October (Fall 1929)—The People vs. Adolphus Rock (February 1930)—From the Niemen River and the River Moy (1930)—A One-room Flat on Bank Street (Early 1930)—Autumn Days (Late 1929)—Of Phil, the Silver Son-in-law (March 1930)—The Laurel in the Pines (Early 1930)—The Color of the Air, III—The Little Magazine *Tambour* (Spring and Summer 1929)—The People vs. Jesús Cortez (April 1930)—Shaw's Farmhouse on Long Lake (May 1930)—Father and Son (Late Spring 1930)— The House on Norwood, in West End (Summer of 1930)—The Evils of Capitalism (Fall 1930)—A Dissenter's Disciple (Fall of 1930)—The Time Now Is... (November 1930)—The Color of the Air, IV—S.S. St. Louis (December 1930)—Parent and Child (May 1931)—The Partnership (Late May 1931)—Novelist and Novice (June 1931)—The Color of the Air, V—Memoir of a Summer in the Woods (June-September 1931)—The Color of the Air, VI—Long View (Fall of 1931)—The Sons of Phil and Max (September 1931)—Apt. C-6, 131 Washington Street (Fall of 1931)—*A Hotel of Charm and Refinement* (Fall of 1931)— Homage to a Call-girl (Fall of 1931)—*The Old Man's Place* (Fall of 1931)—Once Again, the Wandering Jew (December 1931)—The Luckless One (January 1932)—Fish Shape Paumanok (January 1932)—*Contact: An American Quarterly* (Fall 1931)—*When I Became a Man* (Early 1932)—The Dragon Press Dragon (Spring 1932)—Instructor, Translator, Publisher (1932)—The Color of the Air, VII—The Value of a Dollar, I (Summer of 1932)— The Value of a Dollar, II (Summer of 1932)— The Value of a Dollar, III (Summer of 1932)—Aunt Jo (Summer of 1932)—Stepsister Leah (Summer of 1932)—*The Water Wheel* (Summer of 1932)— Hell to Pay (Late Summer 1932)—A Day's Absence from the Sutton (Fall 1932)—The Fiduciary (Late 1932)—L. T.: Why Don't you Practice on a Whore? (December 1932)—The Insulted and Injured (End of 1932)—A Restaurant on 34th Street (End of 1932)—Coda (End of 1932)—The Color of the Air, VIII—First

Novel (Early 1933)—First Review (March 1933)—The Harlem School of Literature (Spring 1933)—With the Compliments of the Author (Spring 1933)—First Letter from *Central Pension* (March 1933)—And Later Reviews (Spring 1933)—Brooks Bothers: Men's Clothiers (August 1933)—The 48th Passenger (November 1933)—The Flat on Central Park West (November 1933)—The Novel about Little Sam (December 1933)—The Color of the Air, IX—What Are You Doing Young Man? (Early 1934)—Farewell to an Olderly Woman (Early 1934)—A Letter from Uncle Dave (March 1934)—From Wandering on a Foreign Strand (Early 1934)—Being of Sound Mind and Memory (May 1934)—Stubborn and Rebellious Sons (May 1934)—A Goshen Far from Egypt (June 1934)—The Quality of Mercy (June 1934)—Of One Who Wrote to Eugene Debs (June 1934)—Harris Friedman (1933-34)—Encounter in a Hospital Hallway (summer of 1934)—The Color of the Air, X—A Long Last Season at the Shore (Summer of 1934)—The Same Pilgrim, the Same Plymouth Rock (Fall of 1934)—Poor Man's Party (End of 1934)—Gone to Sit at the Feet of Mary (Early 1935)—The Painted Woman Goes (Early 1935)—Who Was That Lady…? (Early 1935)—Aunt Rae (Early 1935)—The Color of the Air, XI—An Affair of the Heart (From Early 1935)—Labor Day Weekend (Late Summer 1935)—A Bar or Two of Music from Afar (Summer of 1935)—The Color of the Air, XII—Along a Liffey of Your Own (Summer Of 1935)—*The Old Man's Place* (Fall of 1935)—The Color of the Air, XIII—Another Book (January 1936)—170 West 73rd Street, Apt. 10b (February 1936)—Queer Street, Apt. 10b (February 1936)—Exercise on an Empty Stomach (March 1936)—And Other Valuable Considerations (May 1936)—By the Light of the Dog Star (July 1936)—A Man Called Morris (August 1936).

Note: There are the following misprints:
p.13, l.22—"Summer 0f 1935"
p.157, l.20—"called ''a"

p.159, l.12—"a cup of coffee steam, its vapor"
p.163, l.10—"Carl Rakosi. but"
p.170, l.29—"the same railing as off, the same mistakes"
p.196, l.20—"to made bad worse,"
p.266, l.5—"the comment of a a critic"

Hardcover editions of *The Waters of Darkness* were sold with a 4-page pamphlet laid in: "A Note Concerning John Sanford's Epic Trilogy" by John Martin, publisher of the Black Sparrow Press (see E1k).

The following pieces are repeated from previous books: A Place Called Here (A9); The Apprentice (1927-29) contains an episode revised from Auld Acquaintance (O. B.) 1928 A Poem Set to Music in A12; Adelantado of Florida (A9); A Summer that Began in May (1929) contains an episode revised from Auld Acquaintance (S. L.) 1929 The Pleasures of Sin for a Season in A12; What Will the Duke Say? (A9); In the Kaatskills (A9 & A11); Memoir of a Summer in the Woods (June-September 1931) contains Nathanael West 1903-1940 Miss Lonelyhearts in the Adirondacks (A11) and "Tired Men and Dung" (C9); A Constitutional in Philadelphia (A9); *The Old Man's Place* (Fall of 1931) contains an episode revised from Auld Acquaintance (R. P.) 1931 A Woman Arrayed in Purple in A12; Winter Carnival (A9); L.T.: Why Don't You Practice on a Whore? revised from Auld Acquaintance (L. T.) 1932 Let Her Take Thee with Her Eyelids in A12; In Bronze Above a Doorway (A9 & A11); Marse Linkum (A5 & A9); Painter of the Painted Indian (A9); The Running W (A9); A Bar or Two of Music from Afar contains Auld Acquaintance (H. L.) 1935 A Nine-Page Letter (A12); A Wandering Jew (A9); A Land to Love (A9 & A11).

The Waters of Darkness is noteworthy for its evocations of the early years of the Depression in New York; for its insights into a young man's search to craft an identity for himself as a writer; and for its depiction of the summer J. S. and Nathanael West spent together in the Adirondacks, when J. S. was working on *The Water Wheel* and West was working on *Miss Lonelyhearts*. This summer was crucial in shaping J. S.'s writing for years to come. The short stories he would soon craft drew on settings from, and material acquired during, his stay at Viele Pond. His next three novels would be set in nearby Warrensburg. And, although he had had an affinity for nature, derived from the summers of his youth spent on the Jersey Shore, J. S.'s stay in the mountains deepened his love for America's wilderness, a theme that would imbue his later novels, such as *A Man Without Shoes*, and his non-fiction.

b. First (limited, signed, numbered) edition:

[title page as in A20a]

Collation and pagination identical to A20a, except for p.*291*, which is numbered in red ink, rather than lettered.

Mauve cloth spine; spine label and boards identical to A20a. Clear acetate dust jacket.

Published simultaneously with A20a at $30.00; 150 copies.

Contents: As in A20a.

c. First trade edition:

[title page as in A20a and A20b]

22.8 x 14.9 cm. 1^2 2-3^{16} 4^8 5-12^{16}. Pp.*1-18*, 19-301, *302-308*.

P.*1* publication history; p.*2* blank [except for extension of design elements from title page]; p.*3* title; p.*4* copyright; pp.*5-356* [identical to A20a and A20b, except that p.*291* is not lettered or numbered].

Black cloth spine; spine label and boards identical to A20a and A20b. Clear acetate dust jacket.

Published simultaneously with limited edition at $20.00; 300 copies.

Contents: As in A20a and A20b.

Note: On 1 July 2002, David R. Godine took over unsold copies, offering them at $22.95.

d. First paperback edition:

[title page as in A20a, A20b and A20c]

22.8 x 14.7 cm. Collation and pagination identical to A20c.

Stiff, textured yellowish white paper wrappers printed in mauve, blue, bright red and black; printed down the spine [in black:] JOHN | SANFORD [in red:] THE WATERS | OF DARKNESS [in black:] BLACK SPARROW PRESS. Upper and lower covers identical to A20a, A20b and A20c. Edges cut flush; endpapers; perfect binding; yellowish white wove paper.

Published simultaneously with hardcover edition at $12.50; 2,500 copies.

Contents: As in A20a, A20b and A20c.

Note: The mauve ink on the spine of the paperback edition is highly sensitive to light. Frequently it fades to a mint green color.

On 1 July 2002, David R. Godine took over unsold copies, offering them at $13.95.

A21   A VERY GOOD LAND TO FALL WITH   1987

a. First (limited, signed, lettered) edition:

[grayish mint-green square] | [in black:] JOHN | SANFORD | [in red:] A VERY GOOD | LAND TO FALL | WITH | [at a 30-degree angle:] [grayish mint-green rule extending onto facing page] | [in black:] SCENES | FROM | THE | LIFE | OF | AN | AMERICAN | JEW | [grayish mint-green rule] | [horizontal:] VOLUME 3 | [grayish mint-green square] | BLACK SPARROW PRESS [small black square] SANTA BARBARA [small black square] 1987

22.7 x 14.9 cm. $1^2\ 2^1\ 3\text{-}4^{16}\ 5^4\ 6\text{-}12^{16}$. Pp.*i-ii, 1-14*, 15-296, *297-300*.

P.*i* BY JOHN SANFORD | NOVELS AND OTHER FICTION | [9 titles] | INTERPRETATIONS OF AMERICAN HISTORY | [4 titles] | LETTERS | [1 title] | AUTOBIOGRAPHY | [3 titles on 6 lines]; p.*ii* blank [except for extension of design elements from title page]; p.*1* title; p.*2* [...] Copyright © 1987 by John Sanford | [...] Printed in the United States of America [...] | ISBN 0-87685-714-4 | ISBN 0-87685-715-2 (signed) | ISBN 0-87685-713-5 (pbk.); p.*3* [author's signature in blue ink: John Sanford/Julian Shapiro]; p.*4* blank; p.*5* dedication: To friends, among whom these: | Herbert Ortman [from Lafayette College, and former law partner], Richard Johns [publisher of the little magazine *Pagany*], George | Brounoff [mentor and leader of group of intellectuals during the late 1920s (see Appendix C)], Alan [Pete] Lewis [English professor and member of Brounoff's group], Lynn Riggs [J. S.'s first writing partner in Hollywood; wrote *Green Grow the Lilacs* on which *Oklahoma* was based], | Richard Wentworth [editor at University of Illinois Press who was a proponent of J. S.'s historical books],

Paul Mariani [former literary executor to J. S., biographer of W. C. Williams]—and | Louise Gifford ["hand-me-down" girlfriend of J. S., depicted in *The Water Wheel, To Feed Their Hopes* and the autobiography]. | J. S.; p.*6* blank; p.*7* A Note on the Inserts; p.*8* blank; pp.*9-12* contents; p.*13* fly title; p.*14* blank; pp.15-296 text; p.*297* Printed in October 1987 in Santa Barbara & Ann Arbor | for the Black Sparrow Press by Graham Mackintosh & | Edwards Brothers Inc. Design by Barbara Martin. | This edition is published in paper wrappers; there | are 300 cloth trade copies; 150 hardcover copies | have been numbered and signed by the author; & 26 | copies handbound in boards by Earle Gray have been | lettered & signed by the author. [letter in red ink] | [publisher's sparrow device 1.7 x 1.7 cm.] | p.*298* photo of J. S.; p.*299* author biography; p.*300* blank.

Navy blue cloth spine with a floral pattern in turquoise, silver and gray, with light gray and grayish green paper label lettered down the spine [in black:] JOHN | SANFORD [in red:] A VERY GOOD LAND | TO FALL WITH; light gray paper boards; upper cover has a grayish green geometric pattern extending to lower cover; printed [navy blue square] | [in black:] JOHN | SANFORD | [in red:] A VERY GOOD | LAND TO FALL | WITH | [at a 30-degree angle] [in black:] SCENES | FROM | THE | LIFE | OF | AN | AMERICAN | JEW | [horizontal:] VOLUME 3 | [navy blue square]. All edges cut; endpapers; flat spine. Clear acetate dust jacket. Yellowish white wove paper.

Published 11 December 1987 at $40.00; 26 copies.

Contents: 2200 Miles on *The Chief* (August 1936)—The Town of Our Lady Queen of the Angels (Fall of 1936)—Vignettes (Fall of 1936)—The Color of the Air, I—The War in Spain (1937)—More Vignettes (1936-37)—News from the Front (Early 1937)—Once Again, Vignettes (Early 1937)—The Color of the Air, II—Two

Book Reports by M. Roberts (Early in 1937)—The Smiths: Their Short and Simple Annals (Early in 1937)—A Waiter Named George Portugal (Early in 1937)—Sentences from a Letter to Ruth (Early in 1937)—2214 Canyon Drive (Early in 1937)—The Color of the Air, III—Another Sunday (Spring of 1937)—Light and Shade (Spring of 1937)—The White Sands of New Mexico (Spring of 1937)—The Smith Family Album (Spring of 1937)—A Personal and Political Sequence (Summer and Fall of 1937)—At the Sign of the Lion (Fall of 1937)—More Letters from a Father to a Son (Fall of 1937)—A Short Talk with Maggie—Praiser of Times Past (Fall of 1937)—The Color of the Air, IV—One for the Road (December 1937)—Concerning a Trip to New York (December 1937)—The Old Settlers (Early in 1938)—Persuasion Above a Garage (Spring of 1938)—While Lying on a Glider (Spring of 1938)—The Color of the Air, V—An Original Story (Spring of 1938)—Never Build a House in a Hollow (March 1938)—On the Writing of *Seventy Times Seven* (April 1938)—Entries in a Note-book (April-June 1938)—Concerning a Trip to Reno (June 1938)—"A Series of Lectures by One of Our People" (Summer of 1938)—Where and Why (Late Summer 1938)—The Color of the Air, VI—In the Summer of That Year (June-September 1938)—Whipping-Boy of the Western World—In the Fall of That Year (October 1938)—A New York Sequence (Nov. 1936-March 1939)—The Advice of Counsel (Early December 1938)—The Color of the Air, VII—The Thirtieth Day of the Month (December 1938)—Hard Lines in Boston (March 1939)—Casualty List (Late March 1939)—Transcontinental (April 1939)—Rent $75 per mo. furn. (June 1939)—How One of Its Days May Have Gone (Summer of 1939)—The Nazi-Soviet Pact (Summer of 1939)—Tidings from Near and Far (Fall of 1939)—Letters from the Governor (Fall of 1939)—A Social Evening: four stages (Early in 1940)—The Color of the Air, VIII—That Spring and Summer (1940)—That Fall and Winter (1940)—Bad Days at Year's End (Late 1940)—On a Side-Street in Hollywood (January

1941)—They That Will Be Rich (April 1941)—A Meal Consisting of Words (April 1941)—*The People from Heaven* (Summer of 1941)—A Game That Was Played on a Wall (Late Summer 1941)—What You Gain on the Roundabouts (Fall of 1941)—The Color of the Air, IX—Literature for the Masses (Late Fall 1941)—An Airedale Named Juno (November 1941)—East Wind Rain (December 1941)—Trying to Call Back Yesterday (Pearl Harbor)—A State of War Exists, 1 (January 1942)—A Question Asked and Answered (February 1942)—The Color of the Air, X—A State of War Exists, 2 (March-April 1942)—A Letter from Blanche Knopf (March 1942)—While Sitting with Your Father in the Sun (April 1942)—When I Was a Child (May 1942)—The Color of the Air, XI—The House on Navajo (May 1942)—Dear Frank, you wrote (May 1942)—A State of War Exists, 3 (June 1942)—Letters from Ken McCormick (July 1942)—A State of War Exists, 4 (July 1942)—A State of War Exists, 5 (September 1942)—A Letter from Charles Pearce (November 1942)—A State of War Exists, 6 (October-November 1942)—Round-Trip to Culver City (March 1943)—A Letter from Curtice Hitchcock (April 1943)—Lunch at the Ritz (April 1943)—The Campaign (April 1943)—The Flawed Diamond (May-August 1943)—Pictures of Three Girls (September 1943)—To Nathanael West-1903-1940 (October 1943)—Harcourt Brace Fall Catalogue (October 1943)—*Come, Come to See...*! (October-December 1943)—The Sleeping Dog (January 1944)—A Regiment of Men (March 1944)—*A Man Without Shoes*, Part One (April 1944)—Dr. Gustave Holmgren (May 1944)—Four Acres in Encino (August 1944)—Hath Israel No Sons? (August 1944)—Dr. Gustave Holmgren, cont'd. (October 1944)— Dr. Gustave Holmgren, cont'd. (November 1944)—A Visit from Uncle Dave (December 1944)—Again, the War on the Wall (December 1944)—A Fool in Armor (January 1945)—Dr. Gustave Holmgren, cont'd. (February 1945)—A Member of the Armed Forces (March 1945)—F. D. R. (April 12, 1945)—*A Man Without Shoes*, Part Two (May 1945)—Moving

JOHN SANFORD

Pictures from Buchenwald (May 1945)—An Encino Afternoon, two stages (June 1945)—As One War Ends.... (June 1945)—The Color of the Air, XII— The Color of the Air, XIII—...Another War Begins (August 1945)—The Color of the Air, XIV.

Note: There are the following misprints:
p.21, l.39—missing * before footnote
p.133, l.25—missing close quote at end of line
p. 159, l.16—"you though that"
p.195, l.23—"Yo've been here"
p.234, l.9—"you wondered why. wasn't"
p.258, l.23—"once in a while of"
p.293, l.19—"ash of gras,"

The following pieces are repeated from previous books: Twelve Dozen Girls (A9 & A12); Two Black Caskets and Eleven White (A15); A River of the Air (A15); The School at Carlisle (A15); The Troop Trains (A15); A Gringo: *Do You Speak English* (A9); Rosina Sacco and Luigia Vanzetti (A15); Freight Train on the Southern (A15); Voyages, VII (A9 & A11); Tragic Strip (A9); Shikata Ga Nai (A15); Of One Who Missed the Second Creation (A15); The Revelation (A9); The Ugly Sky (A15). Portions were condensed for *Connexions* as "Maggie" (C43). *Lonelyhearts* reprints brief quotes (see B27).

This volume of the autobiography begins with J. S.'s train trip out to California to start his job as a screenwriter, and it ends with the atomic bombing of Nagasaki. It details J. S.'s courtship with fellow screenwriter Marguerite Roberts, his becoming a member of the Communist Party, and his failed attempts to join the service during World War Two. It covers the period M. R. considered the couple's "best years."

b. First (limited, signed, numbered) edition:

[title page as in A21a]

Collation and pagination identical to A21a, except for p.*297*, which is numbered in red ink, rather than lettered.

Deep green cloth spine; spine label and boards identical to A21a. Clear acetate dust jacket.

Published simultaneously with A21a at $30.00; 150 copies.

Contents: As in A21a.

c. First trade edition:

[title page as in A21a and A21b]

22.8 x 14.9 cm. *1^2 2-3^{16} 4^4 5-11^{16}*. Pp.*1-14, 15-296, 297-300*.

P.*1* publication history; p.*2* blank [except for extension of design elements from title page]; p.*3* title; p.*4* copyright; pp.*5-300* [identical to A21a and A21b, except for p.*297* which is not lettered or numbered].

Royal blue cloth spine; spine label and boards identical to A21a and A21b. Clear acetate dust jacket.

Published simultaneously with limited edition at $20.00; 300 copies.

Contents: As in A21a and A21b.

d. First paperback edition:

[title page as in A21a, A21b and A21c]

22.7 x 14.9 cm. Collation and pagination identical to A21c.

Stiff, textured light gray paper wrappers printed in grayish mint-green, navy blue, black and red; lettered down the spine [in black:] JOHN | SANFORD [in red:] A VERY GOOD LAND | TO FALL WITH [in black:] BLACK SPARROW PRESS. Upper and lower covers identical to A21a, A21b and A21c. Edges cut flush; endpapers; perfect binding; yellowish white wove paper.

Published simultaneously with hardcover edition at $12.50; 2,500 copies.

Contents: As in A21a, A21b and A21c.

Note: On 1 July 2002, David R. Godine took over unsold copies, offering them at $14.95.

A22   A WALK IN THE FIRE   1989

a. First (limited, signed, lettered) edition:

[background geometric design of whitish yellow, extending onto facing page] | [in black:] JOHN | SANFORD | [at 30-degree angle] [in red:] A WALK | IN THE FIRE | [navy blue square] | [in black] [horizontal:] SCENES | FROM | THE | LIFE | OF | AN | AMERICAN | JEW | [at 30-degree angle:] VOLUME 4 | [navy blue square] | [horizontal:] BLACK SPARROW PRESS [square] SANTA BARBARA [square] 1989

22.9 x 14.9 cm. $1^2\ 2^1\ 3^{16}\ 4^1\ 5^{16}\ 6^1\ 7\text{-}14^{16}$. Pp.*i-ii, 1-14, 15-323, 324-328.*

P.*i* BY JOHN SANFORD | NOVELS AND OTHER FICTION | [9 titles] | INTERPRETATIONS OF AMERICAN HISTORY | [4 titles] | LETTERS | [1 title] | AUTOBIOGRAPHY | [5 titles on 10 lines]; p.*ii* blank [except for extension of design elements from title page]; p.*1* title; p.*2* [...] Copyright © 1989 by John Sanford | [...] Printed in the United States of America [...] | ISBN 0-87685-758-6. — ISBN 0-87685-757-8 (pbk.) — ISBN | 0-87685-759-4 (cloth signed) [...]; p.*3* [author's signature in blue ink: John Sanford]; p.*4* blank; p.*5* dedication: to her father and mother | Henry Albert and Decky Wells Smith | for my beloved Maggie [J. S.'s wife, who died four months prior to the book's publication]; p.*6* blank; p.*7* A Note on the Inserts; p.*8* blank; pp.*9-12* contents; p.*13* fly title; p.*14* blank; pp.15-323 text; p.*324* blank; p.*325* [publisher's sparrow device] | Printed in March 1989 in Santa Barbara & Ann Arbor | for the Black Sparrow Press by Graham Mackintosh & | Edwards Brothers Inc. Design by Barbara Martin. | This edition is published in paper wrappers; there | are 300 cloth trade copies; 150 hardcover copies | have been numbered & signed by the author; & 26 | copies handbound in boards by Earle Gray have been | lettered & signed by the author. [letter in red ink]; p.*326* photo of J. S.; p.*327* author biography; p.*328* blank.

Navy blue cloth spine, with an arboreal pattern printed in silvery brown, with brown paper label lettered down the spine in black: JOHN | SANFORD A WALK | IN THE FIRE; cream colored paper boards; upper cover has a brown geometric pattern extending to the lower cover; printed [in black:] JOHN | SANFORD | [at 30-degree angle] [in red:] A WALK | IN THE FIRE | [navy blue square] | [horizontal] [in black:] SCENES | FROM | THE | LIFE | OF | AN | AMERICAN | JEW | [at 30-degree angle:] VOLUME 4 | [navy blue square]. All edges cut; endpapers; flat spine. Clear acetate dust jacket. Yellowish white wove paper.

Published 7 July 1989 at $40.00; 26 copies.

Contents: Gods of Another Olympus (Summer of 1945)—*Little Boy Blues* (August 1945)—Night-flight to a Funeral (August 1945)—The Color of the Air, I—Real Property (October

1945)—... Or the Leopard His Spots (November 1945)—A Smell
of Smoke (November 1945)—Blues for *A Man Without Shoes,* 1
(November 1945)—Misty Morning at Santa Anita (December
1945)—Chief Justice of the Ontra Cafeteria (December 1945)—
The Color of the Air, II—Daniel Webster Smith (January
1946)—On the Sport of Kings (February 1946)—A Day of No
Particular Significance (April 1946)—Harriet Esther Nevins—
Another Obituary (June 1946)—Somebody from Downtown
(Summer of 1946)—*A Swimming Pool?,* You Said (April 1946)—
Won Driving, Second and Third the Same (June 1946)—The
Last of a Poor Misfortunate Boy (July 1946)—Blues for *A Man
Without Shoes,* 2 (Early in 1946)—Blues for *A Man Without
Shoes,* 3 (July-August 1946)—The Color of the Air, III—Father
to the Man (1946)—Pogrom—People's Educational Center
(Fall of 1946)—The Little Red Schoolhouse (January 1947)—
Blues for *A Man Without Shoes,* 4 (March 1947)—A Movable
and Wandering Thing (Spring of 1947)—Maggie's Story (April
1947)—John's Story (May 1947)—Brother and Sister (Summer
of 1947)—Concerning Remission of Sin (Summer of 1947)—Art
as a Weapon (Fall of 1947)—Benjamin Thau (Late in 1947)—The
Color of the Air, IV—Dishonor Among Thieves (Fall of 1947)—
Somebody Else from Downtown—Ruth Borne, Housekeeper—
Art Rowley, Handyman—Dr. Gustave Holmgren, cont'd. (Fall
of 1947)—A Few Questions and Answers (Fall of 1947)—Sendoff
at the Burbank Airport (October 1947)—Are You Now Or Have
You Ever Been...? (October 1947)—A Rainy Evening in Encino
(November 1947)—The La Brea Tar Pits (November 1947)—The
Color of the Air, V—A Man, Desiring... (Fall of 1947)—Writers
Meeting in the Roosevelt Ballroom (End of 1947)—The Louis
Mayer Stock Farm (March 1948)—4912 White Oak Avenue
(March 1948)—Bloodlines (Spring of 1948)—If I Forget Thee,
O Jerusalem (May 14, 1948)—Messalina (June 1948)—A Walk
Between Two Sentences (July 1948)—Dr. Gustave Holmgren,
cont'd. (Summer of 1948)—Figures of Speech (Summer of

1948)—Request from a Stranger (August 1948)—The Color of the Air, VI—*Pshaw*, An Obituary (November 1948)—A Novel Called *The Bandage* (Summer 1948)—White Oak Evening, 1 (Fall of 1948)—White Oak Evening, 2 (Fall of 1948)—Three Sheets of Paper (January 1949)—In a Box at Santa Anita (February 1949)—Concerning the Color of Eyes (March 1949)—The Plantin Press (April 1949)—The Color of the Air, VII—Joseph McCarthy, Rise and Fall (1949)—A Little Local Color (Summer of 1949)—Let Bygones Be (Summer of 1949)—A Pile of Trash (Summer of 1949)—The Plum Tree (1949)—Blues for *A Man Without Shoes*, 5 (July 1949)—An Event of Great Importance (October 1949)—A Short Walk in Graustark (1949)—From Each According to His Ability (December 1949)—Richard Nixon (1950)—The Color of the Air, VIII—Priscilla and Alger Hiss (January 1950)—A Report on the Weather (February 1950)—Joseph McCarthy Again (February 10, 1950)—The Cold Wind as Before (March 1950)—King of the Kindergarten (April 1950)—Blues for *A Man Without Shoes*, 6 (May 1950)—The Big City (June 1950)—The Color of the Air, IX—A Flight of Stormy Petrels (July 1950)—The Earth Was Without Form (July 1950)—Dr. Gustave Holmgren, cont'd. (July 1950)—Won Handily, Second and Third Driving (July 18, 1950)—Dr. Gustave Holmgren, concluded (Late in July 1950)—Thoughts on the Road to Del Mar (August 1950)—Tove Christiansen, Housekeeper (August 1950)—Messalina Made the Pace in Hand (August 7, 1950)—January 12, 1988—Prospectus (September 1950)—Thalberg Building, Third Floor (October 1950)—Seventh Race at Hollywood Park (November 9, 1950)—The Color of the Air, X—January 29, 1988—Fifth Race at Hollywood Park (December 9, 1950)—Back, Briefly, From the Dead (January 1951)—Definitions (January 1951)—Pretty as a Little Red Pair of Shoes (February 1951)—Thalberg Building, Room 243 (February 1951)—The Plantin Press Announces (March 1951)—The House Committee Hearings in Washington (March-April 1951)—The Color of the Air, XI—Scheherezade

(May 1951)—On the Erie (May 1951)—*A Man Without Shoes*, The Book (Late Spring 1951)—*A la Recherche*...(March 8, 1988)—*A Man Without Shoes*, Copy #1 (June 1951)—*A Man Without Shoes*, As Merchandise (June 1951)—*A Man Without Shoes*, As a Weapon (1951)—The Color of the Air, XII—Six Months On, Six Months Off (July 1951)—Report to the Governor (July 1951)—At the Far End of Easy Street (July-August 1951)—Where the Heavy Going Begins (Late Summer 1951)—The Color of the Air, XIII—Metro Conference, No. 1 (August 1951)—The Color of the Air, XIV—A Woman With a Cold Eye (August 1951)—A Note on Retaining Counsel (August 1951)—Sunday, August 19, 1951—Day of Rest (August 19, 1951)—A Stained-glass Window (August-September 1951)—Western Union (August 1951)—The Color of the Air, XV—Again, the Stained-glass Window (August-September 1951)—The House Committee Hearings in Los Angeles (September 1951)—The Color of the Air, XVI—Metro Conference, No. 2 (September 1951)—Again, the Chief Justice of the Ontra Cafeteria (September 1951)—Metro Conference, No. 3 (September 1951)—Two Letters (September 1951)—Metro Conference, No. 4 (September 1951)—Metro Conference, No. 5 (October 1951)—Fragments (October 1951)—Metro Conference, No. 6 (October 1951)—Metro Conference, No. 7 (November 1951)—Metro Conference, No. 8 (November 1951)—Four Days in Encino (November 1951)—July 11, 1988—Metro Conference, No. 9 (November 1951)—Maggie as Merchandise (November 1951)—Metro Conference, No. 10 (November 1951)—Metro Conference, No. 11 (November 1951)—Not With a Bang Not With a Whimper (November 21, 1951)—The Color of the Air, XVII.

Note: There are the following misprints:
p.152, l.12—"Stanley Roses's."
p.156, l.12—"so that there . no"
p.171, l.34—"you're realized"
p.180, l.22—"blew in my last"

p.273, l.8—""""Whom"
p.297, l.30—"at times. sugar"
p.321, l.1-2—two lines have been inserted above the top line of the page

The following pieces are repeated from previous books: A Martial Air at a Hanging (A15); The Last Gentleman (A15); Father to the Man (A15); The *Amistad*, Formerly the *Friendship* (A15); Buckeye Johnny Appleseed (A5 & A9); Poor Mexico, So Far from God (A15); Second Inaugural (A9); A Flood Upon the Earth (A15); Joseph McCarthy, Rise and Fall from Oh God, When I Go Down (A15); The Customhouse Years (A15); Homestead, Pennsylvania (A9); Give a Dog a Bad Name (A9 & A11); The American (A9); No Ashes for Utah (A9); At the Far End of Easy Street was revised from The Private Car *Superb*, Pullman Strike, I, and The Kentucky Abraham in A9; The Black and the Blues (A9); The Gastonia Strike (A15); Castle-Builder in Union Square (A9 & A12); On Refusing to Answer (A15); Gods of Another Olympus is revised from a piece by the same name in *Frank* (C40); Another Obituary reprints "Nathanael West" from *The Screen Writer* (C27); Prospectus reprints a portion of "A Man Without Shoes A Novel by John Sanford" (E1g); The Plantin Press Announces reprints a portion of "The Plantin Press Announces A MAN WITHOUT SHOES" (E1h). *Lonelyhearts* reprints brief quotes (see B27).

A Walk in the Fire begins with two pieces on the atomic bomb and ends with J. S.'s wife, Marguerite Roberts's, departure from her job at Metro-Goldwyn-Mayer. It covers the period that began with the carefree years the couple shared at their Encino house. But, all the while, there is a building sense of foreboding, in part symbolized by J. S.'s struggles to find a publisher for *A Man without Shoes* (A5). Then come the hearings in Los Angeles of the House Committee on un-American Activities, at which both J. S. and M. R. refused to name names. Finally, there is the denouement of meetings with Metro executives, which led to a settlement of M. R.'s contract and termination of her employment after a dozen years.

b. First (limited, signed, numbered) edition:

[title page as in A22a]

Collation and pagination identical to A22a, except for p.*325*, which is numbered in red ink, rather than lettered.

Light yellowish beige cloth spine; spine label and boards identical to A22a. Clear acetate dust jacket.

Published simultaneously with A22a at $30.00; 150 copies.

Contents: As in A22a.

c. First trade edition:

[title page as in A22a and A22b]

22.9 x 14.9 cm. $1^2\ 2^{16}\ 3^1\ 4^{16}\ 5^1\ 6\text{-}13^{16}$. Pp.*1-14*, 15-323, *324-328*.

P.*1* publication history; p.*2* blank [except for extension of design elements from title page]; p.*3* title; p.*4* copyright; pp.*5-328* [identical to A22a and A22b, except for p.*325* which is not lettered or numbered].

Light brown cloth spine; spine label and boards identical to A22a and A22b. Clear acetate dust jacket.

Published simultaneously with limited edition at $20.00; 300 copies.

Contents: As in A22a and A22b.

d. First paperback edition:

[title page as in A22a, A22b and A22c]

22.7 x 14.9 cm. Collation and pagination identical to A22c.

Stiff light yellowish white paper wrappers printed in brown, black, red and navy blue; printed down the spine in black: JOHN | SANFORD A WALK | IN THE FIRE BLACK SPARROW PRESS. Upper and lower covers identical to A22a, A22b and A22c. Edges cut flush; endpapers; perfect binding; yellowish white wove paper.

Published simultaneously with hardcover edition at $12.50; 2,500 copies.

Contents: As in A22a, A22b and A22c.

Note: On 1 July 2002, David R. Godine took over unsold copies, offering them at $13.95.

A23   THE SEASON, IT WAS WINTER   1991

a. First (limited, signed, lettered) edition:

[background geometric design of bluish gray, extending onto facing page] | [in black:] JOHN SANFORD | [red rule extending to facing page] [black square] | [in red:] THE SEASON, | IT WAS WINTER | [black square] [red rule] | [in black, with bluish gray rules following:] SCENES | FROM | THE | LIFE | OF | AN | AMERICAN | JEW | [black square] [red rule] | VOLUME 5 | BLACK SPARROW PRESS [black square] SANTA ROSA [black square] 1991

22.8 × 14.9 cm. $1^2\ 2^1\ 3\text{-}4^{16}\ 4^6\ 5\text{-}12^{16}$. Pp.*i-ii, 1-16, 17-296, 297-304.*

P.*i* BY JOHN SANFORD | NOVELS AND OTHER FICTION | [9 titles] | INTERPRETATIONS OF AMERICAN HISTORY | [4 titles] | LETTERS | [1 title] | AUTOBIOGRAPHY | [5 titles on 10 lines]; p.*ii* blank [except for extension of design elements from title page]; p.*1* title; p.*2* [...] Copyright © 1991 by John Sanford | [...] Printed in the United States of America [...] | Black Sparrow Press books are printed on acid-free paper. | [...] ISBN 0-87685-826-4 (cloth) : — ISBN 0-87685-825-6 (paper) : | — ISBN | 0-87685-827-4 (signed cloth) : [...]; p.*3* [author's signature in blue ink: John Sanford]; p.*4* blank; p.*5* dedication: for | Marguerite Azora Sanford | "Maggie Roberts" | Nov. 26, 1905-Feb. 17, 1989 | with all my love; p.*6* blank; p.*7* epigraph [3 lines from William Bradford]; p.*8* blank; p.*9* [rule] | A NOTE ON THE INSERTS | [rule] | [...] fifteen in all, of which fourteen, written expressly for this volume, are new. [...]; p.*10* blank; pp.*11-13* contents; p.*14* blank; p.*15* fly title; p.*16* blank; pp.17-20 foreword; pp.21-296 text; p.*297* [publisher's sparrow device] | Printed in March 1991 in Santa Barbara & Ann | Arbor for the Black Sparrow Press by Graham | Mackintosh & Edwards Brothers Inc. Text set in | Bembo by Words Worth. Design by Barbara Martin. | This edition is published in paper wrappers; | there are 300 hardcover trade copies; 125 hardcover copies have been numbered & signed | by the author; & 26 copies handbound in boards by | Earle Gray have been lettered & signed by the author. | [letter in red ink]; p.*298* photo of Marguerite Roberts; p.*299* biography of M. R.; p.*300* photo of J. S.; p.*301* author biography; pp.*302-304* blank.

Black cloth spine, with a leaf pattern printed in red, green, yellow and white; pale blue-gray and darker blue-gray paper label printed down the spine [in black:] JOHN | SANFORD [vertical yellow-green stripe] [in red:] THE SEASON, | IT WAS WINTER; pale blue-gray paper boards; upper cover has a darker blue-gray geometric pattern extending to the lower cover; printed [in black:] JOHN SANFORD | [yellow-green rule extending to lower cover] | [in red:] THE SEASON, | IT WAS WINTER | [blue square] [yellow-green rule] | SCENES | FROM | THE | LIFE | OF | AN | AMERICAN | JEW | [blue square] [yellow-green rule] | VOLUME 5. All edges cut; endpapers; flat spine. Clear acetate dust jacket. Yellowish white wove paper.

Published 6 May 1991 at $45.00; 26 copies.

Contents: Foreword by J. S.—The Blacklist (November 22, 1951)—An Afternoon With the Governor (November 22, 1951)—The Color of the Air, I—Photographs and Other Pictures (April-August 1952)—The Color of the Air, II—Maggie's Mother (Summer and Fall 1952)—Changes (Fall-Winter 1952-53)—*The Land That Touches Mine* (Spring of 1953)—The Color of the Air, III—After Nine Years in Encino (Summer 1953)—Last Pictures of the Encino Place (July 1953)—"Without you ...," She Said (Fall of 1953)—Carmel 1: The Chapman House (Fall 1953-Spring 1954)—The Color of the Air, IV—South from Carmel on State 1 (Spring of 1954)—An Obituary for Maggie's Mother (Summer of 1954)—The House on Woodbridge (Late Spring of 1954)—The Blind Airedales (Summer of 1954)—Requiem for an Airedale: Juno XIV (Summer 1954)—The Color of the Air, V—The Importance of Being Ernest (Fall of 1954)—Various Things in Several Seasons (1954-55)—The Color of the Air, VI—Excursion to New York (May-July 1955)—The Color of the Air, VII—Carmel 2: The Warnow House (Fall-Winter 1955-56)—The Color of the Air, VIII—The Humphrey House (January 1956–)—The Color of the Air, IX—The Medicine-men of Beverly Hills (1956-57)—Medication (Early in 1957)—No Iron Bars a Cage (January 1957)—Sunday at 812 Buena Vista Road (Spring of 1957)—His Nora, Your Maggie (Early in 1957)—The Stone Mason (Early in 1957)—Oh, Say Does that Star-spangled...? (Early in 1957)—The Color of the Air, X—Perils in the City (Early in 1957)—We Are Such Stuff (1957-1958)—Out for a Spin (1957)—Again, the Governor in Montecito (Early in 1957)—Little Rock, Then and Now (September 1957)—Glimpses of Family Life (From 1936)—A Natural History of Stoneholme (1956-57)—The Aluminum Moon (October 4, 1957)—The Color of the Air, XI—The Seventh Payment (January 1958)—The Fifty-seventh Week (Late Spring 1958)—Questionnaire (Late Spring 1958)—June 16, 1958 (June 17, 1958)—*Hotel de Dream*, A Screenplay (Late Spring and Summer 1958)—The Color of the Air, XII—European Trip, 1958 (August-December 1958)—The Color of the Air, XIII—Dinner at *The Talk of the Town* (January 1959)—Three Conversations (February 1959)—A Breath of Fresh Air (Late February 1959)—Family Dinner (March 1959)—The Good Treasure of the Heart (March 1959)—Look Away, Look Away (March 1959)—The Color of the Air, XIV—The Academy Awards (April 23, 1959)—John the Sanguine (April 1959)—Miscellany (Summer and Fall 1950)—The Color of the Air, XV—The Month of December (December 1959)—The Fifth Letter (Early 1960)—To Form a More Perfect Union (June-July 1960)—Roberts-1960 (June-July 1960)—The Day (Summer 1960).

Note: There are the following misprints:
p.13, l.10—"(Summer and Fall 1950)"
p.83, l.42—"You're got shortcomings"
p.132, l.4—"yes, """
p.138, l.10-2—regarding M.R.'s play based on *The Land that Touches Mine*, Pryor is described as being changed from a minister to a doctor. However, in the novel, Pryor was a teacher; his brother, the protagonist in *Every Island Fled Away*, was a minister.
p.150, l.30—"He stopped for a pine-cone"
p.189, l.21—"written about," Maggie said. She wasn't"
p.251, l.21—section separator should be deleted
p.255, l.34—"lot of space,"Maggie said"

The piece The Wandering Jew is repeated from A9 & A19.

The Season, It Was Winter is the first book J. S. wrote after the death of his wife of fifty years. The book exposes the bleakness of her loss, combined with the bleakness of the period covered, the blacklist years of banishment. It starts with the Sanfords' embarking on a European trip—less a grand tour than a self-imposed exile from the country that had rejected them. In the Sanfords' flight from their stateside travails, this trip resembles J. S.'s earlier Europe trips. And, as he had twenty years earlier, the couple found their tribulations were awaiting them on their return. Soon they would sell their beloved Encino home, and J. S. would become rootless once more, another way in which the blacklist period echoed the alienation J. S. experienced in his youth. No doubt, the depression that M. R. slipped into after losing her beloved job at M-G-M, a second home to her, evoked for J. S. his mother's decline and death four decades earlier. The book is full of rainy days, far too many for the dry climate of California. However, the book ends on a high note, with M. R.'s hiring by Columbia Pictures as a screenwriter, terminating her time on the blacklist.

This volume also ends J. S.'s association with Black Sparrow Press, which had issued six of his books, the most of any publisher.

b. First (limited, signed, numbered) edition:

[title page as in A23a]

Collation and pagination identical to A23a, except for p.*297*, which is numbered in red ink, rather than lettered.

Dark yellowish green cloth spine; spine label and boards identical to A23a. Clear acetate dust jacket.

Published simultaneously with A23a at $35.00; 125 copies.

Contents: As in A23a.

c. First trade edition:

[title page as in A23a and A23b]

22.9 x 14.9 cm. *1² 2¹⁶ 3¹ 4¹⁶ 5¹ 6-13¹⁶*. Pp. *1-16, 17-296, 297-304.*

P.*1* publication history; p.*2* blank [except for extension of design elements from title page]; p.*3* title; p.*4* copyright; pp.*5-304* [identical to A23a and A23b, except for p. *297*, which is not lettered or numbered].

Black cloth spine; spine label and boards identical to A23a and A23b. Clear acetate dust jacket.

Published simultaneously with limited edition at $30.00; 300 copies.

Contents: As in A23a and A23b.

d. First paperback edition:

[title page as in A23a, A23b and A23c]

22.8 x 14.8 cm. Collation and pagination identical to A23c.

Stiff light blue-gray paper wrappers printed darker blue-gray, black, red, yellow-green and blue; printed down the spine [in black:] JOHN | SANFORD [vertical yellow-green stripe] [in red:] THE SEASON, | IT WAS WINTER [in black:] BLACK SPARROW PRESS. Upper and lower covers identical to A23a,

A23b and A23c. Edges cut flush; endpapers; perfect binding; yellowish white laid paper.

Published simultaneously with hardcover edition at $15.00; 2,550 copies.

Contents: As in A23a, A23b and A23c.

Note: On 1 July 2002, David R. Godine took over unsold copies, offering them at $14.95.

A24   MAGGIE: A LOVE STORY   1993

a. First edition:

MAGGIE | [3 leaf ornaments] | A LOVE STORY | *by John Sanford* | BARRICADE BOOKS | Fort Lee, New Jersey

22.8 x 14.5 cm. $1^4\ 2^6\ 3\text{-}6^{16}\ 7^8\ 8^4\ 9\text{-}11^{14}\ 12\text{-}15^{16}\ 16^8\ 17^{16}$. Pp.*i-vi*, vii-xiv, 1-5, *6*, 7-47, *48*, 49-51, *52*, 53-91, *92*, 93-191, *192*, 193-195, *196*, 197-251, *252*, 253-319, *320*, 321-357, *358*, 359-411, *412*, 413-415, *416-418*.

P.*i* half title; p.*ii* blank; p.*iii* title; p.*iv* [...] | Copyright © 1993 by John Sanford | [...] Printed in the United States of America. | [...] | ISBN 0-942637-97-6 : $22.00 | [...] | 0 9 8 7 6 5 4 3 2 1; p.*v* dedication: To Maggie | 1905-1989 | *Dream of little fat angels* [what the Sanfords' favorite Musso and Frank waiter, George Portugal, used to say to Maggie when they left after dinner]; p.*vi* blank; pp.vii-xii contents; pp.xiii-xiv foreword; pp.1-5 text; p.*6* blank; pp.7-47 text; p.*48* blank; pp.49-51 text; p.*52* blank; pp.53-91 text; p.*92* blank; pp.93-191 text; p.*192* blank; pp.193-195 text; p.*196* blank; pp.197-251 text; p.*252* blank; pp.253-319 text; p.*320* blank; pp.321-357 text; p.*358* blank; pp.359-411 text; pp.*412* blank; pp.413-415 afterword; pp.*416-418* blank.

Grayish white one-quarter cloth (with beige thread woven in) and periwinkle paper boards; stamped in gold [down the spine] [in outlined script:] Maggie [swash M, G & G, with scroll above A through E] A [swash A] Love [swash L] Story [swash S] [in outlined print:] JOHN SANFORD [across the foot of the spine in solid print:] BARRICADE [the two outlined As and a rule above form a barricade] | BOOKS. All edges cut; endpapers. White paper dust jacket printed in greenish blue, black and yellow, with palm trees silhouetted by a setting sun; designed by Sal Alba. Yellowish white wove paper.

Published 1 October 1993 at $22.00; 3,326 copies.

Contents: Foreword by J. S.—The Color of the Air, I—The Latter Days—The Color of the Air, II—The Twain Meet—Plain English—A Nice Jewish Girl—In an Apricot Orchard—What the Right Hand Giveth—A Miscellany—A Year at Musso's—Women—From the Smith Family Annals—Smoke Signals—The Twain Marry—The Color of the Air, III—The Latter Days—The Color of the Air, IV—The Best Years—Nicknames—Two Short Stories—A Parable—Maggie, On Women—More Smoke Signals—Panorama—Whatsoever Ye Shall Ask—At Dave Chasen's—The Best Years, II—The Color of the Air, V—The Latter Days—The Color of the Air, VI—The Power of the Tongue—The Day the Worst Years Began—The Proving Ground—The Worst Years, 1st Half—Black and White Photography—His Zelda, Your Maggie—Steinbeck's Blotters—Minutiae—To the Finland Station!—Mama—*The Land That Touches Mine*—The House in the Olive Grove—All Men and Women are Created Equal—… Qui Mal Y Pense—Visions of the Night—The Color of the Air, VII—The Latter Days—The Color of the Air, VIII—Avowals on Scraps of Paper—Signs of Life—Over a Gin and Tonic—In the Summer of the Year—England—The End of the Worst Years—The Bearded One—A Yearbook—The Color of the Air, IX—The Latter Days—The Color of the Air, X—In the Ninth Year of the Blacklist—Scenes for a Cast of Two—The Airedale Lionheart Juno—Short Sixes Found in a Diary—Grand Tour—*Every Island Fled Away*—*The Old Man's Place*—Warning:—A Few Recollections of That Year—*The $300 Man*—*A More Goodly Country*—Concerning Hal Wallis—Concerning John Wayne—The Color of the Air, XI—The Latter Days—The Color of the Air, XII—...Of Things Past—Birthday Present—Philip D. Shapiro—John, the Space-Man—Joseph Moncure March—Your Father's Children—Old Moving Pictures—About the Wear and Tear of Time—The Color of the Air, XIII—The Latter Days—The Color of the Air, XIV—Amoretto—A Mélange—All Flesh is Grass—Concerning Pearl Arizona—Goodbye, Ben—Two Studies of the Same Character—Being of Sound Mind—A Little Something to Lay at Her Feet—Honoraria—Two Days in September—The Word Made Flesh—The Color of the Air, XV—The Latter Days—The Last Day—Afterword by J. S.

Note: The pieces The Sacco and Vanzetti Jury and Sacco and Vanzetti previously appeared in *Santa Barbara Review* as "Sacco & Vanzetti" (C46). They were reprinted in "The Sacco and Vanzetti Papers" in *American Letters and Commentary* (see C56).

Originally titled *No Friends to Welcome Them* and later *Maggie: A Memoir*, this book was intended as the sixth volume of the autobiography. However, according to J. S., Black Sparrow rejected it as "too anecdotal." J. S. finally placed the book with Barricade, who suggested changing the name to the current title. In the end, Barricade became embittered with J. S. because he had already published excerpts from *Maggie* in *Santa Barbara Review* (C46), thus depriving the publisher of what they considered valuable serialization rights.

Although J. S. viewed *Maggie* as the sixth volume of his autobiography, and it shares some similarities with the Black Sparrow work (i.e., being divided into scenes, and having colors of the air interspersed), this volume is more rightly thought of as a stand-alone memoir. *Maggie* re-covers material contained in previous books, starting with J. S.'s meeting Roberts at Paramount Studios.

Maggie is punctuated with scenes called The Latter Days, which foreshadow Roberts's death. The book ends with her death in 1989.

Physically, *Maggie* is, sad to say, an ugly book. The lettering on the spine is unreadable from any distance. The typeface and design are oafish, reminding one of a large-print book, bloated at its 415-page length. After the wonderful jobs by Capra and Black Sparrow, *Maggie* is a bibliographic disappointment. The public also found it unappealing, with sales during the first five years of a mere 850 copies.

b. First e-book edition (Bloomsbury Reader), [2013]

MAGGIE | A LOVE STORY | *by John Sanford* | [publisher's device with a reversed script B and forward script R] | BLOOMSBURY READER | LONDON • NEW DELHI • NEW YORK • SYDNEY

ISBN: 9781448211630

Published 16 July 2013 at $6.50; number of pages not specified.

A25   THE VIEW FROM MT. MORRIS   1994

First edition:

The View from Mt. Morris | [leaf ornament] | A Harlem Boyhood | [leaf] | Barricade Books Inc. | New York

22.9 x 14.2 cm. 1^1 2-4^2 5^1 6-7^{16} 8^8 9-10^{16} 11^8 12-13^{16}. Pp.*i-v*, vi-viii, 1-13, *14*, 15-19, *20*, 21-37, *38*, 39-61, *62*, 63-107, *108*, 109-129, *130*, 131-145, *146*, 147-151, *152*, 153-231, *232*.

P.*i* title; p.*ii* copyright: [...] | Copyright © 1994 by John Sanford | [...] Printed in the United States of America. | [...] | ISBN 1-56980-018-9 : $22.00 | [...] | First Printing; p.*iii* epigraph: *For water is a movable and wandering thing.* | Blackstone, *Commentaries*; p.*iv* Other John Sanford publications | [20 titles on 27 lines]; p.*v* dedication: To Maggie | 1905-1989 | from the empty room [an allusion to J. S.'s saying to Maggie, "I hate to see you leave a room."]; pp.vi-viii contents; pp.1-13 text; p.*14* blank; pp.15-19 text; p.*20* blank; pp.21-37 text; p.*38* blank; pp.39-61 text; p.*62* blank; pp.63-107 text; p.*108* blank; pp.109-129 text; p.*130* blank; pp.131-145 text; p.*146* blank; pp.147-151 text; p.*152* blank; pp.153-231 text; p.*232* blank.

Reddish fuchsia one-quarter cloth and medium gray paper boards; stamped in silver [down the spine:] Sanford THE VIEW FROM Mt. MORRIS [across the base of the spine:] BARRICADE [the two outlined As and a rule above form a barricade] | BOOKS. All edges cut; endpapers. White paper dust jacket printed in red and black; designed by Edgar Blakeney. Yellowish white wove paper.

Published 1 October 1994 at $22.00; number of copies not known.

Contents: Foreword by J. S.—Birth Certificate—The *Gainsboro*—1905: Clarks, Nebraska—Your Father—The Color of the Air (Einstein)—Your Mother—The Color of the Air (Brownsville)—Your Mother's Mother—1907: Clarks, Nebraska—Your Mother's Father—1909: Clarks, Nebraska—Your Father's Father—Your Father's Mother—The Color of the Air (Matthew Henson)—Your Mother's Socialist Brother—Your Mother's Retarded Brother—Your Mother's Younger Sister—1910: Blanca,

Colorado—Your Uncle Harry—Your Mother's Elder Sister—Your Uncle Harris—Your Father's Elder Sister—The Color of the Air (Mexico)—The *Cabonak*—Shapiro & Levy—The Color of the Air (Triangle Fire)—A Sense of Smell, and Other Senses—1910: Blanca, Colorado—Nathaniel Weinstein—1912 Clarks, Nebraska—The Enemy: Thyself—Photo of a Family of Four—The Color of the Air (Gov. William Sulzer)—A Family of Four No More—203 West 117th Street—1913: Clarks, Nebraska—Mourner's *Kaddish*—Off the Old Head of Kinsale—The Year of Mourning Ends—Full Many a Flower, Two Views—The Color of the Air (Gavrilo Princip)—The Great War—Neighborhood Merchants—Childe Julian, The Boy King—The Color of the Air (Gov. John M. Slaton)—Alvin Levy—The Color of the Air (Verdun)—Harlem's Village Green—À La Recherche du Temps Perdu—P. S. 10—Jacob Mendelson—He Kept Us Out of War—Your Friend, Woodrow Wilson—A Man Named Harry Krakauer—Bar Mitzvah—The Color of the Air (The October Revolution)—Family Discussion—De Witt Clinton Annex—The Color of the Air (The Armistice, Versailles)—Your Cousin Jassie—1920 Fullerton, Nebraska—Jasper, Carl, Stan, and Lenny—The Color of the Air (Sacco and Vanzetti)—Lenny, Stan, Carl, and Jasper—Forsake the Foolish, and Live—The Color of the Air (The Volstead Act)—De Witt Clinton, Main Building—A Visit to the Past—1924: Denver, Colorado—Josie, the Painted Woman—A Last Summer in Long Branch—1926: El Centro, California—One War Ends, Another War Begins—The Nevins Family—Plaintiff and Defendant—1931: Big Bear, California—The Summer of 1920—I Hope and Trust, Julian—1931: Los Angeles, California—Summer's End in Asbury Park—The Path Not Taken—Elegy on Washington Heights—1936: Hollywood, California.

Note: A portion of The *Gainsboro* was reprinted in *Redemption: The Life of Henry Roth* (see B22).

The View from Mt. Morris contains more recollections from J. S.'s early life, filling in gaps in the autobiography. Like the autobiography, it is punctuated by Colors of the Air. In addition, interspersed throughout are pieces called The View from Mt. Morris, which describe photographs of J. S.'s future wife from the same period of the narrative. The effect is to give the impression that, unknown to them, the future couple is steadily working its way toward meeting each other.

Physically, *The View from Mt. Morris* is even more disappointing than *Maggie* was. Whether by accident, or, as J. S. believed, out of vindictiveness over Barricade's falling out with J. S., this book's title page does not list the author's name. In general, the ordering of the front matter appears amateurish and haphazard. Sales were appalling: 435 copies in the first three years.

A26   WE HAVE A LITTLE SISTER   1995

First edition:

WE HAVE A LITTLE SISTER | *Marguerite: the Midwest Years* | John Sanford | *We have a little sister,* | *and she hath no breasts* | *what shall we do for our* | *sister in the day when* | *she shall be spoken for?* | —Song of Solomon 8.8 | CAPRA [publisher's goat head device] PRESS | SANTA BARBARA

22.8 x 14.7 cm. 1^4 2^{16} 3^1 4^1 5^{10} $6\text{-}12^{16}$. Pp.*i-xii*, 1-28, (2 plates), 29-270, *271-272*.

P.*i* also by John Sanford [21 titles]; p.*ii* frontispiece: 1907 photo of Marguerite Roberts and siblings; p.*iii* title; p.*iv* Copyright © 1995 by John Sanford | [...] Printed in the United States of America. | ACKNOWLEDGMENT [J. S. thanks his sister-in-law Bijou for her help with writing this book] | [...] | ISBN 0-88496-399-3 (cloth) | Published by CAPRA PRESS | [...]; p.*v* DEDICATION

[...] To Maggie, then, for Maggie | 1905-1989; p.*vi* THE SMITH FAMILY [names and dates for M. R.'s parents and siblings]; pp.*vii-x* contents; p.*xi* foreword; p.*xii* blank; pp.1-28 text; [2 plates with 10 photos]; pp.29-269 text; pp.270 afterword; pp.*271-272* blank.

Black cloth boards; stamped in brass down the spine: WE HAVE A LITTLE SISTER / JOHN SANFORD / CAPRA PRESS. All edges cut; endpapers; flat spine. White paper dust jacket printed in brownish gray and black, with photo of a very young Marguerite Roberts on the front, and a photo of J. S. by M. R. on the back flap; designed by Frank Goad. Yellowish white wove paper.

Published in September 1995 at $25.00; number of copies not obtainable.

Contents: Birth Certificate—1905: Tannersville, N.Y.—Marguerite's Father—The Color of the Air (Earthquake)—Marguerite's Mother—The Color of the Air (The First Broadcast)—Marguerite's Sister Pearl—Photography Section—Marguerite—Marguerite's Brother Dan—1909: Long Branch, N.J.—Marguerite's Sister Connie—Marguerite's Sister Bijou—Marguerite and her Friends—1912: New York, N.Y.—Marguerite at the Riverbank—Blanca, alt. 7,870, pop. 252—Purdy's Café, John Roach, prop.—Baby Sister—Bijou, a.k.a. Midget—The Outside World from Inside Marguerite—A Short Course in Biology—Grade School, Clarks, Nebr.—Bussy—The Merrick County Fair—The Color of the Air (Teddy Roosevelt)—Marguerite's Very Feminine Body—A Teddy Bear Named Teddy—Concerning Marguerite's Very Feminine Body—The Sewing Machine—1913: Pine Brook, N.J.—Marguerite Astride her Buckskin Pony—Marguerite's Room—The Periodic Smiths—Every Fourth Phase of the Moon—The Color of the Air (Mexico)—Marguerite Solitaire—Marguerite and that which

She Fed on—As Was Said in Eden—Decky, Maid-of-all-Work, Two Scenes—1914: New York, N.Y.—Clothesline—O, Those Golden-Rule Days—A Short Course in Domestic Relations—What God Hath Joined Together—Leviticus—May 7, 1915—The Color of the Air (Flanders)—Concerning Marguerite's Buttons—From Pilger to Olympus, a Round-trip—The Fast Mail to Points West—*Un Bel Di Vidremo*—War—The Color of the Air (Influenza)—A Separate Room—The Color of the Air (Sacco and Vanzetti)—From the Smith Family Annals—The Color of the Air (The Peace Treaty)—Greeley Business College—1921: Pottersville, N.Y.—Marguerite and Leonard—The Greeley Pharmacy—1922: Niagara Falls, N.Y.—Target Practice—A Real Gent—Waiting for a Sign—The Color of the Air (Mussolini)—Leonard: a Further Stage—Reflections on a Reflection—Supper at the Smiths—1923: New York, N.Y.—Round-trip to Denver—Sugar from the Sugar Beet—Incident Beneath the Pines—The Next Day—Sisters: A Dialogue—Concerning Pearls of No Great Price—Department Store—Mainly in Decky's Room—The Flyer—The Last Supper—1925: Long Branch, N.J.—Under Way—At the Water's Edge—The Florence Sweet Shop—The Grand Canyon of the Arkansas—The Monte Cristo Hotel—Crossing Monarch Pass—Gunnison—The Color of the Air (W. J. Bryan)—Montrose, alt. 5,820 ft.—In the *Belvedere* Coffee-shop—Dear Midgie, She Wrote—A Short Talk on the Road—Grand Junction, alt. 4,587 ft.—Conversations with Strangers—The Third Passenger—A Mile-high Dialogue—Glenwood Springs, alt. 5,756—Leadville, alt. 10,152 ft.—Now and Then—The Manitou & Pikes Peak Railway—Homeward Bound—Questions and Answers—Supper at Home—The Mother Wit of Sister Pearl—A Supper Called Dinner—Expedition into Wyoming—A Small Flat on 12th Street—A Talk with Brother Dan—Changes of Season—Where the Gods Still Dwell—1927: At Sea, Aboard the "France"—Caution: This Is a One-way Road—Imperial Valley—El Centro, pop. 3,550—An Exchange of Letters—All Around the

Town—1930: The Wandering Jew—The Hundred Days—1931: Viele Pond—The End of the Hundred Days—1929: West End, N.J.—A Train-ride to the Future—1452 W. 39th Street—The Color of the Air (The Depression)—The Writers Building at Paramount—Afterword by J. S.

Note: The First Broadcast was adapted from Words in Space in A9. The Color of the Air (Sacco and Vanzetti) was reprinted in "The Sacco and Vanzetti Papers" in *American Letters and Commentary* (see C56).

We Have a Little Sister can be seen as a companion book to *The View from Mt. Morris* (A25). In it, J. S. imaginatively reconstructs the early life of his wife, Marguerite Roberts, ending with their meeting in the hallway of the writers' building at Paramount Studios. Interspersed throughout are episodes entitled "The View from Afar Off," which describe photos at the time of J. S. As in the previous book, the effect is that the young J. S. is destined to meet M. R. Also of note is that several of the episodes in M. R.'s life had earlier been adapted for the character Eugenia in *The Land that Touches Mine* (A6).

Sales of *Little Sister* were very poor. By April 1996, only 202 copies had been shipped. A paperback edition of *Little Sister* was announced but never published.

A27   INTRUDERS IN PARADISE   1997

First edition:

[heavy vertical rule next to a column of shaded diamond boxes] [to the left of the base of the rule:] *Intruders | in Paradise* | [at the foot of page, beneath the rule:] JOHN SANFORD

22.8 x 14.5 cm. $1\text{-}2^{16}\ 3^4\ 4\text{-}8^{16}$. Pp.*i-xvi*, 1-25, *26*, 27-107, *108*, 109-173, *174*, 175-203, *204*, 205-209, *210-216*.

P.*i* half title; p.*ii* UNIVERSITY OF ILLINOIS PRESS | *Urbana and Chicago*; p.*iii* title; p.*iv* © 1997 by John Sanford | Manufactured in the United States of America | C 5 4 3 2 1 | [...] | Six of the pieces in this book have appeared before: | [...] | ISBN 0-252-02343-9 (alk. Paper) | [...]; p.*v* epigraph: [small shaded box] *Dance us back the tribal morn!* | —Hart Crane, *The Bridge*; p.*vi* blank; p.*vii* [box] [7 lines describing native inhabitants of the New World] | —legend on an ancient map; p.*viii* blank; p.*ix* dedication: [box] To Maggie | 1905-89 | [11 lines of dialog between J. S. and M. R.]; p.*x* blank; pp.*xi-xiv* contents; p.*xv* fly title; p.*xvi* blank; pp.1-25 text; p.*26* blank; pp.27-107 text; pp.*108* blank; pp.109-173 text; p.*174* blank; pp.175-203 text; p.*204* blank; pp.205-209 text; p.*210* blank; p.*211* Other Books by John Sanford | [22 titles on 23 lines]; p.*212* blank; p.*213* author biography; pp.*214-216* blank.

Deep green cloth boards stamped in gold [across the spine:] [two rules surrounding a geometric design of shaded diamonds] [down the spine:] *Intruders in Paradise* [geometric design] | SANFORD | [across the foot of the spine:] University | of Illinois | Press | [two rules surrounding a geometric design]. All edges cut; endpapers. White paper dust jacket printed in black, red, blue, green, yellow and peach, with a photo of J. S. by Garrett White on the back; illustration by Jan McCracken. Yellowish white wove paper.

Published 20 October 1997 at $26.95; 1,500 copies.

Contents: Scenes of the National Life, 1—Judas in Peru—The First Knee on Canada—The Black Napoleon—Less than Kin and More than Minion—The Framers in Philadelphia—Fling Away Ambition—Scenes of the National Life, 2—The Second Wife of John Brown—The Wife of John Charles Frémont—Good-bye My Fancy—An Odd Little Woman from Nashville—The Ladies' War—Pickett's Charge—Occurrence on the Hill of Bells—The

JOHN SANFORD

Mighty Fallen—Billy the Kid—The Purest Man of Our Race—The Atheist—Full within of Dead Men's Bones—The President Maker—J. A. McN. Whistler—A "Boston Marriage"—Scenes of the National Life, 3—The South Fork Hunting and Fishing Club—Once Upon a Time in Watercolor—Mexico, Stepmother of Mexicans—The White Indian—An Apple that Rolled—Agony in a House of the Lord—With the Instinct of My Race—Modern Art on Lexington Avenue—A Land to Love—A Gringo: Do You Speak English?—The Uncommon Commoner—Viva la Vida—Dancer in the Dark—Mt. Rushmore—With the Voice of Many Waters—Scenes of the National Life, 4—Money Is the Root of All Eval, He Wrote—The Gastonia Strike—The Poor Get Screwed, He Said—Traitor to His Class—For Gene, in Homage—What Hath This Rodent Wrought!—In Much Wisdom Is Much Grief—The God with the Glass Head—The King of Louisiana—Zelda Reconsidered—Scenes of the National Life, 5—They Still Walk, They Still Speak—Speaking Off-the-Record—SS *St. Louis*—Nathanael "Pep" West—The Businessman—aka Little Doovey—Juanito y Evita—The Journey of Death—Beware of Men—The Moor of Princeton—Scenes of the National Life, 6—A Sinner in the Hands of an Angry God—The Old Gang of His—Das Kapital—A Man Named Frank Wills—The Other President from Illinois—A Prudent Wife Is from the Lord—Painter—The Nominee—Kaddish for a Dead Fink—The Waters of the New World—Scenes of the National Life, 7.

Note: The following pieces previously appeared elsewhere: The First Knee on Canada (A4, A9 & A18); The Mighty Fallen, adapted from A9; A Land to Love (A9, A11 & A20); A Gringo: Do You Speak English? (A9 & A21); The Gastonia Strike (A14 & A22); The Poor Get Screwed, He Said (A23); A Traitor to His Class, adapted from A23; The Moor of Princeton (A15). Scenes of the National Life, 1 was revised from "Scenes of the National Life" in *Santa Barbara Review* (C47). They Still Walk, They Still Speak was reprinted in "The Sacco and Vanzetti Papers" in *American Letters and Commentary* (see C56)

University of Illinois Press issued 45 advance uncorrected proof copies, consisting of page proofs bound in laminated covers; the upper cover is the front of the dust jacket. Some copies are comb bound with black plastic, while others are velo-bound with black flat plastic strips.

Published when J. S. was 93 years old, *Intruders in Paradise* returns to the fertile ground of personal interpretations of American history. In this volume, which was originally titled *The New World*, J. S. broadens his scope to include the entire Western Hemisphere. Similar themes to earlier books are sounded: the rape of the land and the enslavement of the masses, particularly the indigenous peoples. The longer pieces are punctuated by Scenes from the National Life, in which J. S. takes on multiple brief topics in succession.

Even though she had been dead for several years, and would not fit in the narratives of most of these pieces, J. S.'s wife, Marguerite Roberts, appears in sections of italicized dialog in several of the segments, acting as an interlocutor for J. S. These bits of dialog prefigure J. S.'s next book, *A Palace of Silver* (A29).

In July 2005, the publisher declared this book out of print, with 518 copies sold.

A28 HAPPY HOLIDAYS FROM   2002
CAPRA PRESS

a. First (signed) edition:

[in script] *Happy Holidays* | *from* | *Capra Press* | [signature in blue ink of publisher] | Bob Bason | [signature in black ink of associate publisher] | Rich Barre

17.8 x 12.7 cm. *1*^{2}. Pp.*1-4*.

P.1 [photo of a star in the night sky above a palm tree, from the cover of Rich Barre's *The Star*]; *p.2* [small photo of J. S. with a possessive arm around M. R.'s shoulders, 2.7 x 1.8 cm., reproduced from the jacket of *A Palace of Silver* (A29)] | [text: the first two paragraphs from A29, with errors uncorrected from page proofs (e.g., *grounds* twice, instead of *rounds* and *grounds*)] | From *A Palace of Silver* by John Sanford, a Capra Holiday 2002 release | [shaky signature of J. S. in black ink] | [three lines with information about the cover photo]; *p.3* title; *p.4* [in red:] CAPRA PRESS FALL 2002/SPRING 2003 TITLES | [in black: 8 titles on 8 lines, the first of which announces *A Palace of Silver* for December 2002 release] | CAPRA [red goat head device, .6 x .7 cm.] [in black:] PRESS | MEMORABLE BOOKS SINCE 1969 | [address and contact information on 3 lines].

Stiff yellowish white paper with one glossy side, printed in blue, green, yellow, black and red; folded at left.

Published in December 2002; distributed gratis; approximately 150 copies.

Contents: first two paragraphs from A29.

Note: This holiday card was sent to friends of the rejuvenated Capra Press.

b. First regular edition

[title page as in A28a]

17.8 x 12.7 cm. [collation and pagination identical to A28a, except for p.2 which is not signed]

Published in December 2002; distributed gratis; approximately 350 copies.

A29 A PALACE OF SILVER   2003

a. First (limited, signed, lettered) edition:

A PALACE OF SILVER | A [swash A] Memoir [swash M] of [swash F] Maggie [swash M] Roberts [swash R] | JOHN SANFORD | FOREWORD BY NORMAN CORWIN | AFTERWORD BY JOSEPH MCBRIDE | CAPRA [publisher's goat head device] PRESS | PUBLISHERS OF MEMORABLE BOOKS SINCE 1969 | SANTA BARBARA

22.9 x 15.0 cm. *1-6*^{16}. Pp.*1-6*, 7-12, *13-14*, 15-153, *154*, 155-175, *176*, 177-180, *181-192*.

P.*1* half title; p.*2* Other Books by John Sanford | Fiction | [9 titles on 11 lines] | Creative Interpretations of History | [5 titles on 6 lines] | Autobiography and Memoir | [10 titles]; p.*3* title; p.*4* Copyright © 2003 by John Sanford | [...] | Printed in the United States of America | [...] | ISBN 0-9722503-6-0 (hc) | ISBN 0-9722503-7-9 (hc numbered) | ISBN 0-9722503-8-7 (hc lettered) | [...] | Edition: 10 9 8 7 6 5 4 3 2 1 | First Edition; p.*5* dedication: For Maggie | who dwells in the gardens | [publisher's ornament] | *We* [swash W] *will build upon her a palace of* [swash F] *silver...* | —SONG OF SOLOMON 8.9 | [ornament] | [6 lines thanking Jack Mearns]; p.6 blank; pp.7-12 foreword; p.*13* fly title; p.*14* blank; pp.15-153 text; p.*154* blank; pp.155-175 afterword; p.*176* blank; pp.177-180 Marguerite Roberts filmography; p.*181* This first edition was printed in October 2002 by | McNaughton & Gunn, Saline, Michigan. [...]; p.*182* blank; p.*183* Two thousand hardcover copies of A Palace of Silver were | printed by Capra Press in October 2002. An additional | one hundred copies have been numbered and signed by | the author and Mr. Corwin. Twenty-six copies in slipcases | were also lettered and signed by both. | This is copy: [lettered in black ink] | [signed in black ink by Norman Corwin] | [signed in black ink by J. S.]; p.*184* blank; p.*185* About Capra Press; pp.*186-192* blank.

Brownish bronze cloth boards stamped in silver down the spine: A PALACE OF SILVER JOHN SANFORD, and across the foot of the spine: [publisher's goat head device] | CAPRA | PRESS; on the upper cover: A PALACE | OF SILVER. All edges cut; endpapers. White paper dust jacket printed in silver, black and brownish gray, with a photo of M. R. and a protective/possessive looking J. S. on the front; photo of J. S. on the back flap; designed by Frank Goad. Yellowish white wove paper. Brownish bronze unprinted cloth covered slipcase.

Published February 2003 at $85.00; 26 copies.

Contents: Foreword by Norman Corwin; A Palace of Silver; Afterword by Joseph McBride; Marguerite Roberts Filmography.

Note: A small number of advance reading copies were issued, which consisted of finished pages of the book bound in unprinted glossy white stiff wrappers.

Portions were previously published in *Tin House* (C52) and the *Los Angeles Times*, as "Where the Heart Is at Peace" (C55), as well as "Happy Holidays from Capra Press" (A28). Joseph McBride's profile and filmography of M. R. previously appeared in *Written By*, the magazine of the Writers Guild.

Sun and Moon Press originally contracted for *Palace* as a Green Integer Book. However, due to publication delays, J. S. terminated the contract. Fortuitously, a revived Capra Press was in the market for new books.

Published in J. S.'s ninety-ninth year, *A Palace of Silver* consists of imaginary dialogues between J. S. and his wife, who had been dead for over ten years by the time of the book's writing. These dialogues take place mostly in the cemetery where

Maggie's ashes are buried, or in the grove behind the Sanfords' home. The book is a revealing portrait of the devastation of old age: the loneliness, the physical decline. Rare is it to have documentation of old age written by one who truly is old. Not wholly somber, this book recalls Samuel Beckett in its literal graveside humor.

The book is handsomely typeset and bound, although its layout has an unfortunate asymmetry, with its preliminary pages crowded toward the front and several blank leaves forlornly empty at the rear. Sales were very poor: fewer than 200 of the trade copies.

b. First (limited, signed, numbered) edition:

[title page as in A29a]

22.9 x 15.0 cm. Identical to A29a, except for p.*183*, which is numbered in black ink, rather than lettered. No slip case.

Published simultaneously with A29a at $65.00; 100 copies.

Contents: As in A29a.

c. First trade edition:

[title page as in A29a & A29b]

22.9 x 15.0 cm. Identical to A29b, except for p.*183*, which is not numbered or signed.

Published simultaneously with the limited edition at $25.95; 2,000 copies.

Contents: As in A29a & A29b.

d. First e-book edition (Bloomsbury Reader), [2013]

A PLACE OF SILVER | *A Memoir of Maggie Roberts* | JOHN SANFORD | [publisher's device with a reversed script B and forward script R] | BLOOMSBURY READER | LONDON • NEW DELHI • NEW YORK • SYDNEY

ISBN: 9781448213269

Published 12 September 2013 at $6.50; 180 pp.

A30 SPEAKING FROM AN EMPTY ROOM: THE SELECTED LETTERS OF JOHN SANFORD   2021

a. First edition:

SPEAKING IN | AN EMPTY ROOM| *The Selected Letters of John Sanford* | [floral ornament] | Edited and with an introduction by Dan Giancola | Afterword by Jack Mearns | Tough Poets Press | Arlington, Massachusetts

21.1 x 14.8 cm. Pp. *1-8*, 9, *10*, 11-15, *16-18*, 19-383, *384*, 385-387, *388*, 389, *390-394*.

Pp.*1* blank; p.*2* Books by John Sanford | [categorical listing of 24 titles]; p.*3* half title; p.*4* blank; p.*5* title; p.*6* Copyright © 2021 by the Literary Estate of John Sanford | Introduction copyright © 2021 by Dan Giancola | Afterword copyright © 2021 by Jack Mearns | Back cover photo by Dan Giancola […] | ISBN 978-0-578-77472-5 | Tough Poets Press | […]; p.*7* dedication: *For Maggie and The Governor* [J. S.'s father] | As Always…; p.*8* blank; pp.*9* contents; p.*10* blank; pp. 11-15 Introduction by Dan Giancola; p.*16* blank; p.*17* fly title; p.*18* blank; pp.19-376 text; pp.377-383

Afterword: My Conciliatory Tone by Jack Mearns; p.*384* blank; pp.*385-387* index of recipients; p.*388* blank; p.*389* acknowledgments; p.*390* blank; p.*391* Publisher's Acknowledgments: Profound thanks are extended to the following for their generous financial support which helped to defray some of the book's production costs [names of Kickstarter campaign contributors]; pp.*392-395* blank; p.*396* CPSIA information [...].

Glossy white stiff paper wrappers printed in white, bronze, black and shades of sepia; lettered down the spine [in white:] SPEAKING IN AN EMPTY ROOM | [in bronze:] THE SELECTED LETTERS OF JOHN SANFORD; lettered on the upper cover [in white:] SPEAKING IN | AN EMPTY ROOM [in bronze:] THE SELECTED | LETTERS OF | JOHN SANFORD | [in black:] Edited and with | an introduction by | Dan Giancola | Afterword by | Jack Mearns; the upper cover reproduces a portion of a 1935 promotional photograph of J. S. that was distributed with review copies of *The Old Man's Place* (A2a); on the bottom cover is a photograph of an aged J. S. at his writing desk by Dan Giancola; edges cut flush; perfect binding. Yellowish white wove paper.

Published 4 January 2021 at $18.99; print on demand.

Note: This volume prints 222 letters spanning the years 1931 to 2003—written to family, friends, fans, and publishers—that reveal J. S. as a working writer. They are full of his personal and professional tribulations, which are frequently intertwined.

I am embarrassed to admit that my afterword contains two errors. For some mystifying reason, I wrote that J. S. had 23 not 24 books published, and I incorrectly listed the year of J. S.'s marriage as 1939, when *Seventy Times Seven* (A3a) came out. In truth, J. S. married Maggie at the end of December 1938.

B. CONTRIBUTIONS TO BOOKS

B1   THE BEST SHORT SHORTS OF 1932   1932

THE BEST | SHORT SHORTS | OF 1932 | *Edited by* | PAUL ERNEST ANDERSON | *and* | LIONEL WHITE | [publisher's G P P device] | G. P. Putnam's Sons | NEW YORK : LONDON | 1932

18.7 x 12.1 cm. xvi, 272 pp.

Orange cloth boards; lettered in black on the spine and upper cover; edges cut; endpapers. Gray paper dust jacket printed in black and orange.

Also issued in light yellowish green cloth with green lettering, with dust jacket unchanged and book otherwise identical.

Published in 1932 at $2.00; number of copies not obtainable.

Contains: "I Let Him Die" 228-234, story, see C12.

Note: This is J. S.'s first appearance in a book, predating *The Water Wheel* (A1) by several months.

B2   NATHANAEL WEST: AN INTERPRETIVE STUDY   1961

[across opposing pages:] [left side:] *An Interpretive Study* [right side:] *by James F. Light | Northwestern University Press*

20.9 x 12.8 cm. xiii, 221 pp., 2 blank leaves.

Black cloth boards; stamped in silver across the spine and in brass on the upper cover; some copies with top edges stained orangish red; edges cut; endpapers. Yellowish white paper dust jacket, printed in grayish green, black and white.

Published in May 1961 at $4.75; 1,500 copies.

Contains: quotations about West 7-8, 33, 34, 61-62, 63-64, 67, 68, 69, 74, 89, 106-107, 131-132.

Note: J. S. stated that he was one of the few people who knew West who was willing to talk to the author for this book.

B3   HELLO, HOLLYWOOD!   1962

DOUBLEDAY & COMPANY, INC. | PRESENTS | THE RIVKIN-KERR PRODUCTION | OF | HELLO, HOLLYWOOD! | A BOOK ABOUT THE MOVIES BY THE PEOPLE | WHO MAKE THEM

23.3 x 14.7 cm. 571 pp., 2 blank leaves.

Black cloth; stamped in silver down the spine, with film spool in blind on the upper cover; top and bottom edges cut; page ends roughly cut; decorated endpapers; yellowish white paper dust jacket printed in black, orange, greenish blue and light green.

Published in 1962 at $6.95; number of copies not obtainable.

Contains: "Nathanael West" 527-530, memoir, see C27.

B4   A RETURN TO PAGANY   1969

[across opposing pages:] [left side:] *A Return to* [right side:] [publisher's device of willow within a fenced enclosure] PAGANY | [thin rule across both pages] | [left side:] *The History, Correspondence, and* | *Selections from a Little Magazine* [right side:] *1929-1932* | *Edited by* STEPHEN HALPERT | *with* RICHARD JOHNS | *Introduction by* KENNETH REXROTH | [left side:] BEACON PRESS [right side:] *Boston*

25.2 x 17 cm. xix, 519 pp., 2 blank leaves [facsimiles throughout text]

One quarter red cloth spine; stamped in white down the spine; blue cloth boards with abstract village in blind on the upper cover; edges cut; endpapers. White paper dust jacket; printed in dark blue and red. (Many copies have a remainder mark of paint sprayed on the top page edges.)

Published in 1969 at $12.50; number of copies not obtainable.

Contains: "An Adirondack Narrative" 390-405, story, see C10; letter to Richard Johns 24 February, 1932, 421; letter to Richard Johns [1933], 506.

B5 NATHANAEL WEST: THE ART OF HIS LIFE   1970

a. First edition:

Nathanael West | The Art of His Life | *by Jay Martin* | [publisher's fish device] | FARRAR, STRAUS AND GIROUX | NEW YORK

21.3 x 13.9 cm. xxi, 435 pp., 10 plates

Light beige cloth boards flecked with darker threads; stamped down the spine in orange and black; edges cut; endpapers. Yellowish white paper dust jacket; printed in black, red and dark beige; photos of West on front and back.

Published 1 January 1970 at $10.00; number of copies not obtainable.

Contains: quotations about West 23, 38, 54, 65, 73, 94, 143, 279; "Book Marks for Today" 145, letter co-written with West, see C8.

Note: J. S. felt that Martin did not quote him extensively enough. He felt Martin used only the positive quotations but not the negative ones. J. S. wrote Martin and asked to have his quotations removed before publication, but Martin did not comply with this request.

b. 21.7 x 13.4 cm. xix, 435 pp., 4 plates. Published in the U. K. by Secker & Warburg in maroon cloth, stamped in gold on the spine; yellowish white dust jacket, printed in brown and yellow; top edges stained maroon. Published May 1970 at £4.50; number of copies not known.

c. 20.7 x 13.5 cm. xxi, 435 pp., 1 blank leaf, 10 plates. Published in paperback edition by Hayden in stiff yellowish white textured wrappers, printed in black, beige and umber. Published 1971 at $4.95; number of copies not obtainable.

d. 21.4 x 13.4 cm. 1 leaf, xxi, 436 pp., 2 blank leaves, 8 plates. Reissued in paperback by Carroll & Graf in stiff yellowish white wrappers, printed in purple, pale yellow and fuchsia, with a photo of West on the upper cover. Published 1984 at $8.95; number of copies not known.

B6 NATHANAEL WEST: A COMPREHENSIVE BIBLIOGRAPHY   1975

Nathanael West: | A Comprehensive Bibliography | By William White | Oakland University | The Kent State University Press

21.6 x 13.7 cm. xi, 209 pp., [3] pp. advts.

Fuchsia cloth boards; stamped in black down the spine; edges cut; endpapers. Issued without dust jacket.

Published 8 April 1975 at $8.00; 2,000 copies.

Contains: "Book Marks for Today" 131, letter co-written with West, see C8.

B7 SOME TIME IN THE SUN   1976

a. First edition:

Some Time | in the Sun | [thin rule] | *Tom Dardis* | Charles Scribner's Sons/New York

23.4 x 14.9 cm. xi, 274 pp., 1 blank leaf

One-third beige cloth spine; lettered in green down the spine; olive cloth boards; edges cut; endpapers. Yellowish white paper jacket, printed in light mint green, darker green, yellow and black.

Published in 1976 at $9.95; number of copies not obtainable.

Contains: photos of J. S. and Nathanael West at Viele Pond 158; quotations about West 159-160, 167, 170.

b. 20.9 x 13.1 cm., xi, 244 pp., 1 blank leaf. Also published in a substantially smaller book club edition, with one-quarter glossy whitish gray cloth spine, stamped in blue-green down the spine; dark blue-green cloth boards; top edges cut, bottom edges roughly cut, page ends trimmed. Most likely published 1976; price and number of copies not obtainable.

c. 23.5 x 15.1 cm. xi, 274 pp., 1 blank leaf. Published in the U. K. by André Deutsch in dark green cloth, stamped in gold on the spine; yellowish white dust jacket, printed in green, yellow, black, and beige. Published 1976 at £5.50; number of copies not obtainable.

d. 19.7 x 12.5 cm. xiii, 297 pp., 1 p. advt., 2 blank leaves. Published in paperback edition by Penguin in stiff yellowish white wrappers, printed in beige, yellow and light green. Published 1981 at $5.95; number of copies not obtainable.

e. 22.8 x 15.2 cm. xi, 274 pp., 1 blank leaf. Reissued in paperback by Limelight Editions in yellowish white paper wrappers, printed in red, yellowish orange, green and blue. Published 1988 at $12.95; number of copies not obtainable.

B8   THE PUSHCART PRIZE II   1977

a. First edition:

[across opposing pages:] [left side:] [3 publisher's flame ornaments] THE PUSHCART PRIZE II: [right side:] BEST OF THE SMALL PRESSES | [left side:] *An annual small press reader assembled with Founding Editors* | [23 names on 8 lines] [right side:] EDITED BY BILL HENDERSON | [publisher's pushcart device] | published by THE PUSHCART PRESS | 1977-78 Edition | [left side:] BEST OF THE SMALL PRESSES [right side:] THE PUSHCART PRIZE, II: [3 publisher's flame ornaments]

23.6 x 15.5 cm. 528 pp.; number of copies not obtainable.

Light bluish gray cloth; stamped in black and light blue across the spine; top edges stained light blue; page ends roughly trimmed; endpapers. Yellowish white paper dust jacket; printed in red and yellow.

Published July 1977 at $12.50; 3,000 copies.

Contains: "Foreword" 473-475, foreword from *Adirondack Stories*, see A10; "The Fire in the Catholic Church" 475-484, story, see A10 and C13.

b. 23.0 x 13.1 cm. 528 pp. Published in paperback edition by Avon in stiff yellowish white wrappers, printed in gray, blue, red and black. Published March 1978 at $5.95; 10,000 copies.

B9   THE INQUISITION IN HOLLYWOOD   1980

a. First edition:

[in shadowed type:] THE | INQUISITION IN | HOLLYWOOD | [not shadowed:] *Politics in the Film Community* | *1930-1960* | Larry Ceplair & Steve Englund | *Anchor Press/Doubleday* | *Garden City, New York* | *1980*

22.3 x 15.35 cm. xvi, 536 pp., 8 plates

Black cloth; lettered in gold down the spine in silver; stamped in blind on upper cover; top and bottom edges cut; page ends roughly trimmed; endpapers; flat spine. Yellowish white paper dust jacket, printed in white, yellow and shades of orangish red.

Published in 1980 at $17.50; number of copies not obtainable.

Contains: quotations [source not identified, presumably an interview] 14-15, 180, 399.

b. 19.6 x 14.8 cm. 544 pp. Published in paperback by University of Illinois Press in stiff yellowish white wrappers, printed in black, red, white and shades of gray. Published 17 July 2003; price and number of copies not obtainable.

B10   A MAN WITHOUT SHOES   1982

[within a red-ruled box:] [in red:] A MAN | WITHOUT | SHOES | [in black:] *A NOVEL* BY JOHN SANFORD | [publisher's sparrow device] | BLACK SPARROW PRESS | *SANTA BARBARA: 1982*

25.3 x 16 cm. xviii, 454 pp., 1 blank leaf

Paper boards printed in beige and brown in a woven wicker pattern; spine of coarse green cloth; beige paper spine label, printed in orangish red; top edges cut, bottom edges roughly trimmed, page ends uncut; endpapers. Tan dust jacket printed in orangish red, brown and black, with black cross-hatching on front and front and back flaps.

Issued in March 1982 at $25.00; approximately 1,500 copies.

Contains: "Author's Introduction" *iii-vii*.

Note: see A5 for a full description of this item.

B11   BLAST 3   1984

[within a thick-ruled yellow box:] [in red:] *BLAST 3* | [thick yellow rule] | EDITED BY SEAMUS COONEY | [thick yellow rule] | CO-EDITED BY | BRADFORD MORROW, BERNARD LAFOURCADE | AND HUGH KENNER | BLACK SPARROW PRESS • 1984

30.3 x 22.6 cm. 357 pp., 4 plates, 3 blank leaves

Greenish yellow textured paper wrappers, printed in black, yellow, red and shades of green; edges cut flush; perfect bound; endpapers. Laid in was a 33-1/3 RPM stereo vinyl 7" single of songs by Michael Ingham.

There was a deluxe edition of 426 copies bound in paper covered boards identical to the wrappers. Twenty-six lettered copies have a brilliant red cloth spine and paper spine label; 400 numbered copies have a black cloth spine and paper spine label; all hardcover copies were issued in an unprinted greenish yellow paper dust jacket. Limited copies are lettered or numbered in red on

p. 357 but are otherwise identical to the paperback edition. The lettered edition was sold at $40.00 and the numbered edition at $30.00.

Published 21 September 1984 at $20.00; 3,504 copies.

Contains: "The Leo Frank Case, 1913-1915" 309-315, historical piece, see A15; "Eugene V. Debs, 1855-1926" 316-321, historical piece, see A15.

B12   S. J. PERELMAN: A LIFE   1986

a. First edition:

S.J. PERELMAN | [thin rule, which loop of J breaks] | A LIFE | [thin rule] | *Dorothy Herrmann* | G. P. PUTNAM'S SONS NEW YORK

22.8 x 14.5 cm. 337 pp. [the page numbering is off, so that the first page is p. 3], 8 plates

Dark gray cloth spine; stamped in silver; grayish white paper covered boards; all edges cut; endpapers. Yellowish white paper dust jacket, printed in brown and black.

Published in 1986 at $18.95; number of copies not obtainable.

Contains: quotations about Perelman 32, 34, 102, 139, 244.

b. 23.4 x 15.4 cm. 338 pp. [the page numbering is off, so that the first page is p. 3], 8 plates. Published in paperback edition by Simon & Schuster as a Fireside book, in stiff yellowish white wrappers, printed in black, shades of orange and gray. Published in 1987 at $8.95; number of copies not obtainable.

c. 21.5 x 13.1 cm. 337 pp. [the page numbering is off, so that the first page is p. 3], 4 plates. Published in U. K. paperback edition by Papermac in stiff yellowish white wrappers, printed in black, red and gray. Published 1988 at £7.95; number of copies not obtainable.

B13   POLITICS AND THE MUSE   1989

[in bold:] Politics And The Muse: | Studies in the Politics of | Recent American Literature | Edited | by | Adam Sorkin | [not bold:] Bowling Green State University Popular Press | Bowling Green, Ohio 43403

22.8 x 15.2 cm. vi, 242 pp.

Red cloth boards; lettered in black on the spine; top and bottom edges cut, page ends trimmed; endpapers. Glossy white paper jacket, printed in royal blue, black, pink and red.

Published in 1989; price and number of copies not obtainable.

Contains: quotations about Nathanael West and the blacklist period 42.

Note: The chapter by Tom Dardis, "The Plight of the Left-wing Writer," presents industry insider details about the publication of *The Land that Touches Mine* (A6a & A6b), as well as how J. S.'s blacklisting nearly scuttled reprinting *The Old Man's Place* (A2c) in paperback in 1957.

B14 FRANK CAPRA: THE CATASTROPHE OF SUCCESS 1992

a. First edition:

[in shadowed script, sloping upward:] Frank | Capra | [underlining swash broken by the p] | [in normal, horizontal print:] THE | CATASTROPHE | OF SUCCESS | *by Joseph McBride* | *Simon & Schuster* | *New York London Toronto Sydney Tokyo Singapore*

23.6 x 14.9 cm. 768 pp., 12 plates

Dark bluish gray one-quarter cloth spine; stamped in fuchsia; pinkish red paper covered boards; all edges cut; endpapers. Yellowish white paper dust jacket, printed in silver, black and purple.

Published in 1992 at $27.50; number of copies not obtainable.

Contains: quotations about Capra and from letters to Capra 459-460, 462-465.

b. 23.3 x 14.9 cm. 763 pp., 8 plates, 2 blank leaves. Published in the U. K. by Faber and Faber in black cloth, stamped in white on the spine; yellowish white dust jacket, printed in black and gray. Published 1992 at £25.00; number of copies not obtainable.

c. 23.5 x 15.5 cm. 768 pp., 8 plates. Published in paperback edition by Simon & Schuster as a Touchstone book, in stiff yellowish white wrappers, printed in black, brown, gray and light green. Published 1993 at $16.00; number of copies not obtainable.

d. 21.4 x 13.3 cm. 763 pp., 8 plates, 2 blank leaves. Published in U. K. paperback edition by Faber & Faber in stiff yellowish white wrappers, printed in black, gray and white. Published 1996 at £12.99; number of copies not obtainable.

B15 RED SCARE 1995

a. First edition:

[in outline:] RED | SCARE | [in normal type:] *Memories of the | American Inquisition | An Oral History* | GRIFFIN FARIELLO | [publisher's gull device in box] | W • W • NORTON & COMPANY | *New York London*

23.4 x 15.2 cm. 575 pp.

One half black cloth spine; stamped in brass; red paper covered boards; all edges cut; endpapers. White dust jacket printed in black, red, yellow and gray.

Published in 1995 at $29.95; number of copies not obtainable.

Contains: "John Sanford" 289-294, interview by Griffin Fariello.

b. 29.1 x 15.3 cm. 575 pp. Published in paperback edition by Avon in yellowish white paper wrappers, printed in red, pale yellow and black. Published May 1996 at $15.00; number of copies not obtainable.

B16   HONNI SOIT QUI MALIBU   1996

PHILIPPE GARNIER | HONNI SOIT | QUI MALIBU | *Quelques écrivains | à Hollywood* | [Sagittarius device for the Stanley Rose Bookshop] | BERNARD GASSET | PARIS

22.6 x 14 cm. 384 pp., 4 plates

Yellowish white paper wrappers, printed in dark grayish blue, silver, white, black and shades of blue; edges cut flush, perfect bound.

Published 1996 at 139FF; number of copies not obtainable

Contains: quotations from an interview with J. S. 53-84, small photo on rear of plate 4, chronology 358-359

Note: in French. See B31 for a full description of this item.

B17   NATHANAEL WEST: NOVELS AND OTHER WRITINGS   1997

Nathanael West | [thin rule] | NOVELS AND OTHER WRITINGS | *The Dream Life of Balso Snell* | *Miss Lonelyhearts* | *A Cool Million* | *The Day of the Locust* | *Other Writings* | *Unpublished Writings and Fragments* | *Letters* | [thin rule] | [publisher's open book device] | THE LIBRARY OF AMERICA

20.0 x 12.0 cm. x, 835 pp., 1 blank leaf.

Copper colored cloth printed in red and gold on spine; all edges cut; decorated endpapers. White paper dust jacket; printed in black, red and blue, with list of volumes in series on verso.

Published in May 1997 at $35.00; 21,543 copies.

An undetermined number of copies were issued in a beige cloth covered slipcase stamped in gold, without dust jacket.

Contains: "To the New York World-Telegram" 769-770, letter co-written with West, see C8.

B18   TENDER COMRADES   1997

a. First edition:

[9 cm. black column in center of page] [unprinted, within column:] [small square] | [within thin-ruled box, at an angle:] PATRICK MCGILLIGAN AND PAUL BUHLE | [in type:] TENDER COMRADES | [horizontal:] [small square] | [in black script within unprinted strip:] A Backstory of the Hollywood Blacklist | [unprinted:] PHOTOGRAPHS BY ALISON MORELY AND | WILLIAM B. WINBURN | ST. MARTIN'S PRESS [small publisher's ornament] NEW YORK

23.5 x 14.9 cm. xxiii, 776 pp.

Black paper boards; lettered in gold on spine; all edges cut; endpapers. White paper dust jacket; printed in silver, black and red.

Published in 1997 at $35.00; number of copies not obtainable.

Contains: photo of M. R. by J. S. 571; "Marguerite Roberts (and John Sanford)" 571-584, interview by Tina Daniell.

b. 23.5 x 15.5 cm. xxiii, 776 pp. Published in paperback edition by St. Martin's as a Griffin book, in stiff yellowish white wrappers, printed in red, black, silver and bronze. Published February 1999 at $19.95; number of copies not obtainable.

B19   SONGS FROM THE ARMY OF   1998
THE WORKING STIFFS

DAN GIANCOLA | [in bold:] SONGS FROM | THE ARMY OF | THE WORKING STIFFS | [not bold:] KARMA DOG EDITIONS | LONG ISLAND, NEW YORK | 1998

13.8 x 9.9 cm. 61 pp., 1 blank leaf.

Yellowish white paper wrappers, printed in black and gray; edges cut flush, perfect bound.

Published May 1998 at $5.95; 1,000 copies.

Contains: 5-line quotation praising the book, on the lower cover.

B20   TAMBOUR VOLUMES 1-8,   2002
A FACSIMILE EDITION

TAMBOUR | Volumes 1-8, a Facsimile Edition | Harold J. Salemson | *Editor* | *Introduction by* | Mark S. Morrisson and Jack Selzer | The University of Wisconsin Press

16.5 x 13.5 cm. v, 91, i, 60, vii, 60, vii, 76, vii, 77, vi, 76, vii, 75, viii, 76, vii, 77, v pp., 3 blank leaves.

Stiff white paper wrappers, printed in purple and pale yellow, with French-fold flaps; edges cut flush; perfect bound.

Published 20 January 2002 at $24.95; 1,042 copies.

Contains: "You, Drum Major" vol. 3 10-15, essay, see C4; "An Old Lady" vol. 4 50-53, story, see C5; "Terpsichore on the Nevsky Prospect" vol. 6 50-56, story, see C6.

Note: These pieces represent J. S.'s earliest published works.

B21   PAYMENT IS EXTRACTED   2002

PUBLICATIONS IN THE HUMANITIES, UNIVERSITY OF JOENSUU | 27 | [in bold:] Payment Is Extracted | Mechanisms of Escape into America in Immigrant | and Post-Immigrant Jewish American Fiction | *Roy Goldblatt* | [not bold:] University of Joensuu | Joensuu 2002

25.0 x 17.4 cm. viii, 252 pp., 2 pp. listing of other books in series.

Stiff white paper wrappers, printed in gray, navy blue, black and shades of blue and yellow; edges cut flush, perfect bound.

Published 28 January 2002 at €20; 140 copies.

Contains: quotations about Albert Maltz and John Howard Lawson 175.

B22   REDEMPTION: THE LIFE OF   2005
HENRY ROTH

REDEMPTION | *The Life of* | Henry Roth | [small ornament] STEVEN G. KELLMAN [small ornament] | [publisher's gull device in box] | W. W. NORTON & COMPANY | NEW YORK • LONDON

23.4 x 15.4 cm. xii, 372 pp., 8 plates

One-third copper and light gray paper boards; stamped in silver on spine; all edges cut; endpapers. Yellowish white paper dust jacket; printed in brass, black and shades of gray.

Published August 2005 at $25.95; 10,000 copies.

Contains: quotations about Mt. Morris from *The View from Mt. Morris* (A25) 46.

B23   TRINITY OF PASSION   2007

a. First edition:

[large vertical left brace enclosing 3 lines of title] [in bold:] Trinity | of | Passion | [not bold:] The Literary Left and | the Antifascist Crusade | [in bold:] ALAN M. WALD | [not bold:] The University of North Carolina Press | Chapel Hill

23.5 x 15.5 cm. xx, 319 pp., 2 blank leaves.

One-third black cloth spine; lettered in silver down the spine; grayish beige cloth boards flecked with black threads; edges cut; endpapers. White paper dust jacket; printed in grayish blue, black and red.

Published 26 February 2007 at $60; number of copies not obtainable

Contains: photo of J. S. taken by Marguerite Roberts 188; quote from a 1989 interview with the author 189.

Note: Alan Wald's chapter, "The Conversion of the Jews," illuminates the process of J. S.'s joining the Communist Party.

Unfortunately, it also contains numerous errors—from placing J. S.'s date of death in 1999, to incorrect publication dates for *The Water Wheel* and *Every Island Fled Away*, to stating that J. S. and M. R. "together ... collaborated on a number of motion pictures" at M-G-M, to saying that M. R. invoked the First Amendment at the HUAC hearings, which is what the Hollywood Ten unsuccessfully did before being jailed for contempt of Congress. Wald also repeats the somewhat common misconception about "Sanford's decision to follow Nathanael West to Hollywood," when in fact the two had been estranged for several years before chancing to meet up again in Los Angeles.

b. 23.5 x 15.5 cm. xx, 319 pp. Published in paperback by University of North Carolina Press, in stiff yellowish white wrappers, printed in grayish blue, black and red. Published 1 August 2014 at $26.00; number of copies not obtainable.

B24   A CLASS OF ITS OWN   2008

A Class of Its Own: | Re-Envisioning American Labor Fiction | Edited by | Laura Hapke and Lisa A. Kirby | [in bold:] Cambridge Scholars | [thin rule] | [bold:] Publishing

20.5 x 14.2 cm. xiv, 321 pp.

Black cloth boards; lettered in silver down the spine; all edges cut; endpapers; flat spine. White paper jacket, printed in black and light brownish yellow.

Published 1 December 2008; price and number of copies not obtainable

Contains: quotations from *The People from Heaven* (A4) 146-149.

B25 DAYBOOK OF CRITICAL READING AND WRITING 2009

[unprinted in green blocks in rough-edged type font:] DAYBOOK | [in bold:] OF CRITICAL READING AND WRITING | [in green strip:] American Literature | [photograph of New York street crowded with traffic] [green image of paperclip attaching green box to top of photo] [4 lines unprinted in box:] daybook, *n.* a book in | which the events of the | day are recorded; *specif.* | a journal or diary | [image of paperclip attaching light green box to bottom of photo] [4 lines printed in box:] [in black:] THE AUTHORS | [each name in dark green, preceded by a black *:] Fran Claggett | Louann Read | Ruth Vinz | [in bold:] Great Source | [not bold:] A Division of Houghton Mifflin Harcourt Publishing | Wilmington, Massachusetts

25.1 x 19 cm. 287 pp.

Stiff yellowish white paper wrappers, printed purple and white over a color photograph of the street scene on the title page.

Published in 2008; price and number of copies not obtainable.

Contains: "Shikata Ga Nai" 168-169, historical piece, see A15 and A21.

Note: This high school English textbook uses the historical piece to illustrate "using vignette as commentary," with a particular focus on its visual imagery.

B26   MISS LONELYHEARTS & THE DAY   2009
OF THE LOCUST

Miss Lonelyhearts | & |The Day of the Locust | NATHANAEL WEST | Introduction by Jonathan Lethem | Afterword by John Sanford | [publisher's device] | A New Directions Book
20.3 x 13.2 cm. xi, 191 pp., 2 blank leaves.

Stiff paper wrappers, half light pink and half light blue, printed in black and white; edges cut flush, perfect bound.

Published 23 June 2009 at $11.95; number of copies not obtainable.

Contains: "Afterword" 187-191, see C49.

B27   LONELYHEARTS   2010

a. First edition:

[in bold:] LONELYHEARTS | [light gray floral ornament with horizontal stem] | [thin rule] | [not bold:] THE SCREWBALL WORLD | *of* | NATHANAEL WEST | *and* | EILEEN McKENNEY | [in bold:] MARION MEADE | [not bold:] [publisher's dolphin device] | HOUGHTON MIFFLIN HARCOURT | BOSTON NEW YORK 2010

22.9 x 15 cm. xvii, 392 pp., 8 plates, 2 blank leaves.

One-quarter greenish blue and three-quarter white paper cloth boards; stamped in silver on spine; all edges cut; endpapers.

Glossy white paper dust jacket; printed in light beige, brown, red and greenish blue.

Published 11 March 2010 at $28.00; number of copies not obtainable.

Contains: quotations from letters about Nathanael West 259, 275 and from *A Very Good Land to Fall With* (A21) and *A Walk in the Fire* (A22) 308, 313-314.

Note: Though Marion Meade only cites J. S. sparingly, her overall view of West as a person seems to hew more toward J. S.'s negative view than had prior biographers'.

b. 20.3 x 13.5 cm. Published in paperback edition by Houghton Mifflin Harcourt as a Mariner book, in stiff yellowish white wrappers, printed in black, magenta, purple, beige, and shades of blue, gray and yellow. Published 10 March 2011 at $22.95; number of copies not obtainable.

B28   AMERICAN NIGHT   2012

a. First edition:

[in bold:] AMERICAN | [gray vertical rule on left side of text extending to bottom of page] | [in shaded bold:] NIGHT | [not bold:] *The Literary Left in the* | *Era of the Cold War* | ALAN M. WALD | The University of | North Carolina | *Chapel Hill*

23.5 x 15.4 cm. xix, 412 pp.

Black cloth boards; stamped in silver on spine; all edged cut; endpapers. Glossy white paper dust jacket; printed in black, gray and red.

Published 15 October 2012; price and number of copies not obtainable.

Contains: quotation about the Communist Party's prohibition of homosexuals from becoming members from *A Very Good Land to Fall With* (A21) 119.

b. 23.5 x 15.4 cm. xix, 412 pp. Published in paperback edition by University of North Carolina Press, in stiff yellowish white wrappers, printed in black, gray and red.

Published 15 October 2012; price and number of copies not obtainable.

B29   REGIONALISTS ON THE LEFT   2013

Regionalists on the Left | Radical Voices from the | American West | Edited by | Michael C. Steiner | UNIVERSITY OF OKLAHOMA PRESS : NORMAN

23.5 x 15.4 cm. xv, 399 pp.

One-quarter red cloth spine, red paper boards; stamped in black on spine; all edged cut; endpapers. White paper dust jacket; printed in red, black and shades of gray.

Published 15 March 2013 at $29.95; number of copies not obtainable.

Contains: 1935 publicity photo of J. S. 282, quote from rear of dust jacket from *The Old Man's Place* (A2a) 284, quote from letter about Nathanael West 294.

Note: Jack Mearns's chapter, "John Sanford's Radical Regionalism: The Universal of the Particular," asserts that—even though J. S. did not identify himself as a regionalist—his themes and writing approach fit well with those of avowed regionalists.

B30   TWO CHEERS FOR HOLLYWOOD   2017

[in staggered large block print resembling the Hollywood Sign:] TWO CHEERS | FOR HOLLYWOOD | [smaller:] JOSEPH MCBRIDE ON MOVIES | [publisher's geological tower device] [in normal print:] Hightower Press | *Berkeley, California* | 2017

25.5 x 17.6 cm. 693 pp.

Stiff, yellowish white paper wrappers, printed in gray, yellow, white and shades of brown; all edges cut flush, perfect bound.

Published 19 September 2017 at $38.50; number of copies not obtainable.

Contains: numerous quotations from J. S., both from J. S.'s books and from personal communications with Joseph McBride 162-183.

Note: A noted Hollywood biographer, McBride originally wrote this piece in 1993 but was unable to find a publisher for it. McBride provides insightful commentary on J. S.'s entire career. The many quotes from J. S. about his own writing and politics are unusually revealing about J. S.'s approach and character. A new introduction to the essay incorrectly states that J. S. died at age 99, rather than dying in his 99th year.

B31   SOUNDRELS & SPITBALLERS   2020

[in light gray, like cut-outs:] SCOUNDRELS | &SPITBALLERS [& and S overlap; top of S is also overlapped by the Sc above] | [in black:] WRITERS AND HOLLYWOOD IN THE 1930S | [in gray:] PHILIPPE GARNIER | [two lines, within square publisher's device, in white:] BLACK POOL | PRODUCTIONS

21 x 13.8 cm. 370 pp., 5 pp. for notes.

Stiff white paper wrappers, printed in white and sepia, with French-fold flaps; edges cut flush; perfect bound.

Published 2020 at $25.00; number of copies not obtainable.

Contains: lengthy quotations from a 1986 documentary interview about Nathanael West 60-68, 70-71, 85; photo of J. S. and West at Viele Pond 64.

Note: This is an English translation of the author's 1996 *Honni Soit qui Malibu* (B16). As the book's title suggests, the author holds a decidedly caustic view of his subjects. Still, his treatment of J. S. is especially and inexplicably vicious. On a factual level, the chapter "The Hollywood Flagellant" is rife with errors. More baffling is how utterly Garnier dismisses J. S. as a person and a writer—e.g., "Sanford...in spite of his artistic ambitions and political gestures, never had the slightest grip on the world around him"; "most of his books give the impression of being about nothing"; "This was precisely the story of his curious life: that of a man from whom nothing was ever asked, but who spent his entire existence explaining himself to the world...in haughty volumes few had bothered to read."

Oddly, Amazon.com does not sell this book yet lists it as a "Pidgin English Edition."

C. CONTRIBUTIONS TO PERIODICALS

1921

C1 SHAPIRO, JULIAN L. *The Clintonian*, 21 (June 1921) 34. Photo, nickname [Jibby], quote [He makes use of gas tank], and activities. [Senior yearbook for DeWitt Clinton High School in New York City. The senior class included writers Countee Cullen and Lionel Trilling.]

1923

C2 JULIAN LAWRENCE SHAPIRO, B.S. *Lafayette Melange* (1923) 143. Listing as a member of the sophomore class, with quote: "Well, ovah in N'York," and hometown of New York. [Yearbook for Lafayette College, Easton, PA.]

C3 SHAPIRO, JULIAN LAWRENCE. *Directory of the Alumni and Students of Lehigh University* (June 1923) 182. Listing as a current student, an arts major and member of class of '25, with address [of his father's law office]. [Though he lasted at Lehigh less than two weeks, J. S. managed to make it into this directory.]

1929

C4 YOU, DRUM MAJOR. *Tambour*, 3 (June 1929) 10-15. Essay, reprinted in *Tambour Facsimile Edition*, 2002 (B20). [J. S.'s first publication is a nearly incomprehensible manifesto on literature, notable for its lauding of William Carlos Williams and his *In the American Grain*. *Tambour* was published by Harold Salemson, whose uncle worked in J. S.'s father's law office.]

C5 AN OLD LADY. *Tambour*, 4 (September 1929) 50-53. Story, reprinted in *Tambour Facsimile Edition*, 2002 (B20). [J. S.'s unkind portrait of his paternal grandmother.]

1930

C6 TERPSICHORE ON THE NEVSKY PROSPECT. *Tambour*, 6 (February 1930) 50-56. Story, reprinted in *Tambour Facsimile Edition*, 2002 (B20). [J. S.'s swipe at friend and mentor George Brounoff.]

1931

C7 PROSE. *The New Review*, 1, 2 (June-July 1931) 135-138. Fiction. [This piece represents a condensation of several sections from *The Water Wheel* (A1).]

C8 BOOK MARKS FOR TODAY [co-written with Nathanael West]. *New York World-Telegram*, 64, 94 (October 20, 1931) 23. Letter complaining about how the columnist had called literary journals that did not pay authors "panhandling magazines." Reprinted in *Nathanael West: The Art of His Life*, 1970 (B5), *Nathanael West: A Comprehensive Bibliography*, 1975 (B6), and *Nathanael West: Novels and Other Writings*, 1997 (B17).

1932

C9 TIRED MEN AND DUNG. *The New Review*, 1, 4 (Winter 1931-32) 395-397. Review of Nathanael West's *The Dream*

Life of Balso Snell. Reprinted in *The Waters of Darkness*, 1986 (A20).

C10 AN ADIRONDACK NARRATIVE. *Pagany*, 3, 1 (January-March 1932) 46-61. Story, reprinted in *A Return to Pagany*, 1969 (B4) and *Adirondack Stories*, 1976 (A10). [The entire run of *Pagany* was reprinted by the Kraus Reprint Corporation in 1966.]

C11 THE FIRST CHAPTER OF A NOVEL. *The New Review*, 2, 5 (April 1932) 86-91. Fiction, reprinted with extensive revisions in *The Water Wheel*, 1933 (A1).

C12 TWO STORIES [I Let Him Die & Jasper Darby's Passion]. *Pagany*, 3, 2 (April-June 1932) 47-55. Stories, which formed the basis for *Seventy Times Seven*, 1939 (A3). "I Let Him Die" was reprinted in *Best Short Shorts of 1932*, 1932 (B1), and both stories were reprinted in *Adirondack Stories*, 1976 (A10).

C13 THE FIRE AT THE CATHOLIC CHURCH. *Contact* 1, 2 (May 1932) 52-64. Story, incorporated into *The People from Heaven*, 1943 (A4) and reprinted in *Adirondack Stories*, 1976 (A10) and *The Pushcart Prize, II*, 1977 (B8). [The entire run of *Contact* was reprinted by the Kraus Reprint Corporation in 1967.]

C14 ONCE IN A SEDAN AND TWICE STANDING UP. *Contact* 1, 3 (October 1932) 37-45. Story, which was incorporated into *The People from Heaven*, 1943 (A4) and reprinted in *Adirondack Stories*, 1976 (A10). [This story was originally slated for the first issue of *Contact*, but editor William Carlos Williams was concerned that its suggestive title would provoke censorship of the new magazine. That Nathanael West did not fight to keep this story in issue number one widened the rift between J. S. and West.]

C15 THE DIME: A CRUEL STORY. *Contempo*, 3, 1 (October 25, 1932) 1, 5. An episode from *The Water Wheel*, 1933 (A1).

1934

C16 HOLLOWAY. *A Year Magazine*, 1, 2 (December 1933-April 1934) 186-193. Prose from J. S.'s abortive novel, variously titled *A Lingering Illness* and *David Holloway* (E6e).

1937

C17 SHAPIRO, JULIAN LAWRENCE. *Lafayette College Alumni Directory* 84, 197. Listing as a member of the class of 1925, address unknown.

1940

C18 TRANSCONTINENTAL. *Black & White* (June 1940) 26-31. Poem, reprinting the historical episode from *Seventy Times Seven*, 1939 (A3). [The entire run of *Black & White* was reprinted by the Greenwood Reprint Corporation in 1968.]

C19 W. WHITMAN : H. MELVILLE. *The Clipper* (August 1940) 9-11. Poem. [J. S. was a member of this periodical's editorial board. Apparently, he was a tough critic: in issue one he was described on the masthead as their "smiling 'No' man." Also in issue one, a piece titled "The Manuscript Marketplace: A Practical Guide for Professional Writers" had this to say about *The Clipper*: "Critical & satirical stories, articles, poems. Literary material honestly felt and truly written. No pay, little glory. But where else can you get it into print?" The entire run of *The Clipper* was reprinted by the Greenwood Reprint Corporation in 1968.]

C20 COLDER TOMORROW AND SUNDAY. *The Clipper* (September 1940) 13-16. Poem about explorer Eric the Red.

C21 I'LL BRING YOU BACK CHICAGO. *The Clipper* (December 1940) 15-18. Poem, reprinted in *The People from Heaven*, 1943 (A4).

1941

C22 THE PEOPLE FROM HEAVEN. *The Clipper* (June 1941) 17-19. Poem reprinted in *The People from Heaven*, 1943 (A4) and *A More Goodly Country*, 1975 (A9).

C23 FIRST KNEE IN CANADA. *The Clipper* (September 1941) 17-18. Poem, reprinted as "The First Knee on Canada" in *The People from Heaven*, 1943 (A4), *A More Goodly Country*, 1975 (A9), *The Color of the Air*, 1985 (A18), and *Intruders in Paradise*, 1997 (A27).

1943

C24 THE LINCOLNS NEVER SHOOT. *Negro Digest* (December 1943) 17-20. Fiction, condensed from *The People from Heaven*, 1943 (A4).

1945

C25 MARSE BROWN. *New Masses*, 56, 5 (July 31, 1945) 7. Poem, reprinted as "Had I So Interfered in Behalf of the Rich" in *A Man Without Shoes*, 1951 (A5), and revised in *A More Goodly Country*, 1975 (A9).

1946

C26 MARSE LINKUM. *New Masses*, 58, 10 (March 5, 1946) 18. Poem, reprinted in *A Man Without Shoes*, 1951 (A5) and *A More Goodly Country*, 1975 (A9).

C27 NATHANAEL WEST. *The Screen Writer*, 2, 7 (December 1946) 10-13. Memorial, reprinted in *Hello, Hollywood!*, 1962 (B3), and *A Walk in the Fire*, 1989 (A22).

1948

C28 SANFORD, JOHN. *Biographical Record of the Men of Lafayette 1832-1948*, 369. Listing (also under Shapiro) with biographical information, including "pract law NYC 28-36; novelist 36—; screen writer Paramount and MGM Studios Calif 3 yrs." It lists novels up through *A Man without Shoes* (A5).

1964

C29 SANFORD JOHN. *Lafayette Alumni Directory*, 65, 464, 465. Listing (also under Shapiro) as a member of the class of 1925, "address unknown."

1974

C30 THE BARK WAS THREE FEET THICK. *Sierra Club Bulletin*, 59, 10 (November-December 1974) 9. Prose, reprinted in *A More Goodly Country*, 1975 (A9).

1976

C31 LETTER FROM THE GRAVE. *Congressional Record—House*, 122, 3 (February 5, 1976-February 18, 1976) 3159.

Prose from *A More Goodly Country* (A9), which Rep. Roncalio (Wyo.) read into the *Record* in honor of the nation's bicentennial. [Ironically, this unflattering portrait paints George Washington—as J. S. portrayed all the Founding Fathers—as an elitist, warning of the dangers of empowering the common man: "You are haunted by the Spectre of Democracy.... I say put this Brute the People down." It was not until years later that J. S. changed his view of Washington and became an admirer.]

1982

C32 MY BOOKS AND BACKGROUND. *The New York Times Book Review* (July 4, 1982) 5. A brief autobiographical sketch, accompanying "Rejection and Resurrection," a review of *A Man without Shoes* by Morris Dickstein, and a photo of J. S. by "Marguerite Sanford." [Interestingly, in this piece, J. S. seems to inflate his relationship with Nathanael West. After meeting on a New Jersey golf course, "[w]e picked up our old friendship, wrote together in hotels and in an Adirondack cabin, published together in the little magazines of the time and even came to Hollywood together in the mid-30's." This last statement is most curious, as J. S.'s and West's friendship was essentially over by 1933, when *Miss Lonelyhearts* and *The Water Wheel* were published, years before either writer separately journeyed to Hollywood.]

1985

C33 AN INTERVIEW WITH JOHN SANFORD. *Concept*, 26 (June 1985) 22-30. Photo of J. S. and interview by Julia Meredith and Alex Capri.

C34 IN MEXICO-TO DIE FOR ONE'S COUNTRY. *Concept*, 26 (June 1985) 30. Prose reprinted from *A More Goodly Country*, 1975 (A9).

C35 AN INTERVIEW WITH JOHN SANFORD: AN AMERICAN CLASSIC. *The Literary Review*, 28, 4 (Summer 1985) 544-554. Interview by Robert W. Smith. Also issued as a separate offprint (see A17). [This issue has a drawing of J. S. on the upper cover.]

C36 FROM *THE COLOR OF THE AIR*. *The Literary Review*, 28, 4 (Summer 1985) 555-563. Initial scenes of the autobiography, reprinted in *The Color of the Air*, 1985 (A18).

C37 THE UGLY SKY. *Santa Barbara News-Press* (August 9, 1985) A15. Historical piece, reprinted from *The Winters of that Country*, 1984 (A15).

1986

C38 INTERVIEW WITH JOHN SANFORD. *Home Planet News*, 6, 1 (Fall 1986) 5. Interview by Sesshu Foster.

C39 THE COLOR OF THE AIR: SCENES FROM THE LIFE OF AN AMERICAN JEW. *Jewish Spectator*, 51, 4 (Winter 1986) 53-58. Initial scenes of the autobiography, 1985 (A18).

1987

C40 GODS OF ANOTHER OLYMPUS. *Frank*, 8/9 (Winter 1987/88) 44-49. Photo and historical poem reprinted in *A Walk in the Fire*, 1989 (A22).

1988

C41 AN INTERVIEW WITH JOHN SANFORD. *Connexions*, 11 (1988) 28-30. Interview by Lillian Chodorow. [Also in this issue is a festschrift to J. S. by William Kunstler, Elaine Kendall, Chodorow,

Donald Pearce and John Martin, as well as reviews of *A Very Good Land to Fall With* (A21) by Kendall and Shelly Lowenkopf.]

C42 CA INTERVIEW. *Contemporary Authors*, 123 (1988) 345-349. Interview by Jean W. Ross.

1989

C43 MAGGIE. *Connexions*, 14 (1989) 28-35. Autobiography, adapted from *A Very Good Land to Fall With*, 1987 (A21).

1991

C44 SEASONED WITH SAGE AND TIME. *Santa Barbara News-Press*, Scene section (July 5, 1991) 7-8. Photo and interview by Susan Gulbransen. [There is also a photo of J. S. on the cover of the tabloid-format section.]

1992

C45 A LYRIC OF BEAUTY. *Los Angeles Times Book Review* (July 26, 1992) 11. Letter defending the poetry of Archibald MacLeish.

1993

C46 SACCO & VANZETTI. *Santa Barbara Review*, 1, 1 (Spring/Summer 1993) 27-30. Prose, reprinted in *Maggie: A Love Story*, 1993 (A24).

1994

C47 SCENES OF THE NATIONAL LIFE. *Santa Barbara Review*, 2, 1 (Spring/Summer 1994) 6-11. Prose, reprinted in *Intruders in Paradise*, 1997 (A27).

1995

C48 LEGACY OF FEMALE SCREENWRITERS. *Los Angeles Times* (March 12, 1995) F13. Letter defending women screenwriters.

1997

C49 REMEMBERING WEST. *Los Angeles Times Book Review* (August 3, 1997) 6. Review of *Nathanael West: Novels and Other Writings* (B17) in the form of a memoir. Reprinted in *Miss Lonelyhearts & Day of the Locust*, 2009 (B26).

C50 GOOD-BYE MY FANCY. *Los Angeles Times Book Review* (December 7, 1997) 2. Review of *Dreamland: America at the Dawn of the Twentieth Century*, a book of photos, by Michael Lesy.

1999

C51 THE LONG SHADOW. *Los Angeles Times Book Review* (June 13, 1999) 6. Review of *Full Moon*, a book of photos from the Apollo missions, by Michael Light.

2000

C52 A PALACE OF SILVER. *Tin House*, 1, 3 (Winter 2000) 73-80. Initial section of the memoir, reproducing J. S.'s typescript, reprinted in *A Palace of Silver*, 2003 (A29). [Also in this issue is a profile of J. S. by Neil Gordon.]

2001

C53 Letter. *Lafayette Alumni Quarterly* (May 2001) 25. Letter, reminding the college there are still people from the class of '25 around.

C54 THE FORTY-EIGHTH PASSENGER. *American Letters and Commentary*, 13 (2001) 17-23. Story. [A reworking of an unfinished novel (see E6e).]

2002

C55 WHERE THE HEART IS AT PEACE. *Los Angeles Times* (July 31, 2002) E3. Memoir, reprinted in *A Palace of Silver*, 2003 (A29). [This excerpt accompanies a profile of J. S. by Tim Rutten.]

C56 THE SACCO AND VANZETTI PAPERS. *American Letters and Commentary* 14 (2002) 125-152. Prose reprinting all J. S.'s separate writings about Sacco and Vanzetti, with the exception of the sections of *A Man Without Shoes*. This is the first occasion the individual pieces had been gathered; they are arranged chronologically. As in C52, J. S.'s manuscript pages are reproduced.

"Doomsday for a Deemster" reprints Judge Webster Thayer-Doomsday for a Deemster, "The District Attorney" reprints The Sacco and Vanzetti Case-The District Attorney, "Blues for Two Dead Italians" reprints Sacco and Vanzetti, II-Blues for Two Dead Italians, and "Blues for Two Greenhorns " reprints Sacco and Vanzetti, I-Blues for Two Greenhorns, all from *A More Goodly Country*, 1975 (A9). "Don't Cry, Dante," "Last Words for Scorning Men," and "After the Crucifixion" are reprinted from *View from this Wilderness*, 1977 (A11). "August, 1927" is reprinted from *To Feed Their Hopes*, 1980 (A12). "The Bridgewater Trial, 1920" reprints Bartolomeo Vanzetti and Rosina Sacco and Luigia Vanzetti from *The Winters of that Country*, 1984 (A15). "Twelve Good Men and True" reprints The Sacco-Vanzetti Jury and "Vindication" reprints Sacco and Vanzetti from *Maggie: A Love Story*, 1993 (A24). "On the Brockton Streetcar" reprints a Color of the Air from *We Have a Little Sister*, 1995 (A26). "They Still Walk, They Still Speak" is reprinted from *Intruders in Paradise*, 1997 (A27).

[Remarkably, even though he had completed law school, J. S. reported having never heard of the Sacco and Vanzetti case until the evening the pair was executed (see *The Color of the Air*, A18, pp. 191-192). Following his political awakening, J. S. became highly motivated to atone for his shameful ignorance by devoting more words to Sacco and Vanzetti than to any other historical figures.]

2003

C57 HIS WAY WITH WORDS. *Los Angeles Times* (March 8, 2003) E24. Memoir, printing "Sonia: 1929" and " Harriet 1: (1881-1914)" from *A Dinner of Herbs* (see E6k). "Sonia: 1929" reprints "The Pleasures of Sin for a Season" from *To Feed Their Hopes*, 1980 (A12). [This excerpt accompanies an appreciation of J. S. by Tim Rutten.]

2010

C58 A PERSONAL HISTORY OF AMERICA: TALES OF THE MANMADE SEASONS. *Legal Studies Forum*, 34, 1 (2010) 3-304. The entire issue of this legal-turned-literary journal is devoted to J.S.'s work. It reprints a total of 131 historical pieces, arranged chronologically: 56 from *A More Goodly Country* (A9), 13 from *View from this Wilderness* (A11), 25 from *To Feed Their Hopes* (A12), 33 from *The Winters of that Country* (A15), 1 from *A Walk in the Fire* (A22), and 3 from *Maggie: A Love Story* (A24). The volume also includes "Writing and Publishing *A More Goodly Country*" from *Maggie: A Love Story* (A24) and *A More Goodly Country: A New Introduction* (A13).

[This issue also includes an afterword, "John Sanford: Writer & Lawyer" by Jack Mearns.]

D. TRANSLATIONS

Spanish

D1. [I Let Him Die]. *Revista de Occidente.* [In letters to Angel Flores (1/18/33 & 1/28/33), J. S. mentioned an offer from Flores to have Guillermo de Torre translate "I Let Him Die" (C12) into Spanish. I can find no evidence that this translation was done or published. Apparently, Flores also hinted that *The Water Wheel* (A1) would be translated into Spanish, as well (letter from J. S. 4/30/33).

Swedish

D2. MILITARUTBILDNING. *Folket I Bild*, 11 (30 Maj-13 Juni, 1986), 20-21. Translation by Olav Jonason of a section from *A Man Without Shoes* (A5), accompanying a photo of J. S. and a review of *Man* by Per Petterson.

E. MISCELLANEA

E1. PAMPHLETS, BROADSIDES AND CARDS (not listed in sections A and B)

a. invitation to J. S.'s *bris*, 3 June 1904

Card. 8.8 x 11 cm. Printed in black script on stiff yellowish white paper: *New York, June 3rd, 1904 | You are cordially invited to attend | the Brith Milah of our son on Tuesday | June 7th, 10:30 A. M. | Mr. & Mrs. Philip D. Shapiro | 2 West 120th Street*; number of copies not known. A portion of this was reprinted in *The Color of the Air* (A18).

b. invitation to J. S.'s *Bar Mitzvah* [1917]

Card. 5.8 x 10 cm. Printed in black on stiff yellowish white paper: Mr. PHILIP D. SHAPIRO | REQUESTS YOUR PRESENCE AT THE BAR-MITZVAH SERVICES OF HIS SON | JULIAN | TO BE HELD AT | CONGREGATION MOUNT ZION | No. 39 WEST 199TH STREET, NEW YORK | ON SATURDAY, JUNE 2ND, 1917 | AT 9.30 A. M.; with matching envelope; number of copies not known. This was reprinted in *The Color of the Air* (A18).

c. The Dragon Press announces The Water Wheel a novel by Julian L. Shapiro To Be Published March 15, 1933 [self-printed, 1933].

Pamphlet. 21.8 x 13.8 cm. 4 pp. Printed in black on tan paper; folded at left.

Promotional pamphlet for J. S.'s first novel (A1), printed in a run of about 1,000 copies; describes the book and reprints critical praise from Samuel Putnam, William Carlos Williams and Manuel Komroff. J. S. had family and friends give him lists of friends and acquaintances, to whom he sent these pamphlets, and from whom he collected subscriptions for the book.

d.   The Water Wheel by Julian Shapiro [Duffield & Green, 1933].

Broadside. 39.9 x 30.6 cm. Printed in black on beige paper.

Promotion printed by *The Water Wheel's* (A1) distributor for display at bookstores; most likely only a few copies printed. It gives a brief description of the book, excerpts critical praise and has photos of the book and a dashing J. S. striding along the waterfront in Mentone, France.

e.   Peach-Tree Stables [self-printed, c. 1940]

Pamphlet. 15.8 x 10.5 cm. 4 pp. Printed in bluish red on bluish gray textured paper; folded at left.

Advertisement for stables Marguerite Roberts opened for her horse-trainer brother Dan Smith to operate. Text by J. S. About 500 copies printed and few distributed.

f.   Liberty Book Club News [Liberty Book Club, December 1947].

Pamphlet. 20.3 x 14 cm. 4 pp. Printed in black on yellowish white paper; folded at left.

Newsletter announcing second edition of *The People from Heaven* (A4b), with reviews by Eve Merriam and Charles Humbolt and a note from S. A. Russell, chairman of the editorial board; number of copies not obtainable.

g. A Man Without Shoes A Novel by John Sanford [Plantin Press, September 1950]

Pamphlet. 24.7 x 16.2 cm. ii, 16 pp. Printed in black and red on yellowish white paper; unopened signatures folded at top and left. Grayish blue un-printed wrappers, string tied at left.

Prospectus for *A Man Without Shoes* (A5), printed by Saul Marks for J. S. to sample the typeface. About 4 to 6 copies printed. J. S. did not like the round Bembo print, so Marks changed the typeface. The prospectus contains the first three sections of the novel, "Father's Name," "Mother's Name" and "Date of Birth," as well as three historical pieces, Buckeye Johnny Appleseed, Marse Linkum and Paul Bunyan and Friend. A portion of this pamphlet is reproduced in *A Walk in the Fire* (A22).

h. The Plantin Press Announces A MAN WITHOUT SHOES [self-printed, March 1951]

Pamphlet. 19.9 x 12.3 cm. 4 pp. Printed in black and red on yellowish white paper; folded at left.

Promotional pamphlet commissioned by J. S. to take subscriptions for the self-published *A Man Without Shoes* (A5); number of copies not known. It describes the book physically and discusses how the title relates to the protagonist's political awakening. It lists the Sanfords' White Oak address in Encino for the Plantin Press. A portion of this pamphlet is reproduced in *A Walk in the Fire* (A22).

i. This Is John Sanford [Prentice-Hall, 1967].

Pamphlet. 21.6 x 13.9 cm. 8 pp. Printed in black and gray on yellowish white paper; folded and stapled at left.

Promotional pamphlet for *The $300 Man* (A8); number of copies not known. Contains a profile of Sanford, decrying his inability to find an audience, as well as quotes of criticism of his earlier novels. Photo of J. S. on p.*1*.

j. Capra Press proudly announces publication of View from this Wilderness American Literature as History by John Sanford [Capra Press, 1977]

Card. 13.9 x 10.5 cm. Published 1977; number of copies not known. Printed in blue on stiff light yellow textured paper, bottom edge uncut.

Promotional card for *View from This Wilderness* (A11).

k. A Note Concerning John Sanford's Epic Trilogy Scenes from the Life of an American Jew [Black Sparrow Press, 1986].

Pamphlet. 19 x 11.2 cm. 4 pp. Published June 1986; 2,000 copies. Printed in black and light gray on yellowish white paper; folded at left.

Black Sparrow's John Martin writes a publisher's appreciation for J. S.'s autobiography, initially planned for three volumes. This was laid into hardcover copies of *The Waters of Darkness* (A20).

l. We are pleased to announce publication of John Sanford's latest book We Have a Little Sister Marguerite: The Midwest Years [Capra Press, 1995]

Card. 10.1 x 15.2 cm. Published 1995; number of copies not known. Printed in black on stiff light yellow textured paper. Promotional card for *We Have a Little Sister* (A26): "This portrayal of life and values gone by makes this a book of valuable Americana that otherwise would have been lost."

E2. RADIO

a. J. S. made a radio address during World War Two, which he later divulged was "full of Communist propaganda," for which he was "yelled at." Date unknown.

b. Four actors recorded the entire *A Man without Shoes* (A5), which was broadcast on KPFK radio, Los Angeles. Date unknown.

c. J. S. recorded *View from this Wilderness* (A11), for KPFK radio, Los Angeles. It was broadcast Thanksgiving Day 1978. J. S. recalled that he read "badly."

d. J. S. recorded a two-part interview with Michael Silverblatt for his *Bookworm* show on KCRW, Santa Monica, CA. Broadcast 20 & 27 September 1993.

e. J. S. was interviewed by National Public Radio's *Morning Edition* for a segment about restoring credits to blacklisted screenwriters. This program aired 2 October 1997.

E3. ORIGINAL FILMS

a. "Sapphire," a film taking place in New Orleans, co-written with Joseph Moncure March on assignment at Paramount Studios in 1936. At the time the script was completed, Cecil B. DeMille had just directed "The Buccaneer." "Sapphire" was never produced.

b. "The People Against Johnny Doe," a detective film, in mid-1937, while at Paramount. Never produced.

c. "Exclusive," co-written with Joseph Moncure March at Paramount. The film was released in August 1937; both J. S. and March received "book credits" for working on the script but no screen credit.

d. "The Shining Hour," written on assignment for Joseph Mankiewicz at M-G-M in December 1937. Never produced.

e. "Sit Down and Fight," an original screenplay about a sit-down strike at a factory. Never produced.

f. "Honky Tonk," co-written with wife, Marguerite Roberts, is J. S.'s only movie credit. Starring Clark Gable and Lana Turner and directed by Jack Conway, it was released by MGM in 1941. It is available on VHS tape and DVD from MGM/UA Home Video.

J. S. credited M. R. with writing 90% of the script for this film. Still, MGM was so impressed with the writing team's product that they offered J. S. a straight two-year contract, which would have represented J. S.'s first paying job since 1937. However, J. S. recalled M. R.'s saying to him, "If you stay here, you'll never write those books." She sent him home, where he completed *The People from Heaven* (A4), while she continued to write for the screen, supporting him with her earnings for the rest of his life.

g. "The Battle of Russia," an army training film in the *Why We Fight* series, was written for Frank Capra's company in the Army Signal Corps, 1942.

J. S. wrote the original version of this script in the Library of Congress in Washington, DC, where Capra's company was quartered. Capra promised J. S. an officer's commission, however that commission never materialized, likely due to J. S.'s Communist

Party membership. J. S. several times tried to volunteer for the war effort, but every time he was rejected. The film was rewritten by Anthony Veiller and released in 1943. Later, Capra's loyalty to America was questioned in part due to the favorable presentation of the Soviet Union in this film (see Joseph McBride, *Frank Capra: The Catastrophe of Success*, B14).

h. "Know Your Allies—Russia," an army training film, was written for Frank Capra's company in the Army Signal Corps, 1942. Never completed.

i. "The Land that Touches Mine," a 1960 screen adaptation of the novel by the same name (A6), was never produced.

j. "The Forty-ninth State," an original screen story, was never produced.

E4. FILM ADAPTATIONS

a. *The Old Man's Place* (A2) was made into a motion picture called *My Old Man's Place*. It was produced by Cinerama in 1972. Adapted for the screen by Stanford Whitmore and directed by Edwin Sherin, it stared Arthur Kennedy, Mitchell Ryan, William Devane and Michael Moriarty. Originally titled *Glory Boy*, the story was updated to the Vietnam era and transplanted to northern California. J. S. recalled that this film opened in a small theater in New York and closed four days later. The picture was released on video by Prism Entertainment in 1988 but is now out of print.

E5. MUSICAL ADAPTATIONS

a. "An American Cantata"

An American | *Cantata* | AN ADAPTATION OF JOHN SANFORD'S | TO FEED THEIR HOPES | *by Elaine Kendall* |

and | *Elaine Moe* | *With Original Music by* | *Dennis Poore* | *Lyrics by* | *Elaine Kendall* | [4-line disclaimer] | [publisher's lion device] | SAMUEL FRENCH, INC. | [2 lines of addresses] | *LONDON TORONTO* [1989]

20.9 x 12.9 cm. *i*, 61 pp., [3] pp. advts. Stiff yellowish white wrappers, printed in red and blue; wire stapled at left. Published 19 January 1989 at $6.50.

On verso of title leaf: Book Copyright ©, 1989, by John Sanford, Elaine Kendall, Elaine Moe | and Dennis Poore. | Lyrics Copyright © 1984, by Stepping Forward Music | [...] | ISBN 0 573 68793 7.

Note: Originally titled "Quiet Long Enough," this adaptation of *To Feed Their Hopes* (A12) premiered at the Quaigh Theatre in New York on 21 February 1986.

E 6. PROJECTS NOT PUBLISHED

a. "The White Cassock" (May 1931)
Story written during J. S.'s second trip to Europe and submitted to *The Criterion*. Rejected by T. S. Eliot.

b. "Six Miles of Dirt Road" (May 1933)
Story submitted to Richard Johns for *Pagany*; also planned for submission to the *Dragon Yearbook 1933* (see E6d). The only copy was destroyed when Johns's Connecticut home burned down in November 1933.

c. "An Extra Week without Pay" (Fall 1933)
Story accepted by *Pagany*, but the magazine folded before the story could come out in print. Later J. S. submitted this to *Lion & Crown*, a Columbia University student publication that also printed material by non-students. Eugene Joffe was

planning to issue a manuscript edition, in which all material would be written in long-hand on special paper and printed in holograph. This issue of *Lion & Crown* apparently never appeared.

d. *Dragon Yearbook 1933* (1933)
Announced in the dust jacket copy for *The Water Wheel*, this volume was to be a compendium of contemporary writings. An advertisement in *Pagany* said the book was scheduled for spring publication and would include contributions from, among others, Blackmur, Tate, Winters, Fadiman, Baker, Caldwell and Shapiro. J. S. took an active editing role, collecting pieces and forwarding them to Angel Flores at the Dragon Press. However, the Press failed about the same time *The Water Wheel* was issued, and the *Yearbook* never came out.

e. *The Lingering Illness/The Forty-eighth Passenger/David Holloway.*
Begun in December 1933 and abandoned in the summer of 1934, this novel was based on an acquaintance who had apparently committed suicide by jumping off a ship. A. & C. Boni had a contractual option to publish J. S.'s next three novels after *The Old Man's Place* (A2a). They orally rejected this book in December of 1935. J. S. revised the manuscript several times, but never to his satisfaction. A portion of this effort was published as "Holloway" in *A Year Magazine* (see C16). J. S. would return to this topic decades later (see C54).

f. [biography of Ernest Hemingway]
When J. S. contracted with Knight Publishing for *The Old Man's Place* (A2a) in 1935, he also agreed to write what would have been the first biography of Hemingway. The first substantial biographical study of Hemingway was Robert M. Coates's cover story for *Time Magazine* in 1937, although most accounts

cite Malcolm Cowley's 1949 *Life Magazine* piece.[1] In 1949, J. S. returned Knight's advance.

g. *The Big Train*
Planned as a sequel to *A Man Without Shoes*, it was abandoned in the mid-1950s, as J. S. found himself unable to write while his wife was on the blacklist. The title referred to the United States, with each state representing a car in the train.

h. *The Little Sister Spoken For*
Begun in 1996 and abandoned in 1998, J. S. conceived of this book as a third-person account of his marriage. The book ballooned to over 1,700 manuscript pages, before J. S. grew disenchanted with the book's lack of focus and terminated the project.

i. *A Citizen of No Mean Country*
Left unpublished at the time of J. S.'s death, this book tells his father's life story from his father's perspective. While the first half of the book is compelling, the later half—once the father moves out to California to be with his son—loses direction. The book concludes with an excerpt from J. S.'s eulogy read at his father's funeral.

j. *A Little Sister Spoken For*
This reworking of E6h is a sequel to *We Have a Little Sister* (A26), beginning with their meeting in the hallway of the writers building at Paramount Studies. It presents the first five years of the Sanfords' relationship, told from Maggie's perspective.

k. *A Dinner of Herbs*
In this memoir, J. S. returned to a fertile theme: women. Each vignette represents a girl or woman he had known.

---

1 Roza, Mathilde (2011). *Following Strangers: The Life and Literary Works of Robert M. Coates*. Columbia, SC: University of South Carolina Press.

APPENDIX A: INDEX OF HISTORICAL PIECES

Note: Much of J. S.'s writing contains historical elements that are integral to the narrative and can be considered part of the text. Other historical pieces, even in his novels, are typographically set off from the rest of the text. This appendix provides an index to the subjects of the historical pieces in J. S.'s novels, in his quintet of historical books, and as colors of the air in his autobiographical work. Appendix A includes pieces that are about historical characters, including fictional characters, and events. Pieces about family members and personal acquaintances appear in Appendix B.

Adams, Henry – *A9* 207-208, *A11* 116-117
Adams, Mrs. Henry – *A12* 51-52
Adams, Mrs. Virgil – *A12* 101
Adams, John Quincy – *A9* 113-114
Adams, Sam – *A11* 52-53
Agee, James – *A11* 180-181
Aguinaldo, Emilio – *A15* 209-213
Aiken, Conrad – *A11* 181-183
Alamo, The – *A9* 102-104
Albers, Clara – *A12* 40-41
Alger, Horatio, Jr. – *A11* 98
Alonso, Alicia – *A27* 102-105
Altgeld, John – *A9* 188-189
Amistad Case – *A15* 114-117, *A22* 60-63

Anderson, Sherwood – *A11* 139-140
Andrada, Mariana – *A12* 64-65
Appleseed, Johnny – *A5* 218-220, *A9* 111-112, *A22* 83-85
Armory Show, The – *A27* 95-97
Arnold, Mrs. Benedict – *A12* 21-22
Ashley, Lady Brett – *A12* 117-118
Astor, John Jacob – *A9* 115, *A18* 153-154
Astor, Nancy – *A12* 140
Atomic Bomb – *A9* 281, 281-282, *A15* 314-315, *A21* 289-290, 291
    Hiroshima – *A9* 279-280
    Nagasaki – *A15* 316-318, *A21* 293-296
Audubon, John James – *A9* 121-122

Bacon, Nathaniel – *A15* 44-45
Baker, Josephine – *A12* 185
Banford, Isabel – *A12* 41-42
Beach, Sylvia – *A12* 167-168
Beecher, Henry Ward – *A9* 159
Beerbohm, Florence Kahn – *A12* 145-146
Berkeley, Martin – *A24* 253-254
Berkman, Alexander – *A9* 239
Bernstein, Aline – *A12* 157-158
Berryman, John – *A11* 183-184
Bierce, Ambrose – *A11* 108-109
Billings, Warren K. – *A15* 249-252
Billy the Kid – *A27* 53-54
Bisbee Deportations, The – *A9* 231-232
Bison, The – *A15* 188-189, *A22* 131-133, *A23* 24
Blakelock, Ralph A. – *A9* 112-113, *A18* 135
Bloor, Ella Reeve – *A12* 150-151
Blues, The – *A27* 112-113
Blumfield, Minnie – *A12* 186-187
Booth, John Wilkes – *A9* 149-150, *A18* 211
Boston Massacre – *A15* 67-70

Boston Tea Party – *A15* 71-74

Bourne, Randolph – *A9* 235-236, *A11* 149

Braddock, Gen. – *A3a* 151-156, *A3b* 122-126, *A9* 73-74, *A15* 62-63, *A20* 75-76

Brady, Mathew – *A9* 145

Brann, William Cowper – *A11* 119

Brisbane, Arthur – *A11* 128

Broun, Heywood – *A11* 155

Brown, John – *A5* 225-226, *A9* 131-132, *A15* 141, *A27* 31-32

Bryan, William J. – *A9* 196-197, *A26* 142-143, *A27* 100

Bryant, Louise – *A12* 134-135

Buchenwald – *A21* 283

Bunyan, Paul – *A5* 251-256, *A9* 174-179, *A11* 71-76

Burial Practices, Indian – *A27* 4-5

Burr, Aaron – *A27* 23-25

California [in *Roan Stallion*] – *A12* 108-109

Capitalism – *A27* 183-184

Capone, Al – *A15* 294

Capote, Truman – *A24* 353-355

Capra, Frank – *A27* 69

Cardozo, Benjamin N. – *A11* 130-131

Caribbean, The – *A27* 202

Carrington, Margaret – *A12* 49-50

Castro, Fidel – *A23* 228-229, *A27* 119-121

Cather, Willa – *A9* 270-271, *A11* 140-141, *A12* 123-124, *A27* 84-88

Catlin, George – *A9* 158, *A20* 210

Cereno, Benito – (see Melville, Herman)

Chamber, Whittaker – (see Hiss, Priscilla & Alger)

Chaplin, Charlie – *A9* 281-282, *A21* 291, *A24* 53-54

Chapman, John – (see Appleseed, Johnny)

Chivington, Col. – *A3a* 156-161, *A3b* 126-130, *A9* 143-144, *A15* 151-154

Chopin, Kate – *A11* 118, *A12* 65-66

Christianity – *A27* 113
Civil War – *A4* 200-201, *A5* 265-266, 280-281, 283-285, *A9* 139-140, 140-141, 146-147, 147-149
    Draft – *A15* 143-145, 148-150
    Fort Sumter – *A9* 135-136
    Pickett's Charge – *A27* 44-47
Clappe, Louise (Dame Shirley) – *A12* 67-68
Clemens, Olivia Langdon – *A12* 66-67
Clemm, Maria – *A12* 31-32
Cobb, Ty – *A24* 49-50
Cohn, Roy – *A23* 81-82, *A27* 175
Colt, Samuel – *A9* 105
Columbus, Christopher – *A4* 45-56, *A9* 16-25, 25-27, *A11* 25-29
Comic Strips – *A9* 273-274, *A21* 209, *A27* 110
Comingore, Dorothy – *A12* 163-164
Computer, The – *A27* 136
Comstock, Anthony – *A9* 224-225
Coney Island – *A27* 28-29
Constitutional Convention – *A9* 83-84
Coolbrith, Ina – *A12* 115-116
Coolidge, Calvin – *A9* 253
Coronado, Francisco de – *A9* 30-31, *A18* 19
Corruption, Government – *A15* 93-94
Cotton, John – *A9* 53
Coughlin, Father Charles – *A15* 346
Coxey, Gen. Jacob – *A9* 191-192
Crane, Hart – *A9* 264, *A11* 167-168, *A21* 200-201
Crane, Stephen – *A9* 197, 201, *A11* 125, *A12* 72
Crane, Mrs. Stephen – (see Stephen Crane)
Crawford, Joan – *A12* 187-188
Crazy Horse – *A9* 161-162, *A18* 264
Crèvecoeur, J. H. St. John de – *A11* 63
Crockett, Davy – *A11* 68-71
Crockett, Emma – *A12* 37-38

Croly, Herbert – *A11* 129
Crosby, Caresse – *A12* 178-179
Cullen, Countee – *A11* 173-174
Cummings, E. E. – *A11* 160-161
Curley's Wife [in *Of Mice and Men*] – *A12* 129
Custer, George Armstrong – *A3a* 148-151, *A3b* 120-122, *A5* 260-262, *A9* 162-163, *A23* 156-158
Custer, Mrs. George Armstrong – *A12* 46-47

Dare, Virginia – *A5* 282-283, *A9* 32-33, *A12* 3-4, *A18* 32-33
Davies, Marion – *A12* 162-163
Day, Mary Anne – *A27* 31-32
Debs, Eugene – *A5* 220-221, *A6a* 185-186, *A6b* 207-208, *A9* 240-241, 255-256, *A15* 280-287, *A27* 121-124
Declaration of Independence – *A9* 80-81, *A18* 86
Deerfield, MA – *A9* 64-65, *A18* 66-67
Deming, Philander – *A11* 100
Depression, The – *A9* 260, 266, *A15* 303-306, *A26* 266-267, *A27* 27
    Dust Bowl – *A27* 4
De Soto, Hernando – *A9* 31-32 *A20* 35-36
Díaz, Porfirio – *A27* 80-83
Dickinson, Emily – *A9* 169, *A11* 95-96, *A12* 54-55, *A27* 27
Dixieland – *A9* 234-235, *A22* 234-235
Donner Party, The – *A9* 110, *A20* 147
Dorr Rebellion – *A15* 138-140
Dos Passos, John – *A11* 165-166
Downey, Ella – *A12* 100
Drake, Francis – *A15* 20-22
Dreiser, Theodore – *A11* 136-137
Drug Addiction – *A27* 111
Duncan, Isadora – *A9* 256-258, *A12* 111-112
Dyer, Mary – *A12* 9-10

Eakins, Mrs. Thomas – *A12* 128

Eaton, Margaret O'Neale – *A27* 40-44
Eddy, Mary Baker – *A9* 215-217, *A11* 114-116, *A12* 73-75
Edison, Thomas – *A27* 2
Edwards, Jonathan – *A11* 50-51
Ehrlich, Leonard – *A11* 177-178
Einstein, Albert – *A9* 206-207, *A20* 253-254, *A23* 251-252, *A25* 15
Electricity – *A27* 137-138
Eliot, John – *A11* 39-40
Eliot, T. S. – *A9* 174, *A11* 164-165
Ellis Island – (see Immigration)
Emerson, Ralph Waldo – *A11* 77-78
Emmett, Dan Decatur – *A15* 142
Ericson, Leif – *A9* 13, 14-16
Evangelists – *A27* 111-112, 207

Faulkner, William – *A11* 166-167
Feininger, Lionel – *A27* 69-70
Fink, Mike – *A15* 98-101
Fitzgerald, F. Scott – *A9* 272-273, *A11* 163-164
Fitzgerald, Zelda – *A12* 142-143, *A27* 131-134
Foote, Mary Hallock – *A12* 60-61
Ford, Henry – *A9* 244, 255, *A15* 299-300, *A27* 114-115
Ford, Mary Litogot – *A12* 110
Forrest, Gen. N. B. – *A9* 142, *A15* 155-161
Forrester, Marian – *A12* 122-123
Frank, Leo – *A9* 222-224, *A15* 232-239, *A18* 109-110, *A25* 125-126
Franklin, Benjamin – *A9* 88-89
Frémont, Jessie Benton – *A27* 32-36
Frick, H. C. – *A9* 239
Frome, Zenobia – *A12* 82-84
Frost, Robert – *A11* 137-138
Fuller, Alvan T. (see Sacco-Vanzetti case)
Fuller, Margaret – *A9* 106-107, *A12* 36-37

Gardner, Mrs. Jack – *A12* 107-108
Garland, Hamlin – *A11* 124
George, Henry – *A11* 112
Gibbs, Josiah Willard – *A9* 204
Girard, Stephen – *A15* 106-107
God – *A4* 149-157, *A9* 67-71
Goldman, Emma – *A9* 271-272, *A12* 144-145, *A22* 297-298
Gould, Jay – *A9* 183
Graham, Billy – *A24* 317-318
Grant, U. S. – *A9* 167-168, *A15* 195-196
Gravestones – *A27* 1, 29
Green, Hetty – *A9* 226-227, *A12* 94-95
Greenglass, David (see Rosenberg Case)

Hale, Emily – *A12* 161, *A24* 193-194
Hale, Nathan – *A15* 75-77, *A22* 32-33
Hamilton, Alexander – *A9* 84-87
Hanna, Marcus Alonzo – *A27* 61-63
Harding, Warren – *A9* 250-251, *A15* 273
Harper's Ferry – *A9* 130, *A18* 174-175
Harriot, Thomas – *A11* 31-32
Harris, Joel Chandler – *A11* 93-94
Hatteras, Cape – *A27* 203
Hawkins, John – *A15* 26-28
Hawthorne, Nathaniel – *A9* 62-63, *A11* 46-48, *A12* 17-19, *A20* 57-58
Hay, John – *A11* 101-107
Haymarket Riots – *A6a* 125-126, *A6b* 139-140, *A9* 169-170, 170-173, *A15* 197-202, *A18* 284
Hearn, Lafcadio – *A11* 113-114
Helms, Jesse – *A27* 179-180
Helper, Hinton Rowan – *A11* 94-95
Hemings, Sally – *A12* 23-24

Hemingway, Ernest – *A9* 200-201, *A11* 170, *A12* 192-193, *A23* 90-91, 181-182
Hemingway, Grace – *A12* 151-152
Hemingway, Hadley Richardson – *A12* 119
Henry, John – *A5* 251-256, *A9* 174-179, *A11* 71-76
Henry, Polly Ann – *A12* 39-40
Henson, Matthew – *A25* 39-41, *A27* 89-95
Hill, Joe – *A9* 219-220, *A22* 219-220
Hiroshima – (see Atomic Bomb)
Hiss, Priscilla & Alger – *A22* 147-149
Homeless – *A27* 109-110
Homer, Winslow – *A9* 214, 215, *A11* 113, *A27* 75
Hoover, J. Edgar – *A15* 341-342, *A27* 175-176
House UnAmerican Activities Committee – *A15* 326-327, *A22* 321-323, *A27* 176-177
Houston, Talahina – *A12* 33-34
Howe, Fanny Quincy – *A12* 105-106
Howells, William Dean – *A11* 99-100
Hudson, Henry – *A9* 36-37, *A15* 31
Hudson River – *A27* 27-28, 208-209
Hurston, Zora Neale – *A12* 158-159
Hutchinson, Anne – *A9* 48-50, *A12* 7-9

Immigration
    Chinese – *A9* 153-155
    Ellis Island – *A9* 187-188, *A23* 192-193
    Jewish *A9* 184-186
Imperialism, American – *A15* 208
Impressment – *A15* 64-66
Indentured Service – *A15* 34-35
Indian Wars – *A15* 36-41, 111-113, 118-124
Indians, American Persecution of – *A3a* 148-166, *A3b* 120-134, *A4* 110, *A6a* 15, 33, *A6b* 15, 35
Influenza – *A26* 77-78

Information Age – *A27* 206
Ingersol, Robert – *A27* 59
Irving, Washington – *A9* 87, *A11* 76-77, *A20* 101-102
I. W. W. John – *A24* 7-10

Jackson, Andrew – *A9* 107-110
Jackson, Helen Hunt – *A11* 98
Jackson, Rachel – *A27* 38-39
James, Henry – *A9* 226, *A11* 97, 109-110
Jamestown – *A4* 66-72, *A9* 33-36
Japanese-American Relocation – *A15* 312-313, *A21* 222-223
Jazz – *A9* 206
Jeffers, Robinson – *A11* 151-152
Jefferson, Thomas – *A9* 95-98, *A11* 58-59
Jennie Gerhardt – *A12* 77-78
Jesuits – *A4* 112-118, *A9* 44-48, *A18* 48-49, *A27* 9-13
Jewett, Sarah Orne – *A9* 214, *A11* 113, *A12* 69-70, *A27* 64-66
Johnson, Sarah – *A12* 15-16
Johnstown Flood, The – *A27* 72-75
Juarez, Benito – *A27* 48-51

Kahlo, Frida – *A27* 100-102
Kazan, Elia – *A23* 143-144
Keller, Helen – *A12* 175-176
Kennedy, John F. – *A27* 180-182
King, Martin Luther – *A15* 329-334
King Ranch, The – *A9* 166-167, *A20* 224-225
Kristallnacht – *A21* 133-134
Ku Klux Klan – *A15* 182-187
Kurowsky, Agnes von – *A12* 192-193

Labor
    Centrailia Outrage – *A15* 260-264
    Child – *A15* 190, *A27* 3

Ford – *A15* 296-298
Los Angeles Times, Bombing of the – *A15* 219-222
Ludlow Massacre, The – *A15* 247-248, *A21* 46-47
Strikes – *A9* 181-182, *A15* 92, 214-215, 292-293, *A22* 165-166, 264-265
West Virginia Coal Field Wars – *A15* 225-227
Wheatland, CA, Riot – *A15* 228-231

Lamar, Ruby – *A12* 126
Lanier, Sidney – *A11* 107
Lardner, Ring – *A11* 148
Lazarus, Emma – *A11* 110-111, *A12* 55
Lay, Benjamin – *A9* 74-76
Lear, Tobias – *A27* 16-19
Lee, Robert E. – *A9* 136, 157
Lehr, Elizabeth Drexel – *A12* 139
Leisler, Jacob – *A15* 50-51
Le Jenue, Père Paul – *A11* 41-44
Lenin, V. I. – *A9* 233, *A15* 274-276
Leonids – *A27* 1-2
Lewis, Meriwether – *A11* 64-66
Lewis, Sinclair – *A9* 249-250, *A11* 145-146
Lincoln, Abraham – *A5* 221-223, *A9* 92-93, 133-134, 134, 138-139, 145-146, 151, 151-153, *A11* 89, *A15* 180-181, *A18* 194, *A20* 189-190, *A22* 116-117
  Gettysburg Address – *A9* 141-142
  Lincoln-Douglas Debates – *A9* 127-130
Lincoln, Mary – *A9* 150-151, *A12* 44-45
Lincoln, Robert Todd – *A27* 83-84
Lincoln, Nancy Hanks – *A12* 27-28
Lindbergh, Charles – *A9* 259-260, *A15* 328
Little Bighorn – (see Custer, George)
Little Rock, AR – *A23* 165-166
Livingston, Robert – *A15* 55-57
Lloyd, Henry Demarest – *A11* 111-112

Lobbyists – *A9* 156
London, Jack – *A11* 134-135
Long, Huey – *A9* 267, *A27* 129-130
Longfellow, Henry Wadsworth – *A11* 78
Longworth, Alice Roosevelt – *A12* 195-196
Longworth, Nicholas – *A15* 146-147
Louverture, Toussaint – *A27* 14-16
Lovejoy, Elijah P. – *A9* 105-106, *A18* 118
Lowry, Malcolm – *A11* 181-183
Luhan, Mabel Dodge – *A12* 155-156
Lusitania – *A27* 107
Lynching – *A15* 240-243, 277-279
Lyndon, Phillis – *A12* 15

MacArthur, Douglas – *A15* 307-311
MacLeish, Archibald – *A11* 159-160
Madison, James – *A11* 55-56, *A27* 19-23
Maddow, Ben – *A27* 198-201
Maggie – *A12* 61
Maguire, Molly – *A12* 35
Mahan, Alfred Thayer – *A11* 122-123
Maine, State of – *A9* 214, *A11* 113
Maine, U. S. S. – *A9* 198, 218-219, *A27* 59-61
Manhattan Island – *A27* 205
Marin, John – *A9* 213-214
Marshall, James – (see Sutter's Mill)
Marshall, John – *A11* 60-62
Martí, José – *A27* 55-58, 208
Mary, Virgin – *A12* 13-14
Mason, Capt. John – *A11* 40-41
Mather, Cotton – *A9* 65-66
Mather, Increase – *A11* 44-46
McCarthy, Joseph Raymond – *A15* 324-325, *A22* 133-134, 150-151 *A23* 89-90

McCourt, Elizabeth – *A12* 130-131
McCullers, Carson – *A12* 172-173
McKinley, Ida Saxton – *A12* 68-69
McKinley, William – *A9* 196-197, *A15* 208
McPherson, Aimee Semple – *A12* 141
Meir, Golda – *A12* 197
Mellon, Andrew – *A27* 157-158
Melville, Herman – *A9* 91-92, *A11* 83-84, *A15* 203-204, *A22* 145-146
Merriwell, Frank – *A27* 70-71
Mexico – *A26* 47-48
    Mexican-American War – *A15* 125-127, *A22* 101-103
    Mexican Revolution – *A23* 132-134, *A25* 63
Mickey Mouse – *A27* 124-125
Mi Lai Massacre (see Vietnam War)
Millay, Edna St. V. – *A11* 156-157, *A12* 146-148
Mississippi River – *A5* 265, *A9* 27-28, *A27* 203
Mitchell, Maria – *A12* 56
Molly Maguires, The – *A9* 164
Monk, Maria – *A15* 128-137
Monroe, Harriet – *A12* 136
Monroe, James – *A9* 94-95
Monterey, Carlotta – *A12* 176-177
Mooney, Tom – *A9* 228-229
Moore, Marianne – *A11* 152-153, *A12* 180-181
Morgan, J. Pierpont – *A9* 138
Morrow, Elisabeth – *A12* 170-171
Morton, Thomas – *A11* 37-38
Mount Rushmore – *A9* 274-275
Mulholland, William – *A15* 288-290
Munson, Audrey – *A12* 93
Mussolini, Benito – *A26* 100-101
Myers, Gustavus – *A11* 130

Nagasaki – (see Atomic Bomb)
Narváez, Pamphilo de – *A15* 15-16
Naval Warfare – *A15* 95-97
Nixon, Richard M. – *A15* 347-348, *A22* 144-145, *A24* 249-250
Nixon, Thelma (Patricia) – *A27* 187-189
Nolan, Philip – *A1* 170-177
Norris, Frank – *A11* 131-133
Norse Exploration – *A15* 13-14
North America – *A9* 13, *A20* 17
North, Oliver – *A24* 359-361

O'Connor, Flannery – *A12* 169-170
O'Hara, John – *A11* 178-179
O. Henry – *A11* 127
O'Keeffe, Georgia – *A12* 189-190, 190-191
O'Neill, Eugene – *A9* 241-242, *A11* 157
Oppenheimer, J. Robert – *A24* 197-199, *A27* 164-167
Ortiz, Juan – *A15* 17-19
Oswald, Lee Harvey – *A27* 176
Otis, James – *A11* 54-55

Paine, Thomas – *A9* 93-94, *A11* 56-58
Palmer Raids – *A9* 238
Panama Canal – *A9* 205
Parker, Dorothy – *A12* 171-172
Parkman, Francis – *A11* 79
Parrington, Vernon L. – *A11* 133-134
Passenger Pigeon – *A12* 85-86, *A15* 244-246, *A21* 63-66
Patton, George, Jr. – *A24* 321-323
Pearl Harbor – *A9* 275, *A21* 204-205
Peron, Juan & Evita – *A27* 160-163
Personal Ads – *A27* 136-137
Photographs, Women in – *A12* 40, 91, 127-128, *A27* 2

Pinzer, Maimie – *A12* 102-104
Phagan, Mary – (see Frank, Leo)
Plath, Sylvia – *A12* 168-169
Plymouth Plantation – *A9* 42-43, 43-44, *A15* 32-33
Poe, Edgar Allan – *A9* 120-121, *A11* 80-81, *A20* 167-168
Poe, Mrs. Edgar Allan – *A12* 30-31
Pokahontas – *A4* 66-72, *A9* 33-36, 37-39, *A12* 4-7
Ponce de Leon, Juan – *A9* 28-30
Popular Music – *A27* 206-207
Porter, Katherine Anne – *A11* 158-159, *A12* 188-189, *A23* 238-240
Pound, Ezra – *A9* 282-283, *A11* 146-148, *A23* 118-120
Prescott, William Hickling – *A11* 30
Prynne, Pearl – (see Nathaniel Hawthorne)
Pullman Strike – *A9* 192-193, 193-194, 194-195, *A15* 205-207
Putnam, Ann – *A12* 16-17

Quakers – *A9* 53-54

Race Riots
    Brownsville, TX – *A15* 216-218, *A25* 21-22
    Chicago, IL – *A15* 257-259
    Tulsa, OK – *A15* 265-266
Racism – *A6a* 51, *A6b* 53-54, *A9* 104, 242-243, 248-249, *A18* 103
Radio – *A9* 210, *A26* 14
Railroads – *A9* 156-157, *A15* 191-194, *A18* 242
Rand, Ayn – *A12* 172
Reagan, Ronald – *A27* 186
Reed, John – *A9* 221-222, *A11* 150-151, *A20* 270-271, *A27* 97-98
Remington, Frederic – *A9* 212-213
Republicans – *A27* 69
Revolutionary War – *A9* 79-80, *A15* 78-83, 84-88
Roberts, Susan & Betsy – *A12* 24-25
Robeson, Paul – *A15* 343-345, *A27* 171-173
Rockefeller, John D. – *A9* 132-133

Roosevelt, Eleanor – *A9* 278-279, *A12* 193-194
Roosevelt, F. D. – *A9* 276-277, 277, 278, *A21* 281-282
Roosevelt, Sara Delano – *A12* 196
Roosevelt, Theodore – *A6a* 155-156, *A6b* 173-174, *A9* 198-200, 202-203, 205, *A11* 121-122, *A22* 201-203, *A26* 37, *A27* 105-106
Rosenberg Case – *A12* 154, *A15* 319-323, *A23* 59-61, *A27* 158-160
Rowson, Susanna – *A11* 67
Russell, Mrs. Ada – *A12* 152-153
Russian Revolution – *A25* 147
Rutledge, Ann – *A12* 30
Ryder, Albert Pinkham – *A9* 230-231

Sacajawea – *A12* 28-30
Sacco-Vanzetti Case – *A9* 247-248, 258, 259, 265-266, *A11* 153, 154, *A15* 269-272, 291, *A21* 151-152, *A24* 1-4, 403-404, *A25* 161, *A26* 79-80, *A27* 67-68, 139-140, 140-141
Sacco, Mrs. Nicola (Rosina) – *A12* 113-114
Sage, Russell – *A9* 179-180
Salem Witch Trials – *A4* 124-130, *A9* 55-60, 60-61, *A12* 16-17
Sandburg, Carl – *A11* 142-143
Sandino, Agusto Cesar – *A23* 45-47, *A27* 117-119
San Francisco Earthquake – *A26* 8
Saratoga – *A27* 3-4
Scarlet Letter, The – (see Hawthorne, Nathaniel)
Scott, Dred – *A5* 223-224, *A9* 126-127
Scottsboro Case – *A15* 301-302, *A21* 171-172
Sequoia Gigantea – *A9* 160-161, *A27* 5, 52-53
Simpson, Wallis Warfield – *A12* 143
Sinclair, Upton – *A11* 141
Slaton, Gov. John M. (see Frank, Leo)
Slavery – *A4* 81-85, 169-176, 200-201, *A6a* 89-90, *A6b* 97-98, *A9* 40-42, 77-79, 98-101, 123-124, 130, *A15* 23-25, 29-30, 42-43, 46-49, 52-54, 58-61, *A27* 69
Smedley, Agnes – *A12* 156

Smith, Bessie – *A12* 135
Smith, Capt. John – *A4* 66-72, *A9* 33-36
Smith, Lydia Hamilton – *A12* 48
Spanish American War – *A6a* 155-156, *A6b* 173-174, *A9* 198-200, *A22* 201-203
Spanish Civil War – *A9* 269-270, *A24* 93-95
Spanish Conquistadors – *A3a* 161-166, *A3b* 130-134
Sports – *A27* 206
Statue of Liberty – *A9* 276, *A12* 53-54
St. Clare, Evangeline – *A12* 38-39
St. Louis, SS – *A27* 142-146
Steffens, Lincoln – *A11* 150
Stein, Gertrude – *A11* 138-139, *A12* 173-174
Steinbeck, John – *A11* 174-176
Steunenberg, Frank – *A9* 211-212
Stevens, Thaddeus – *A9* 155, *A12* 48
Stevens, Wallace – *A11* 143
Stewart, Mrs. Cornelia Clinch – *A12* 52-53
Stieglitz, Alfred – *A27* 29-30
Stock Exchange, The – (see Wall Street)
Stowe, Harriet Beecher – *A9* 122-123, *A11* 86-87, *A12* 43
Streetcar, Horsedrawn – *A27* 2
Sullivan, Louis – *A9* 254, *A22* 248, *A27* 70
Sulzer, Gov. William – *A25* 89
Sumner, Charles – *A9* 125
Sunday, Billy – *A9* 267-269
Surratt, Mrs. Mary – *A12* 45-46
Sutter's Mill – *A5* 247-251, *A9* 116-119, *A27* 68

Taney, Roger – *A11* 87-88
Taylor, Edward – *A11* 48
Teapot Dome – *A15* 273
Tekakwitha, Katharine – *A12* 11-13
Telegraph – *A27* 4

Teller, Edward – *A27* 168-171
Temple, Charlotte – *A12* 25-26
Thaw, Harry K. – *A9* 209-210
Thayer, Judge Webster (see Sacco-Vanzetti Case)
Thomas, Clarence – *A27* 192-197
Thompson, Dorothy – *A12* 162
Thoreau, Henry – *A9* 137, *A11* 90
Thorpe, Jim – *A15* 223-224, *A21* 86-87
Tilton, Mrs. Theodore (Elizabeth) – *A12* 62-63
Timrod, Henry – *A11* 91
Toklas, Alice B. – *A12* 174-175
Toomer, Jean – *A11* 161-162
Tourgée, Albion Winegar – *A11* 91-93
Triangle Factory Fire – *A9* 217-218, *A12* 78-79, 79-80, *A21* 30-31, *A25* 71
Trilling, Lionel – *A11* 176-177
Truman, H. S. – *A9* 281
Turner, Frederick Jackson – *A11* 125-126
Turner, Nat – *A15* 108-110
Twain, Mark – *A9* 189-191, *A11* 84-86, *A22* 186-187
Tweed, Boss – *A9* 164-166

Unknown Soldier, The – *A9* 245-246
Unknown Woman, United States – *A12* 98-99

Valverde, Fray Vincente de – *A27* 6-9
van Winkle, Rip – (see Irving, Washington)
Vanderbilts, The – *A9* 168-169
Vanzetti, Bartolomeo – (see Sacco-Vanzetti Case)
Vietnam War – *A15* 349, *A27* 177-178
  Mi Lai Massacre – *A15* 335-340
Villa, Francisco (Pancho) – *A9* 251-252, *A21* 125-127, *A27* 98-99
Volstead Act – *A25* 167

Wall Street – *A9* 244-245, *A15* 295, *A27* 125-126, 127-128
Ward, Nancy – *A12* 26-27
Ward, Nathaniel – *A11* 32-33
Warhol, Andy – *A27* 189-191
Washington, Booker T. – *A11* 119-120
Washington, George – *A5* 257-260, *A9* 71-73, 76-77, 81-82, 90-91, 261-263, *A15* 89-91, *A20* 128-129, *A22* 44-46
Washington, Martha – *A12* 20-21
Watergate Break-in, The – *A27* 184-185
Welty, Eudora – *A12* 177-178
West, Nathanael – *A11* 171-173, *A27* 146-156
West Point – *A27* 28
Wharton, Edith – *A12* 137
Wheatley, Phillis – *A11* 82-83
Whistler, J. A. McN. – *A27* 63
Whitman, Walt – *A9* 184, *A11* 108, *A27* 37-38
Whitney, Eli – *A15* 102-105
Whitwell, Mrs. Prudence – *A12* 14
Wiggins, Ella May – *A15* 292-293, *A22* 264-265
Williams, Abigail – *A12* 16-17
Williams, Eunice – *A12* 19-20
Williams, Roger – *A11* 49-50
Williams, Tennessee – *A23* 102
Williams, William Carlos – *A11* 144-145
Wilson, Edmund – *A11* 162-163
Wilson, Edith Bolling – *A12* 160
Wilson, Woodrow – *A9* 221, 229-230, 236-237, *A11* 120-121
Winthrop, John – *A9* 50-52, *A11* 34-36
Wister, Owen – *A11* 123
Wolfe, Thomas – *A11* 169, *A24* 99-101
Woolman, John – *A11* 81-82
Woolson, Constance Fenimore – *A11* 97
Woolworth, Frank Winfield – *A15* 267-268

World War I – *A15* 253-254, 255-256, *A21* 105-106, *A25* 153, *A26*
    65, 82-83
    Bonus Army, The – *A15* 307-311
    Sarajevo – *A25* 109
    Verdun – *A25* 131
Wright Brothers – *A9* 203-204
Wright, Frank Lloyd – *A9* 160
Wright, Richard – *A11* 179-180

Young, Lucy – *A12* 165-167

Zapata, Emiliano – *A27* 76-80
Zenger, John Peter – *A11* 51-52

APPENDIX B: INDEX OF PIECES ABOUT FAMILY MEMBERS AND ACQUAINTANCES

Note: Appendix A indexes pieces about historical individuals, characters and events. Appendix B indexes pieces about family members and personal acquaintances from J. S.'s quintet of historical books. Scenes about family members and friends from the autobiography, where these scenes are integral to the text, are not indexed.

Ackerman, Rosie (aunt's cook) – *A12* 148-149
B., O. [Brounoff, Olga] – *A12* 120-121
Blauvelt, Miss (teacher) – *A12* 86-87
Dress Form – *A12* 80-81
G., L. [Gifford, Louise] – *A12* 114-115
G., P. [Greenwald, Phyllis] (elementary schoolgirl) – *A12* 76-77
Gruenberg, Sarah (aunt) – *A12* 57-59
L., H. [Levine, Hazel] – *A12* 133
L., I. [Lennart, Isabel] – *A12* 179-180
L., S. [Lubart, Sonya "Sonny"] – *A12* 121-122
Lang, Ellen (grandmother's servant) – *A12* 132
Neighbor of J. S. – *A12* 70-72
Nevins, Mrs. Abraham [Leah] (grandmother) – *A12* 88-89
P., R. [Phillips, Romaine] – *A12* 124-125

Roberts, Marguerite (wife) – *A12* 75, 198
Rosenthal, Josephine [Aunt Jo] (father's second wife) – *A12* 181-183
S., D. U. [Smith, Dorothy Ursula] – *A12* 106-107
Sanford, Marguerite – (see Roberts, Marguerite)
Shapiro, Harriet [Chai Esther] (mother) – *A9* 284-285, *A12* 87-88
Shapiro, Ruth (sister) – *A12* 95-97
T., L. [Tobias, Lenore] – *A12* 127
Unknown Girl, Carmel Highlands – *A12* 138-139
Unknown Girl, Harlem – *A12* 92
Unknown Woman, Harlem – *A12* 81-82
Unknown Woman, Long Branch – *A12* 97-98
Unknown Woman, Santa Barbara – *A12* 184
Unknown Woman, Washington Heights – *A12* 89-90

APPENDIX C: "THE MASTER'S" CIRCLE: 1926-1933

John Sanford's early childhood was marked by cycles of abundance and deprivation. At the time of Sanford's birth in 1904, his father, Philip Shapiro, was a successful attorney. Sanford was born in *The Gainsboro*, a beautiful new apartment building at the foot of Mt. Morris Park, in the newly-developed fashionable Jewish neighborhood of Harlem. But the Wall Street Panic of 1907 wiped Philip out. The Shapiro family abandoned *The Gainsboro* for *The Cabonak*, whose name Sanford always associated with the embarrassment of the decline in his family's fortunes. In 1912, Sanford's mother, Harriet's, heart began to fail. Soon, all money went for doctors' visits and trips to mountain resorts for rest. There were long separations from her family, as the Shapiros descended through a succession of rooming houses and cheap hotels.

When Harriet died in 1914, the destitute Shapiros were forced to move into the apartment of her parents, where Philip and his two children shared a single room. That home was dominated by Sanford's boorish grandfather and his shrewish Aunt Rae. By 1920, Philip's practice had revived. He remarried and moved to a new apartment taking Sanford's sister with him. However, Aunt Rae had poisoned Sanford against his stepmother, and—despite Philip's entreaties—Sanford refused to join their household.

Sanford's youth was characterized by loneliness, alienation, and guilt, both over his mother's death and his rejection of his father. Even while his mother was alive, Sanford had experienced a rootless wandering. But, after her death, though he had a steady place to live, he was homeless. Sanford's mother had promoted his education early, taking him to the library and buying him books. In fact, until the end of his life, Sanford treasured the first book she gave him, *Patriotic America: A Young Folks' History of the United States*, which teemed with the characters that would captivate Sanford's writing throughout his career. Harriet's death scarred Sanford deeply, for he was now different from the other children, who had mothers. Although he had skipped grades early on because of his academic prowess, after his mother's death, whatever motivation he had had in school evaporated.

Although Sanford had stated in his senior yearbook a plan to attend the University of Pennsylvania, he did not graduate high school, because he failed English his final semester. Lafayette College in Pennsylvania was one of the few schools that would admit Sanford without a diploma. Though he spent but a year at Lafayette, Sanford would feel an abiding connection to the school, even attending the Class of '25's 25th reunion in 1950. At Lafayette, he also formed an enduring friendship with Herbert Ortman, who would one day become Sanford's law partner when they joined Philip Shapiro's practice. Ortman's early support of Sanford's writing was crucial to the budding author. After reading some of Sanford's earliest attempts in 1928, Ortman told Sanford he'd "be crazy" to give up writing. Ortman was also key in that in 1926 he helped Sanford reestablish contact with one of Sanford's childhood acquaintances, the "Master" of the Master's Circle. And it was Ortman who perpetuated the nickname Sanford had received at Lafayette—Scotty.

The Master was George Brounoff, with whom Sanford had gone to kindergarten in Harlem. Brounoff's father, Platon, was a pianist and composer, who was rumored to be the illegitimate son of Anton Rubenstein. In the 1910s, Platon wrote the opera *Titanic* about the infamous ship's sinking. However, audiences were not yet ready for an opera about so recent a tragedy; its failure was something from which Platon never recovered. George Brounoff himself was an accomplished pianist, but he was not able to memorize music, which barred him from a performing career. He did, however, make a little money accompanying dance classes, which Sanford dramatized in "Terpsichore on the Nevsky Prospect" (see C6). Brounoff was something of a dandy, wearing a derby and Brooks Brothers clothing, even though he was supported financially by his sister, Olga, a chorus girl with the Zeigfeld Follies.

Brounoff was highly knowledgeable about art and music. He held court on these topics at salons in his apartment or klatches in Childs' Deli where the group gathered. Only after the Master had delivered his expatiation were the others permitted to converse. Once Sanford reconnected with Brounoff and joined his circle, it became clear how little Sanford knew of culture. His shame over this deficit impelled him into a crash course of reading and attending performances.

The other indelible influence on Sanford was Nathanael "Pep" West. Sanford and West—then known as Nathan Weinstein—had met as children in Harlem, when West lived in the *De Peyster*, the building Sanford frequented to visit his cousin, son of Aunt Rae. Sanford recalled the young West as aloof and bookish, above such childish pursuits as games of marbles in the dust. West and Ortman had attended summer camp together. But it was through a chance meeting on a New Jersey golf course in 1925 that West and Sanford rekindled their acquaintance.

This meeting on the golf course is a fitting metaphor for the intersection of these young men's lives. Here were two Jews playing a gentile game, a game usually played in groups, by themselves. Sanford, as we already know, was deeply alienated. Although he was by now pursuing in earnest a degree at Fordham

Law School, he was not passionate about his chosen career. And though he continued to have a warm relationship with his father, Sanford still refused to live with him. When the two met on the golf course, Sanford proudly told West that he was studying law. But West's answer dazzled Sanford: he was writing a book. That phrase, "writing a book," opened up an entirely new world.

At first blush, it might seem that West was the more accomplished of the two. But, West—who had already begun to call himself "West"—was alienated, as well, particularly from his Jewish heritage. Certainly, he had a command of literature far beyond his years. But his academic career was no less spotty than Sanford's. West dropped out of high school and was admitted to Tufts University under suspicious circumstances. A semester later, using a transcript from a different Nathan Weinstein, he transferred to Brown University, from which he received a bachelor's degree.[1]

That golf course meeting spawned a symbiotic relationship that filled deep needs for both young men. Sanford was eager for inspiration, eager to make up for the intellectually arid years since his mother's death. And West, too, must have been needy, in this case for an acolyte. West may have been writing a book; but, in 1925, he was far more poseur than auteur. The undiscerning Sanford would be the perfect receptive audience for this dilettante's discourses on literature and the arts. Sanford recalled frequent long walks together through New York City as West lectured him. Later, Sanford would read proof four times with West for West's first novel, *The Dream Life of Balso Snell*. So momentous was the encounter on the links in altering the course of his life that Sanford once told West he considered it his birthday, a confession whose unabashed sentiment drove West to

---

1 Martin, Jay (1971). *Nathanael West: The Art of His Life*. New York: Farrar, Straus & Giroux (B5).

exclaim, "Jesus Christ, Scotty!" and hurry off the bus they were riding in together.

Sanford brought West into Brounoff's circle. Other members included three Brounoff friends. Sammy "Little Sam" Ohrstein taught math at Morris High School in the Bronx. Later, he apparently committed suicide by jumping off a ship. Sanford would unsuccessfully try to develop Ohrstein's story into a novel (see E6e), finally returning to it in his last published short story (see C54). Alan "Pete" Lewis was always with Brounoff; they knew each other from their years at the College of the City of New York. Lewis was a Communist and one of the few people at Sanford's City Hall wedding in 1938. Sam "Big Sam" Levy had spent a couple of years in China. He was a lawyer who worked for *Zitz Weekly*. Sanford recalled that he was in over his head intellectually and was continually baited by West. Bess Hein was Levy's girlfriend, who was later stolen by Brounoff.

Olga Brounoff, George's sister, was a member. Sanford often met her at the stage door after her Ziegfeld performances and walked her back to Childs' where the circle gathered. Olga and Sanford had a mutual attraction, but they never became romantically involved. Olga pleaded with Sanford in 1927 not to sail for England, in his rash and ultimately fruitless attempt to study law at Oxford; she knew that if he went their relationship could never flower. By the end of 1928, Olga was dead of abdominal adhesions at the age of 23. The story of their near-relationship forms a portion of Sanford's first novel, *The Water Wheel* (A1), which was dedicated to Olga.

Sanford brought several people into Brounoff's circle. Ortman played bridge with the group for a while but then faded out. West, though, became a regular participant, inviting a friend from Brown, Ike Orleans; Orleans later taught at Yeshiva University. Sanford also introduced his cousin Mel Friedman to Brounoff. Friedman married a non-Jew and was mourned as dead by his parents. He worked for the Haddon Craftsmen and would later place with publishers and design Sanford's first two novels. Friedman brought in Ed Swann, whose girlfriend, a married woman, Brounoff also stole. Sanford's sister, Ruth, attended occasionally. She fell for Brounoff when he visited the Shapiro family at the Jersey Shore in 1929; but Ruth's feelings were unrequited. Lastly, Sanford introduced Jesse Greenstein, whom he had met on the Jersey Shore in 1927. Greenstein went on to become an astrophysicist and the chair of the Physics Department at Cal. Tech. Sanford lived in Greenstein's apartment while revising *The Old Man's Place* (A2) during the summer of 1935.

Sanford maintained lifelong, if sometimes tumultuous, friendships with Brounoff, Ortman, Lewis, Friedman and Greenstein. But Sanford's friendship with West had withered years before West was killed in a car accident in 1940. Yet, until the end of Sanford's days, his relationship with West bedeviled him. On the one hand, Sanford felt enduring gratitude to West for changing the course of his life; without West, Sanford never would have become a writer, moved to Hollywood, or married Marguerite Roberts. On the other hand, Sanford never got over the sting of slights he felt West had inflicted on him. Sanford vacillated between attitudes of thankfulness and bitter resentment.

While West humored Sanford's pretensions toward being an author, West did not introduce Sanford to his important connections. Sanford never met West's friend Edmund Wilson, and he only met William Carlos Williams when Williams asked West to introduce them. Although Sanford had brought West into Brounoff's circle, Sanford felt West did not reciprocate: West had an independent social world to which Sanford was not admitted. In fact, Sanford recalled late in life that West only summoned Sanford when West was otherwise unoccupied; Sanford intuited that he was not at liberty to initiate contacts with West. And, though Sanford read proof with West on *Balso Snell* four times, West never asked for Sanford's opinion of the work; Sanford concluded later that his opinion was of no consequence to West.

One gets a sense that West viewed Sanford as tolerable, but something of an embarrassment. Some of this attitude may have had to do with West's efforts to conceal his Jewishness. Did West believe that Sanford would speak in some way or make some crude gesture that would tip off others that they were Jews? Or was the dark West worried that, next to the fair-haired Sanford, his Semitic features would stand out?

Two incidents crystallized Sanford's resentment toward West. In the summer of 1931, Sanford and West rented a hunting cabin together in the Adirondacks where they could write. West was working on *Miss Lonelyhearts*, and Sanford was writing *The Water Wheel*. After weeks of hearing each other typing in adjoining rooms, West finally asked, for the first time, to read what Sanford was writing. Sanford proudly offered West the manuscript. But the next morning, when West handed it back, he made no comment on the writing. West merely said the Olga Brounoff character was identifiable, and that "simply isn't done." After all that time, to have his hopes of his mentor's approval dashed by such a dismissive comment. Sanford was crestfallen.

The second incident occurred in early 1932. West was co-editing the revived *Contact* magazine with Williams. Sanford's "Once in a Sedan and Twice Standing Up" was slated to appear in the much-anticipated inaugural issue. However, Williams became concerned that the issue's racy content would provoke censorship from postal authorities. He decided to hold Sanford's story, with its salacious title, until issue three (see C14). Williams had offered to keep the story in issue one, if Sanford would change the title. Even though Sanford had his heart set on appearing in issue one, because of the critical notice he thought the little magazine's debut would receive, he balked at the title change. And, even though it was Sanford's own self-described "mulish" refusal to alter his title that kept him out of issue one, Sanford still blamed West for not sticking up for him by urging Williams to delay another writer's piece instead.

The aged Sanford still expressed a mixture of ire and bafflement over these perceived slights by West. He himself could find no reason for what he viewed as his friend's at least passive betrayal. However, though Sanford always pooh-poohed the idea, it is not unimaginable that West felt threatened by Sanford's writing. Not until that summer of 1931 did *Balso Snell* appear, a book that did not exactly set the publishing world on fire. So, when West read the draft of *The Water Wheel*, he had little more in print than did his pupil. From reading *The Water Wheel*, it would be clear that Sanford was not merely a pretender: he had at least nascent talent. That revelation could not help but destabilize the dynamic of their friendship: the teacher was in danger of being equaled or exceeded by his follower.

There is some evidence that at least one contemporary individual saw jealousy as a motive behind a threatened West's behavior. A letter from Sanford to the Dragon Press's Angel Flores (ca. late 1932 [unfortunately, Flores's letters do not seem to have survived]) suggests someone was working behind the scenes to damage Sanford's standing with Williams: "About my reputation and integrity, upon consideration I find that I haven't got either, so you can forget about writing to Williams to learn who my defamer is. But I see that I get jocular again . in [sic] all seriousness, I'd give a lot to know who told Bill all those lies. I never tried to injure him, a fact you well know." Could that defamer have been West?

A second letter to Flores (11/15/32, in which Sanford intentionally eschewed apostrophes) suggests the publisher believed Sanford's detractor was West, and the motive indeed was jealousy: "About Pep: All right, then, silence, but I reserve the right to stew about a bit in my quietude. I dont think hes jealous at all (I cant see what he has to be jealous about, for hes pretty good in his own right), but I most certainly do believe him to be a malicious, selfseeking opportunist. I shall be thinking that hereafter, though quietly, as you suggest."

Finally, the friends' competition came to a head. Near the end of 1932, the Circle was gathered, as usual, at Childs'. And as usual, after Brounoff had finished imparting the evening's wisdom, West was baiting Big Sam Levy. Only this time, Sanford stood up for Levy against his tormentor. Sanford described the scene thusly in *The Waters of Darkness* (A20, p. 165), referring to himself in the second person, as "you":

> "Let him alone," you say.
> Why? you've often wondered since. Were you shielding Sam or picking a quarrel with Pep? Were you nobly for the underdog or meanly against the dog on top? What moved you—pity for Sam or the sleeping fire come awake?
> [...]
> "Why don't you quit, Pep? Go after someone your size."
> "Someone like you, do you mean?"
> "Yes," you say. "Someone like me."
> "But, Scotty," he says, "I'd be afraid to match wits with you. You might show me up for what I am."
> "What you are, Pep, is a sheeny in Brooks' clothing.... A sheeny in Brooks' clothing, Mr. West," you say. "I knew you when your name had two syllables."

This exchange signaled an end to whatever outward vestiges remained of their friendship.

In late 1936, when Sanford moved to Hollywood to begin work writing for motion pictures, he discovered that West was working as a screenwriter, also. The two of them saw each other with regularity—at Musso and Frank's restaurant, the Stanley Rose book shop, movie theaters, or parties among the Hollywood set. Sanford recalled one time playing pool with West, William Saroyan and John Fante. Their encounters were cordial but restrained; the rupture in their friendship four years past would never be mended.

A pair of letters aptly illustrates the intensely polarized feelings Sanford had about West. On 8/2/39, Sanford wrote a scathing letter to Jesse Greenstein's wife, Nonie, in which he explained his refusal to read *The Day of the Locust*:

> I haven't read West's book because I simply can't tolerate the man. It's the God's honest truth that he's the only human being on the face of the earth that I really detest…. There's nothing in the world that he stands for on the same footing that I do, and it would be impossible for me to read anything of his, however good, with an open mind; I know the living body of the 'writer' too well to lose myself in his prose – and it never was that good.

Sanford added that West's fiction was full of characters who were crushed and crippled by life, whom West sadistically depicted with the "brutality of the occasional vindictive bully – who is yellow." He went on to say:

> No man that I've ever known has less pity for the insulted and injured, less nobility in the face of a life that constantly tends toward making man seem ridiculous. It is a bad thing that life makes some spines look like a corkscrew; it is a contemptible thing that one of the lucky ones jeers at the result; and in Pep's literature there's always some hunchback who has to pay double, once to life and once to Mister West.

Sanford's simmering resentment toward West is palpable.

Yet, after West's death a little more than a year later, Sanford wrote contritely to the Greensteins (1/2/41) to retract his previous letter:

> I deeply regret anything I may have said about him, for when all's said he was responsible for my starting to write.... In addition to that... he was good to me and generous, and almost nothing that's connected with my past is vacant of him.... I'm really sorrier about the whole thing than I know how to say.

And in 1946, Sanford tearfully eulogized West as a dear friend (once again referring to himself as "you"):

> And remembering how you wept after reading about him in the paper that day, you find yourself wanting to say, now, after six years: "Pep, old kid, I hope you won't mind if... Well, I mean if you'll promise not to... That is, please don't be embarrassed if I tell you... But, damn it, Pep, you don't like it when people are sentimental, so you'll have to understand what I'm trying to say without my saying it. And you do understand, don't you, kid? You do understand that I ...." (see B3, p. 530)

For changing his life, Sanford felt West was owed a debt that could never be repaid.

www.ingramcontent.com/pod-product-compliance
Lightning Source LLC
Chambersburg PA
CBHW032224080426
42735CB00008B/700